Post-Truth

Also by Evan Davis

Made in Britain
Public Spending

Post-Truth

Why We Have Reached
Peak Bullshit
and What We Can
Do About It

EVAN DAVIS

Little, Brown

LITTLE, BROWN

First published in Great Britain in 2017 by Little, Brown

1 3 5 7 9 10 8 6 4 2

Copyright © Evan Davis 2017

The moral right of the author has been asserted.

Extracts from 'Beyond Lying: Donald Trump's Authoritarian Reality'
(*New York Times*, 4 November 2016) on p. 157 reproduced by
kind permission of Jason Stanley.
Extracts from 'A new theory for why Trump voters are so angry' (*Washington
Post*, 8 November 2016) on pp. 116–7 reproduced by kind permission of Jeff Guo.

A CIP catalogue record for this book
is available from the British Library.

Hardback ISBN 978-1-4087-0331-1
C-format ISBN 978-1-4087-0333-5

Typeset in Minion by M Rules
Printed and bound in Great Britain by
Clays Ltd, St Ives plc

Papers used by Little, Brown are from well-managed forests
and other responsible sources.

MIX
Paper from
responsible sources
FSC
www.fsc.org   FSC® C104740

Little, Brown
An imprint of
Little, Brown Book Group
Carmelite House
50 Victoria Embankment
London EC4Y 0DZ

An Hachette UK Company
www.hachette.co.uk

www.littlebrown.co.uk

For all those people to whom I have ever
lied, nearly lied, economised with facts
or been phoney, insecure or pretentious.

This is for you.

I fear there are too many of you to mention by name.

And for Guillaume
To whom I am incapable of being anything other than
completely honest.

CONTENTS

Introduction   ix

Section 1: What

1. Truth, Post-Truth and Post-Fact   3
2. Nonsense and Gibberish   30
3. Gestures and Phoney Behaviour   53
4. Bullshit: The Theory   67

Section 2: Why

5. Hidden Messages   91
6. Being Human   121
7. Short-Termism   159
8. Culture and Norms   185

Section 3: How

9. Limits to the Power of Persuasion   215
10. Better Bullshit   246
11. The Discerning Listener   273

Final Words   298

Notes   303
Acknowledgements   333
Index   337

INTRODUCTION

Bullshit old and new

Back in May 2013, a former speech writer for Hillary Clinton and Barack Obama gave a commencement address to the graduating students of Pitzer College in Claremont, Southern California. Jon Lovett was only thirty years old at the time, but had not only spent three years working in the White House; he had been the head writer on an NBC sitcom (*1600 Penn*) and had also worked as a stand-up comedian. Few people better understand the rules of modern communication, in politics or beyond, than him.

The subject of his speech to the students that day was *bullshit*. He was not a fan. He described it as 'one of the greatest threats we face'.

> We are drowning in it. We are drowning in partisan rhetoric that is just true enough not to be a lie; in industry-sponsored research; in social media's imitation of human connection; in legalese and corporate double-speak. It infects every facet of public life, corrupting our discourse, wrecking our trust in major institutions, lowering our standards for the truth, making it harder to achieve anything.[1]

I think we all know how he felt. We are assailed by the stuff all day, from the moment we get up and turn on the radio next to our bed, to the emails we get at work, to the ads we try to avoid as we surf the web, to the pretentious restaurant menus that we encounter when we want a special night out, or the distortions of history laced into the plotlines of movies that purport to be 'inspired by real events'.

But the bullshit to which Mr Lovett was referring is particularly a product of that special class of modern professional communicator: the people who are paid to craft messages and explain things to us. They turn out to be the worst offenders when it comes to mangling the message in a way that obscures the plain truth. Political spin and obfuscation; clumsily drafted corporate press releases; the weasel words and excuses of mediocre bureaucrats; the faux-friendly signage that tries to boss us around in our daily lives; exaggerated distortions we read in newspapers desperate to arouse our interest.

Jon Lovett referred to the numerous books on the subject. One is called *Your Call Is Important to Us: The Truth About Bullshit*.[2] 'There is so much bullshit that one hardly knows where to begin,' the author, Laura Penny, wrote, her title making the point that we are assaulted by it in all corners of our lives. I doubt anyone will disagree with the simple proposition that professional bullshit is a pervasive and important phenomenon. And I should know, because I work in the bullshit industry: I interview politicians on TV and chat with chief executives on the radio. And we who work in the media world have to sell our programmes to our audiences, and that sometimes means trying to make them sound big even if the material is small or medium. My job is to listen to bullshit, to try to expose it and to manufacture my share of it too.

In his speech, Jon Lovett implored the students to strive for truth in their lives, to speak up when they see something wrong and not to be afraid to get into people's faces. And he went on:

> I believe we may have reached 'peak bullshit'. And that increasingly, those who push back against the noise and nonsense; those who refuse to accept the untruths of politics and commerce and entertainment and government will be rewarded. That we are at the beginning of something important.

Well, as I say, Jon Lovett gave his speech in 2013 and he was right to say that we were at the beginning of something important, but he was wrong as to what that was. Within a few years all the everyday bullshit to which we had become so accustomed was overtaken by a new kind of politics, and a new kind of bullshit to accompany it. I was as surprised as anyone else. In 2013, I had already started thinking about this book and I agreed with Lovett that we had reached peak bullshit, that the public had grown cynical of nonsense; become habituated to the tiresome techniques of the professional spinners; could see through exaggeration and deception; and would reward those who demonstrated authenticity and honesty. And then there it was: the reaction came and it was not the emergence of a new breed of plain-speaking, common-sense honest politician; rather, it was an international wave of populist politicians who smashed through the old conventions of political obfuscation, and who introduced us to a new style of communication replete with attention-grabbing propositions that have no basis in fact or expert judgement at all. To take one random example, Donald Trump made the claim that old-style CFC-infused aerosol hairsprays were never damaging to the ozone layer when the gases were released inside an apartment building.[3] He is not the only one to specialise in this form of assertion. In 2013, before Trump was barely a politician, the Czech president Miloš Zeman was pontificating on the effects of smoking: 'I myself only started smoking when I was twenty-seven years old, when my body had fully developed, and tobacco could no longer harm it. So let me recommend your children to do the same: wait until the age of twenty-seven, and then smoke without any risk whatsoever,' he said on a visit to a Philip Morris cigarette factory, to the despair of health professionals.[4]

And then along came the term 'post-truth', an expression of frustration and anguish from a liberal class discombobulated by the political disruptions of 2016. It was in that year, one could say the great political schism to divide Western societies switched from being a left–right one to being about liberalism and populism, each with different priorities, values and tribal allegiances. Post-truth came to refer to a number of different things; the liberals' use of the phrase was obviously fuelled by Donald Trump's election campaign, but that was just a small part of it. In the UK's EU referendum campaign, both sides were said to have used extreme exaggeration or direct falsehood in order to draw attention to the issues that favoured their side of the argument.[5] These were not off-the-cuff stream-of-conscious-ness meanderings, but claims that were carefully calculated to get attention, and some stretched the norms that have tended to discipline political campaigns in Britain. Surprisingly, some deceptions were peddled by intelligent and generally honest people, who felt it opportune to mislead because the penalties of so doing were outweighed by the benefits.

The cluster of post-truth worries extended to other phenom-ena too: fake news stories spread online (a consequence of a technology that ironically makes it easier for non-reputable sources of news to get attention); conspiracy theories, such as the bizarre claim that a Washington DC pizzeria was the base of a child sex ring run by Hillary Clinton and her aide John Podesta; wilful and sometimes offensive provocation online or in print; and finally, a certain scepticism of expert opinion.[6]

It's not hard to see why the term post-truth emerged; there were genuine changes in the way public discourse was conducted, and they were accompanied by a widespread liberal terror at everything that was happening in the world. But this book is not about the politics of 2016 or the presidency of Donald Trump; it is about honesty and communication. And although the political convulsions of 2016 are real and are connected to concerns about the abuse of facts, it is important to sit down, take a deep breath and pause for reflection on the degree to which lying is uniquely a feature of our era. For all the extremes of our time, the post-truth phenomena are rooted in styles of communication that we are familiar with and we all use. It might be tempting to think, just as Jon Lovett did in 2013, that we have now reached some kind of uniquely dysfunctional era in public and private communication, but it is useful to remember what came before the post-truth era. It was preceded by the modern marketing techniques of the twentieth century, which saw messages so perfectly crafted as to be no longer grounded in reality. Or go back further: do you think there was no bullshit in the court of Henry VIII? Or in the medieval Catholic Church? Read Anthony Trollope's *The Way We Live Now*, published in 1875, for a compelling account of Victorian-era mendacity and nonsense. (In Chapter 1, Lady Carbury implores three different editors to commission good write-ups of her first book, referring to the corrupt system of reviews: 'To puff and to get one's self puffed have become different branches of a new profession.'[7])

Or take the Soviet Union. Deprived of the enormous

advertising industry that we have, it lacked the PR professionals and sharp-suited, slick political consultants we know and love, yet there were still endless government messages telling the citizens how well things were going. Poster depictions of implausibly fit characters in strident poses against utopian backdrops; slogans such as 'We will fulfil and over-fulfil Stalin's new five-year plan with honour!' or 'Forward to a new, powerful rise of socialist transport!' and 'Let's vote on merit!' (in a country with single-candidate elections). These Soviet government messages were bullshit by any measure.[8]

So, to inject some perspective into the current debate, the purpose of this book is to provide a first-principles look at mendacity and nonsense, both in the post-truth era and – if I may coin a phrase – in the pre-post-truth period too. I still agree with the central argument of Jon Lovett's commencement address, that we have too much bullshit, but we are not going to get far in improving public discourse without understanding it. So my mission here is to try to set out why bullshit is so ubiquitous, why it sometimes 'works' and why it often goes too far. In short, my aim is to explain why bullshit has an appeal, and how we can get the best from the bullshit-ridden dialogue we have.

This is not a narrow study of the alt-right, or of Donald Trump or the EU referendum, but it is relevant to all of these. Throughout, I adopt a very broad notion of bullshit: I take it as any form of communication – verbal or non-verbal – that is not the clearest or most succinct statement of the sincere and reasonably held beliefs of the communicator. On this account, lying is bullshit; trying to deceive without lying is bullshit; and the myriad forms of padding that are designed to impress, obfuscate or attract attention are also bullshit. Flannel and waffle, distracting decoration or flamboyance, artifice and insincerity, pure nonsense and gibberish all come under my definition. I'm taking it as a far broader concept than that which is deployed by some (notably the philosopher Harry Frankfurt, whose essay 'On Bullshit' first made the word and the topic a respectable subject of study).[9] But I do think the wider definition matches the vast swathe of things to which the word bullshit is applied in common usage. The book is replete with examples of things that meet my definition, but I'm happy to concede that there can even be good bullshit as well as bad.

The central question

The issue at the heart of this book, and the underlying concern about a post-truth society, is why there is so much bullshit. My interest in this subject has partly been ignited by a career in broadcasting, but also by a background in economics. It is not well known, but over the last five decades economists have begun to appreciate that information plays a huge part in the effective functioning of markets. The fact that there are asymmetries of knowledge – that sellers may know more than buyers about the quality of the items being traded – really matters. So economists have studied the theoretical conditions in which it is possible to believe what you are told. However, being economists, they often make the assumption that we are all rational: that if someone has an incentive to lie to us, we would never be so silly as to trust them.

This rational model is interesting, but it struggles to explain the sheer volume of nonsense that we observe, so much of this book is devoted to explaining the *irrational* appeal of bullshit. There are two related mysteries: why would anyone be taken in by the stuff if it is blatant nonsense, or if the claims made are highly likely to be worthless? And if no rational person would be taken in by it, why on earth is so much breath wasted on producing it? If we can't answer those questions, then we'll never understand why bullshit is so resilient, defying all attempts to outlaw it.

These two mysteries make bullshit an intriguing topic. The 'your call is important to us' refrain, to which we have all been exposed, surely doesn't make us think our call is important. Does the company saying it think we are fooled by it? I doubt that too, yet call centres persist in repeating it. There must be something more subtle going on for this kind of behaviour to persist.

Or take the ingenious but hollow brand slogans to which we have become habituated: 'Happiness is a cigar called Hamlet', Mr Kipling makes 'exceedingly good cakes' and 'A Mars a day helps you work, rest and play'. I think we are streetwise enough to know that these are not to be taken literally. We know what a Mars bar is and what it does for us. The advertising might induce us to buy more of them, but I doubt it was ever because we believed Mars bars help us work, rest or play.

This central curiosity of bullshit – why so much of it exists even when it is transparently drivel – is well illustrated by an anecdote in Robert Service's *A History of Modern Russia*.[10] Some time under the rule of President Brezhnev, a young woman is stopped from distributing pamphlets of protest next to Lenin's Mausoleum. But on inspection her pamphlets are found to contain only blank pages. When she is asked to explain, she replies, 'Why bother writing? Everybody knows.'[11] Everybody knows the reality of life in the Soviet Union, there is no need to spell it out. But when everybody knows something is the case, what is the role of communication in trying to promote it or hide it? In the Soviet example, the 'why bother writing?' question should most pertinently have been asked of the propagandists themselves. Why did they bother trying to push the party line when their work appears to have had almost no effect? As Robert Service says, 'Citizens had their own direct experience of Soviet history and politics, and were in an excellent position to pass a private judgement on the words of party propagandists.'[12] Instead of making people feel good about the Soviet state, all the effort expended in poster design simply made people feel bad about the authorities who were apparently deluded. It was, at best, slightly worse than useless. The end result, to quote Service again, is that 'the state was regarded with suspicion by practically everybody'.[13] Indeed, even the propagandists knew they were wasting their time: a survey of them in the Moscow of the 1960s found only one in eleven thought that their Marxist-Leninist message was actually being absorbed into the personal convictions of their audiences. 'And so this most politicizing of states had induced a pervasive political apathy.'[14]

There are two reactions to the observation that talking nonsense is potentially futile. One is to condemn it, and say it should be resisted as it achieves nothing but undermining trust and increasing cynicism. The other reaction is to ask whether it might have some other underlying purpose, beyond direct per-suasion. In this book, I'll follow both of these paths. One thesis is that in many walks of life, such as politics and business, our culture is rather like that of the former Soviet Union in being characterised by a pervasive tendency of those in authority to overstate their case. They bombard us with messages that are disconnected from reality as we see it. In the Soviet case, it was the reality that was shameful; in ours, it is the communicators.

But we also have to recognise that the bad habits of modern communication evolved for a reason. It clearly makes sense not to be truthful at times, and until we know when and where deception and discretion have a role we will not have much idea why the two have become habitually used to excess. In short, to see why professional communicators don't always see it as their job to be candid, we have to ask what the pressures are that drive them not to be.

A small amount of introspection will probably demonstrate the point: the more you observe yourself, the more you realise genuine frankness is not the norm but the exception. We are all economical with the truth in our daily and professional lives, often with benign intent. In the last week you may have told the odd white lie, you may have hidden your ignorance in a conversation, embroidered an anecdote you were telling, offered encouragement or sympathy to someone who didn't deserve it ... or maybe you have lied in a less benign form, exaggerating an expense claim to ensure that the unallowable cost of a bottle of wine is reimbursed to you. As we strive to identify the habits of communicators from the understandable to the indefensible, let's not just assume this is a book about other people. It is to a very large extent about us all.

Structure of the book

The book has three sections. The first sets out the multifarious forms in which bullshit comes, and the problem it represents. The common but simplistic view of it is encapsulated by the dictionary definition: the verb *to bullshit* is 'to talk nonsense to someone, typically in an attempt to deceive them'. A classic case would be the deceit of a snake-oil salesman. A travelling vendor passes through town, trying to sell a magic remedy by lying about its composition and falsely suggesting it has curative powers. He is a bullshit-spouting quack, but will move on to the next town before any foolish purchaser realises his potion is useless. I imagine this is what most people think bullshit in the post-truth era is all about: the lying politician trying to sell us snake-oil remedies to complex problems or cynical corporations pretending to do good, when they are really only interested in making money. But this example of deceit captures only a fraction of the bullshit that is showered upon us every day. Beyond old-fashioned lying there are multiple varieties of not-quite-lying-but-nevertheless-trying-to-mislead. Then it is often the case that the people talking nonsense have persuaded themselves that what they are saying is true, so they are not lying in the literal sense of the word; we all have a strong capacity to delude ourselves, and if it is convenient to believe something we will often come round to believing it. On top of this, bullshit can be *a*-factual in the sense that it is neither true nor false; it bears no relation to facts at all. And finally, it even comes in the form of actions, rather than words, that are designed to signal something not quite true.

The second section of the book consists of four chapters that try to explain the phenomenon. It does not take the view that to understand is to forgive, but it does try to understand. It offers four kinds of explanation of bullshit. First, sometimes a false statement is subtly revealing of a truth, because the choice of false statement says something honest about the communicator. This perhaps accounts for some of the appeal of Donald Trump, who, it has been noted, was taken seriously but not literally by his supporters.[15] Secondly, we are not rational beings and so sometimes communication can exploit our psychological foibles to manipulate our thinking and feelings. Thirdly, there is an argument over time horizons. The truth usually emerges, given long enough; but in the short term, it may be possible to fool enough people for a sufficient time to score an advantage. And fourth, in a society where a culture of bullshit is the norm, it may be irresistible to conform for even the most straightforward and honest person.

Between them, these four chapters are designed to show that communication can be informative even if it is not true; it can be persuasive even if it is not informative; it can be effective in the short term even if it is not persuasive in the long term. And if everyone is doing it, it can be irresistible even if it is not effective.

The final section looks at how we can raise our game, protect ourselves against manipulative attempts to deceive, and improve public discourse. It firstly argues for communicators to be more modest in their goals. While bullshit can have an impact, what it can't do is sustainably convince most people that false propositions are true, when contrary evidence is there to be seen. You may say that your product is good, but that doesn't make it good, and it won't be believed that it's good if consumers are able to make their own judgement. So stop trying. The hard sell has become overused, and has worn out.

This section also argues that there is a strong link between open-mindedness and honesty; that gullibility is often a result of too strong a hope that something is true. Finally, it suggests that societies are particularly vulnerable to temporary epidemics of credulity when people stop caring about where the evidence lies, and instead ask, whose side is that communicator on? It is no coincidence that concern about a post-truth era came at a time of unusually extreme division and tribalism in the West. The unsettling breakdown of the traditional left–right spectrum, the anger at elites, the rise of identity politics – all are conducive to claim and counter-claim. A certain number of people seem to hold views not because they think the evidence supports them, but because they feel that professing a belief in them can serve as an expression of group allegiance and loyalty. Those who want a less bullshit-prone society had better worry about the cause of the divisions, as much as they do the symptoms.

SECTION ONE

WHAT

The many forms which mendacity and
nonsense can take, in a post-truth
world and the era that preceded it

1

Truth, Post-Truth and Post-Fact

Bullshit in the form of mendacity

Facts and lies

You may remember the murders in Soham in Cambridgeshire in 2002. Two young girls, ten-year-old Holly Wells and Jessica Chapman, went missing on a Sunday afternoon in August, having enjoyed a barbecue and then gone to buy some sweets together. Thirteen days later, after a period in which Britain had been gripped by the case and news channels had covered little else, their bodies were found six miles away from where they had last been seen.[1]

The last man to have spoken to the girls was a caretaker at a local college, Ian Huntley. The police began to suspect that he might have been involved in their disappearance, and searching his property and the school where he worked they found compelling evidence against him. He was charged with murder three days after the bodies were recovered.

Huntley went to trial the next year and admitted to having killed the girls, but in court he argued the deaths had been accidental. In his defence he concocted one of the most elaborate and implausible stories in modern criminal history. He claimed that he had encountered the girls near his house that afternoon and that Holly had a stubborn nosebleed. He had taken them both upstairs to his bathroom in an effort to help. This is how the Press Association reported Huntley's barrister's account of what happened:

> Mr Huntley was getting pieces of tissue or toilet paper, putting them under the cold tap to cool them and handing them to Holly, and on one of his turns from getting the wet tissue he slipped and it seems that he may well have banged into her as she was sitting on the edge of the bath, and she went backwards ... When Holly went in the bath, which had roughly 18 inches of water in it because Mr Huntley was going to wash his dog, Jessica stood up and started screaming 'You pushed her, you pushed her'. And he then turned towards Jessica and either with one hand or two, he's not sure, put his hands out towards Jessica, his memory is over her mouth, to stop her screaming. For how long he was in that position he can't say. But he was then conscious that Jessica was no longer supporting herself on her feet. He let go and she went to the ground. He then turned round to the bath and Holly was lying in the bath, apparently dead. He lifted Holly out of the bath, put her on the floor, looked for signs of breathing and found none. He turned his attention to Jessica, he looked for signs of breathing and found none.[2, 3]

Most people reading this can appreciate that it all sounds absurdly implausible. In fact, I think we may call this lying at its purest. It is a credit to the British legal system that, for the duration of the trial, Huntley's account was mostly treated without public derision, because a defence case needs to be given respect until the jury has reached its verdict. But it is telling that in order to spare the embarrassment of the barristers who have to spout such obvious nonsense as a matter of professional obligation, we dress them in wigs and gowns in court, thus drawing a distinction between their real selves and their legal personas. Their fancy dress says, 'I'm offering this account on behalf of my client, but that doesn't mean I believe it any more than you do.'

Now, when it comes to direct lies like this, *facts* are key. The lie has a clear relationship to the facts, in that it is wholly opposed to them. And for many, direct lies are central to fears that we are in a post-truth age; indeed, the term post-fact has been used almost interchangeably with post-truth. One worry is that public figures are happy to assert facts that are simply not true, or to talk about alternative facts. The other fashionable concern is that fake news stories (i.e., lies) are shared across social media before anyone notices that the original source is far from reliable. The news website BuzzFeed looked at some of the successful fake stories of 2016:

> The top-performing fake news story identified in the analysis is a hoax from October that claimed President Obama had banned reciting the Pledge of Allegiance in schools. It was published by ABCNews.com.co, a fake site made to look like *ABC News* that scored six hits in the top 50. The Obama hoax generated more than 2.1 million shares, comments, and reactions on Facebook in just two months.[4]

Others included in the BuzzFeed Top 50 were:

- Woman arrested for defecating on boss' desk after winning the lottery
- Obama passed law for grandparents to get all their grandchildren every weekend
- Pro-Lifers Declare: 'Ejaculation is Murder, Every Sperm Cell Is A Life'
- Daycare Busted Running Toddler Fight Club, Parents Outraged

Whatever the motivations of the writers of these particular false stories, and I assume some were intended as a joke, the interesting cases are those in which facts are deliberately asserted with the intention that they should be believed to be true, in the full knowledge that they are not.

But while facts (or falsehoods) like these appear straightforward, in public discourse they turn out to be a more complicated phenomenon than post-fact anxieties acknowledge. There are certainly such things as facts, and no one should persuade you otherwise. But aside from quite banal facts ('the sun is shining') we always have to use judgement in deciding what is a fact and what to believe: we have to apply a judgement as to the weight of evidence in its support relative to the weight of interpretation put on it.

So for example, is it a fact that Ian Huntley's account of the dreadful events that occurred in his house was a lie? None of us were there; we can't be sure he was lying; we simply think his account was too far-fetched to be plausible, and given all the other evidence available about his character and behaviour, it seems reasonable to say he was making it up. And if we ask why we need to know whether he was lying, it is to determine guilt and apply punishment; certainly the evidence was sufficiently convincing to convict. But it is still a matter of judgement, even if in this extreme case the judgement was a straightforward one.

Similarly, most of us take it as a fact that CFC gases destroy the ozone layer, not because we have observed this ourselves but because people we trust have told us so. Some people take it as a fact that Brexit is bad for the British economy, but it is really only correct to say that most expert and business opinion believes Brexit is bad for the British economy, which is different from saying it actually is. Again, judgement almost always plays a part in our decisions as to what is a fact and what is true. Facts may be *probably* true, or *partly* true, or possibly true in some contexts but irrelevant in others. I think of them as like beams used in construction: that a beam is made of steel is important, but when inserting one to support a building the question is not simply what material it is made of, but whether it is capable of bearing the weight that is being loaded upon it. Debates over which interpretation of the facts is the right one are often less about truth and more about the proportionality of the facts cited in making the case set out.

And because judgement plays a part in assessing this, we have to be aware that much of the mendacity we encounter does not come in as obvious or extreme a form as the example from Ian Huntley or from the cases of fake news. Those are simply at one end of a spectrum of factual deception, but there are many other more nuanced types of mendacity elsewhere on that scale. Without necessarily asserting a statement that is false, people will try to persuade us to believe something that is not true, not quite true or not the whole truth.

Perhaps the reason that these softer forms of deception are so prevalent is that Western societies have made the legal and reputational penalties for flagrant lying very high, and so in most public discourse the outright untruth is worth avoiding. In the UK parliament, deliberately telling a lie is a resignation matter for a minister; outside parliament, it is invariably a matter of disgrace. In court, perjury is a serious criminal offence; and advertisers are prevented from lying, even though it is expected they will offer a one-sided view of their product.[5] So by and large, deceivers don't mind being misleading, just as long as they are not caught telling a fib. And fortunately for the modern communicator, it turns out that lies are often unnecessary anyway: a remarkable amount of powerful deception can be practised without any lies being told.

In this chapter, we'll take a brief tour of the different forms of mendacity in which facts are at issue, even though no direct lie is peddled. In the next chapter we will look at a number of different varieties of nonsense where the precise facts uttered or their veracity tend to be unimportant or irrelevant to the speaker. But for now, we deal with assertions that do have a relationship with the facts, even if it is a rather dysfunctional one.

The near-lie: using the right words to give a wrong impression

If the pure Ian Huntley-type lie is number one in the taxonomy of forms of bullshit, the *near-lie* has to be number two. The words 'I did not have sexual relations with that woman' would, to most of us, seem to be pretty clear, and to exclude any form of sexual contact. When President Bill Clinton looked into the camera and uttered those nine words about his relationship with Monica Lewinsky, was he lying? Possibly he was, but at the very least he was demonstrating the art of picking your words carefully in order to mislead. He later explained that he was interpreting sexual relations as meaning sexual intercourse:

And I believe that is the definition that most ordinary Americans would give it ... I'll bet the grand jurors, if they were talking about two people they know, and said they have a sexual relationship, they meant they were sleeping together; they meant they were having intercourse together.[6]

This is probably one of the most famous examples of the near-lie, and one that comes as close as it is possible to be to bare-faced deception.

As it happens, the lawyers making the original case against Clinton were not stupid; they had wanted to pin him down on the precise meaning of 'sexual relations'. They were acting for Paula Jones, a woman who had filed a lawsuit against him for sexual harassment and assault, and they wanted to show that there was a pattern to Bill Clinton's behaviour. The lawyers submitted a tight definition of sexual relations for Mr Clinton to look at:

For the purposes of this grand jury session, a person engages in 'sexual relations' when the person knowingly engages in or causes contact with the genitalia, anus, groin, breast, inner thigh, or buttocks of any person with an intent to gratify or arouse the sexual desire of any person. 'Contact' means intentional touching, either directly or through clothing.

The President was then asked to reiterate his denial of a sexual relationship:

Q: ... And so the record is completely clear, have you ever had sexual relations with Monica Lewinsky, as that term is defined in Deposition Exhibit 1, as modified by the Court? ...

A: I have never had sexual relations with Monica Lewinsky.

After that encounter, it became clear that Mr Clinton had practised oral sex with Monica Lewinsky, and back at the Grand Jury hearing after he had admitted as much, he was asked how he could not have been lying when he said that he had not had sexual relations as defined by Deposition Exhibit 1.

Q: Well, the grand jury would like to know, Mr President, why it is that you think that oral sex performed on you does not fall within the definition of sexual relations as used in your deposition.

A: Because that is – if the deponent is the person who has oral sex performed on him, then the contact is with – not with anything on that list, but with the lips of another person. It seems to be self-evident that that's what it is. And I thought it was curious.

Again, he says he was not lying, but he was being careful in his choice of words. On the precise definition offered, Monica Lewinsky had sexual relations with him, but he did not have sexual relations with her.[7]

Anyone reading this can see the President had engaged in deceit, but was pulling out all the stops to maintain that he had fallen short of a certain legal line. You might sympathise with him given that his political opponents were throwing vast resources at trying to impeach him on grounds irrelevant to his ability to serve as President, but the deceit was there for all to see. For some, the ingenious deceptions of the kind Bill Clinton engaged in deserve a word of their own; Max Black's essay 'The Prevalence of Humbug' offers this definition: 'HUMBUG: *deceptive misrepresentation, short of lying, especially by pretentious word or deed, of somebody's own thoughts, feelings, or attitudes.'*[8]

Call it whatever you will; for me, the distinction between the lie and the near-lie of the Bill Clinton variety is so fine that it is barely worth drawing, but the distinction *is* drawn and great importance is attached to it. On it can rest honour, a career or a jail sentence. And the distinction is often vitally important psychologically to those who engage in deception. Rather than a 180-degree distortion of facts, there is a 160-degree distortion and that 20-degree difference offers succour to the deceiver that they have not crossed some crucial line in the sand. Deceivers do not want to act in a morally reprehensible manner; they just want to get away with their deceit. As part of the mental process of self-justification that we all engage in when we do something wrong, the near-lie offers comfort. It assuages guilt, allowing the perpetrator the self-respect of being able to say to themselves that no lie was told. Let's admit it: we have all been there, we have all taken advantage of that distinction at some point or other.

Now the example of Bill Clinton choosing his words carefully gets you to the classic near-lie, but when you look at some of the great deceptions of recent times, you find they often come in the form of the lie that isn't quite a direct lie. My guess is that Volkswagen, entangled in a scandal over false emissions readings for its diesel cars, would never have fabricated inaccurate data from scratch. That would have been to have gone too far. But at least some company insiders were happy to install 'defeat devices' in the cars, knowing they would accurately record misleading data.[9] They might as well have made figures up, but they probably told themselves the emissions tests were known to be unrealistic anyway. All car manufacturers use tricks like over-inflating tyres and removing wing mirrors in order to improve fuel consumption during the tests.[10] Is it really so different to use other methods to game the test results? Is there such a difference in ethics between cheating using the routine methods of other manufacturers, and this particular and more ingenious form of using a defeat device? It is with these kinds of internal conversations that major deceptions often begin – always conforming to the moral clarity of the prohibition on a barefaced lie, but taking advantage of the huge grey area that exists between acceptable and unacceptable forms of misleading.[11, 12]

Similarly, when the Vote Leave campaign in the British EU referendum emblazoned their buses with the claim 'We send the EU £350 million a week' they did not make the figure up completely; it was not a lie in the Ian Huntley sense. Rather, they had in mind that one measure of Britain's EU subscription worked out at £350 million a week.*[13] It was the notional amount that Britain *would* pay in the absence of a discount taken off in recognition of special British circumstances. This £350 million is one of the most famous 'lies' in British political campaigning, but there was at least a figure that it related to. And despite every attempt by the authorities and the media to clarify why that figure was wholly bogus – because it was not paid to the EU in any form, ever – it still appeared to acknowledge that there was such a figure as £350 million a week. Once that was conceded, then it just appeared to be a technical matter of ordinary campaign argument about whether this figure or some other figure was the better one to be using. That wasn't the first deception in a political campaign, but the prominence it was given and the mendacious defences made of it in the face of perfectly reasonable critiques certainly took campaign deception in the UK to new extremes. And yet, and yet. The campaign all along believed it had given itself a sliver of justification that

---

* I discuss the £350 million claim in more detail in Chapter 11.

meant it was all just part of the rough and tumble of a political campaign.

Bill Clinton, Volkswagen and the Vote Leave campaign are all in the same category. All were highly conscious of the facts and each knew that the facts mattered; each was very different from Ian Huntley in that they carefully tried to maintain a thread of connection to the truth, but in doing so they ended up demonstrating more ingenuity and cunning than Huntley ever could with his implausible court testimony. Those who avoid the direct lie by careful deception can never argue that the resulting deceit is accidental or incidental. When exposed as mendacious, there is nowhere for them to hide.

Economy with the truth: selective facts

The third in this taxonomy of forms of deception does not require any form of misstatement or near-misstatement of facts; it just requires the absence of relevant information. The phrase 'economical with the truth' was invented to describe it.

The phrase has a long history – Edmund Burke used it in a letter in 1796 ('Falsehood and delusion are allowed in no case whatever: but, as in the exercise of all the virtues, there is an economy of truth. It is a sort of temperance, by which a man speaks truth with measure that he may speak it the longer').[14] Mark Twain played with the notion of economy in truth, noting 'Truth is the most valuable thing we have. Let us economise it.'[15] But the phrase leapt into the popular idiom far more recently, during the *Spycatcher* trial of November 1986 in which the British Cabinet secretary Sir Robert Armstrong (later Lord Armstrong of Ilminster) was dispatched to the New South Wales Supreme Court as a witness in a case initiated by the British government to suppress publication of *Spycatcher*, a former insider's exposé of life in the British secret service. It wasn't the British establishment's finest hour. Armstrong was in a hopeless position and faced an effective opponent in the form of Malcolm Turnbull, the thirty-two-year-old counsel for the author of the book.* Armstrong's hilarious intellectual and verbal contortions have become legendary: including, for example, a moment when he refused to admit to the existence of SIS (the Secret Intelligence Service, or MI6). Reminded by Turnbull that he had already acknowledged that Sir Dick White had been its chief, Armstrong replied, 'I acknowledge the existence of MI6 at the time Sir Dick White was head of it. I do not wish to go any further than that. So MI6 did exist, but only until Sir Dick retired in 1969.'[16]

The specific episode in court that led to the use of the phrase 'economical with the truth' derived from an exchange surrounding a letter the British government had written to the publisher of *Spycatcher*, asking for a copy of the book and rather disingenuously omitting to mention that they had seen galley proofs of the book some weeks before (because those had been provided in confidence). Here is the subsequent exchange:

Turnbull: So that letter contains a lie, does it not?

Armstrong: It contains a misleading impression in that respect.

Turnbull: Which you knew to be misleading at the time you made it?

Armstrong: Of course.

Turnbull: So it contains a lie?

Armstrong: It is a misleading impression in that respect, it does not contain a lie, I don't think.

---

* Turnbull would go on to become Prime Minister of Australia.

Turnbull: And what is the difference between a misleading impression and a lie?

Armstrong: You are as good at English as I am.

Turnbull: I am just trying to understand.

Armstrong: A lie is a straight untruth.

Turnbull: What is a misleading impression – a sort of bent untruth?

Armstrong: As one person said, it is perhaps being economical with the truth.[17]

Armstrong had Edmund Burke in mind when he said this, and is entitled to draw the distinction – as Bill Clinton did – between lying and misleading. But unfortunately for Armstrong, the general public have chosen to interpret 'economical with the truth' more broadly: in common usage it is not equated with 'selective with the facts'. Of this, we can be reasonably sure, because the phrase was analysed in tortuous legal detail by the linguist Alan Durant for a 1992 libel case. At issue was essentially how libellous it was to accuse someone of being 'economical with the truth'. Durant conducted a thorough study of the phrase (including a survey of a hundred people, stratified across different age bands and socio-economic groups) and found as follows:

The phrase may have started life as a polite, even subtle, euphemism, but subsequently became a transparent figurative expression meaning to deceive or lie, especially the concealment of discreditable or unprofessional conduct by people in public office. While Lord Armstrong has continued to maintain that the expression means 'leaving unsaid things which might be embarrassing and which ought to be kept secret from the public', even the interviewer to whom he originally offered this opinion went on to report, 'To most people it is a Civil Service euphemism for telling lies'.[18]

The phrase understood in this broader form was famously picked up by the MP Alan Clark in another court case in 1992, where he charmingly admitted to an extremely serious previous lie (on oath) by confessing that he had been 'economical with the *actualité*'. While the words 'economical with the truth' might have come to be seen as amusingly synonymous with lying, the concept of being selective with the facts is obviously distinct. And on the scale of deceptions it is generally regarded as less serious than the lie or the devious avoidance of a lie. That is per-haps because missing out a fact can more plausibly be presented as accidental or sincere.

When it comes to low-grade mendacity of the kind we are bombarded with every day, economy with the truth is the default form. It has become so commoditised that those who engage in it probably don't even recognise that they are doing it. Just by way of illustration, let me describe a particularly needless (and inevitably futile) example concerning a sensible decision by Transport for London (TfL) in 2009 to redesign the Circle line on the London Underground. The line was no longer going to be a circle: it was now going to be a circle with a piece of string attached to it (making what has variously been described as a 6, a lasso or a teacup). The old Circle line would join the non-circular Hammersmith and City line and the two would operate as one. Trains would no longer go round and round the circle; they would start at the far end of the piece of string (at Hammersmith), go up the string into the circle and round one lap, before going into reverse, back round the circle and then down the piece of string, ending at Hammersmith again.

This was actually a relatively modest timetable change, as

the Circle and Hammersmith and City lines were linked and shared rolling stock. It made sense as TfL needed more trains on the Hammersmith and City section, which had got much busier. And the circular nature of the old Circle line was causing problems as well. It had long been apparent that the absence of a terminal point meant that any problems caused by defective trains caused far greater delays than they did on linear routes. All this could be solved by unravelling the circle to give a proper start and end point. The decision to alter the timetable in this way is the kind of decision taken by managers and bureaucrats all the time. That is what they do. In the public sector, they are meant to weigh up the evidence and then do what they think is in the public interest. They are kept on their toes by their political masters, to whom they are accountable, and they get reported in the press when they do things badly. By and large they are left to get on with their job as long as it all goes right.

But as with so many decisions, while they are in the overall public interest, they are not unambiguously so. In this case, to obtain the benefit of extra trains on the section of the line to Hammersmith inevitably meant fewer trains on other parts. A significant increase in service frequency for the eight stations on the Hammersmith branch implied a slight reduction in services to the twenty-seven stations elsewhere – from one train every eight-and-a-half minutes to one train every ten.[19] Officials quite reasonably decided that the overall public interest was served by re-apportioning trains to where they were needed. But how do you think the news of the changing timetable was communicated? Once the decision to reconfigure services had been taken, the public had to be told, so a poster campaign was launched to alert travellers to what was coming up. Here's what the posters said:

The new extended Circle Line:

- A more reliable service
- Fewer delays
- More trains to Hammersmith

Note that the poster succeeds in stretching the *two* benefits of the new service (the more reliable service and extra trains to Hammersmith) to *three* bullet points, the first two of which say the same thing using different words. Unfortunately, nowhere on the poster did the copywriters find room to devote a bullet point to the one significant disadvantage, that there would be fewer services on other parts of the Circle line. So in effect, what purported to be an informative poster in fact only informed the public of the good news.

Why on earth would they choose to communicate the changes in this partial way? It wouldn't have been difficult to be honest – it wasn't that complicated to explain. The truth could still have been encapsulated in three short bullet points:

- A more reliable service
- More trains to Hammersmith
- Small reductions in other services

One can only wonder why TfL would not have chosen to tell it like this. You might think it is obvious that bureaucrats will want to present the news in as flattering a light as possible. But just ask yourself why. After all, they didn't have to *sell* the service to anybody; the decision to make the changes had already been taken and approved – there was no referendum on it, no need to campaign on the issue. There are no rival Circle lines to steal customers away. This was simply meant to be information from benevolent public servants. And anyway, it was not as if they could hide the consequences of their decision. Once the reduction in services took effect passengers would surely notice it, so what possible benefit could there be from disguising it for just a few weeks ahead of time?

Unsurprisingly, once the new service had gone into operation, complaints that waiting times had increased did surface. Andrew Bosi, chairman of the Capital Transport Campaign, was quoted in the *Evening Standard* as saying, 'What makes this particularly irritating is the way Transport for London marketed the change as though it was a vast improvement.' In other words, it was not TfL's decision that was wrong, it was the exaggerated case made for it.[20]

To me, this case not only exemplifies economy with the truth at its most gratuitous, but also demonstrates the power of social habit to govern the decisions made by professional communications teams. The desire among politicians, businesses and media to sell their wares by focusing on their upsides rather than their downsides is so pervasive that even when there is no need to sell at all it feels wrong simply to communicate in a straightforward way. We'll return to this point, but it stresses the difficulty of breaking out of the mindset of selling rather than simply telling once it is entrenched.

Spin: a favourable interpretation of the facts

The fourth item in this survey of categories of bullshit is spin. The term can of course be used very broadly to describe everything in this chapter, but I have a particular use of it in mind: to spin is to present a favourable interpretation of the available facts. On this meaning, spin is not about the facts as much as about how they are joined up. Spin might work by putting too much weight on particular facts, or exaggerating them, or it might involve a phoney interpretation of some pieces of data. But it is not exactly false. Indeed it may be true, but simply not quite the whole truth. Spin is the routine activity of the many press officers and special advisers who work in government, and who more or less see it as their job to make the news appear good rather than bad.

The most basic form of spin I would encounter in my career as an economics journalist related to the interpretation of economic figures. The figure for UK economic growth in the fourth quarter of 2010, for example, was far worse than anyone expected. Instead of growing by up to half of one per cent, as experts had anticipated, the economy shrank by the same amount.[21] It was a fraught time as the new government had put the country on a strict and controversial diet of government-deficit reduction, which might have been held responsible for the apparent economic slowdown. Step forward the then Chancellor of the Exchequer, George Osborne, to explain it was the weather that did it. Unusually strong snow in December suppressed activity, he said.[22] Mr Osborne's opponents took a different view, and blamed him and his policies. Both sides were spinning, but it must be acknowledged that both sides of the argument had some merit. The statisticians who collated the growth data had themselves pointed out that the snow had made a difference.[23] So neither side in this spinning tussle necessarily disagreed as to the three material facts: December had been very snowy; the government had cut back spending, thus reducing demand in the economy; growth had dried up. The purpose of each side was to place an emphasis in the public mind on their preferred interpretation of those facts.

Almost all political events of significance are spun. Someone makes an attempt to write history with a particular angle – typically favourable or unfavourable. The skill of the spinner is to take the most challenging piece of bad news and tell you why it is actually good. The most extraordinary recent act of political betrayal in the UK was the undermining of Boris Johnson's attempt to lead the Conservative Party (and thus become Prime Minister) by his colleague, friend and campaign manager Michael Gove. In the course of a few hours, Mr Gove went from backing Boris to instead denouncing him and standing for the leadership himself.[24] The spinners on each side were quickly put to work. The obvious interpretation of the sequence of events was that Gove was not only capricious, but that he was disloyal and not to be trusted.[25] That was the interpretation quickly offered by his opponents, but Mr Gove had his own team to spin on his behalf. He was true to his own beliefs, they explained. What was a man of principle to do, having come to the opinion that Johnson was not up to the job? Mr Gove was not ambitious; he was selflessly devoted to public service. If he had been planning to run for Prime Minister all along, he would never have gone about it that way. And so on and so on.[26, 27]

But politics is not alone in being a profession in which spinning has an important role. When companies announce their financial results, they take professional advice on how to refine the message they send to their investors. The investor relations industry exists in part to help companies shape the story they want to tell their shareholders about what the latest figures mean.

And spin exists because there are often two legitimate versions of events, and different people will have different interests in which version is generally believed. The glass can be half-full or half-empty; we can blame guns for killing people, or we can blame people; abortion is the death of a foetus or the choice of a woman. India's Prime Minister Narendra Modi is a nationalist who oversaw an atrocity while a state governor, or a reformist Prime Minister who has mellowed with age. Those ratings figures for a TV programme can be falling, or they can now be falling more slowly than they were before. In most cases, an honest broker would lay out an interpretation that has a bit of 'on the one hand' and 'on the other hand'. The world of spin, though, is a binary one, so even-handedness is abandoned and the hard sell put in its place.

This again makes the point that the way in which facts are used or abused in public discourse is less about their conforming to the criterion of simple truth or falsehood, and more about their deployment in an intelligent and reasonable way. It is precisely because the facts are not generally at issue when it comes to spin that it is so hard to resolve an argument between two competing accounts. There is something particularly wriggly and annoying about an interpretation of events that sounds too self-serving to be credible, but which is nevertheless consistent with the facts as we know them. The spinners are often too good at their art: they are the Latin lovers of the communications world, irresistible but usually too smooth to be trusted.

It is worth saying that the mainstream media likes to think of itself as presenting the news without much spin, but news would be meaningless for most consumers in the absence of it. You wouldn't expect corporate financial results to be presented without some guidance as to whether the figure is good, bad or indifferent; no economic figure would be useful to the average newspaper reader without some interpretation; events in international diplomacy require deconstruction. The key challenge for correspondents who aim to be as impartial as humanly possible is to make sure that the spin they apply is not partisan and gives due weight to the body of expert opinion on the subject. It should also be clear in a report (by the tone, and the form of coverage) whether the reporter is giving a fact, an impression, an obvious interpretation or a personal hypothesis.[28]

There is one particular area where the media, through spin, creates its own special form of mendacity. It is what I would call bullshit through disproportion. A fact is reported, the fact is true, a legitimate interpretation is placed on that fact – but then it is puffed up to a magnitude well beyond anything it deserves. In exaggerating its importance, the media is being misleading because it is applying an implied form of spin that says this story is big, when it isn't.

Good examples often relate to excessive controversy being applied to innocuous public pronouncements that can be interpreted in an unflattering way. A former governor of the Bank of England, the late Eddie George, was caught in this kind of trap back in 1998. He was at a lunch of regional newspaper executives and was talking about the right level of interest rates in the UK. His difficulty was that the north of England generally needed lower rates, while the booming south needed them higher. He was asked whether he thought job losses in the north were an acceptable price to pay for curbing inflation in the south. His answer was as follows:

> Yes, I suppose in a sense I am. It's not desirable, but the fact is we can only seek to affect through monetary policy the state of demand in the economy as a whole. It's only through monetary policy that we can determine what happens to the labour market as a whole.[29]

This was an honest and reflective response to the question, and one which also offered a plain statement of an entirely obvious feature of a single currency across the UK: that monetary policy is a compromise between the varying needs of different regions. But of course, it was the perfect cue for a row about the apparently callous decisions being made by a remote London elite. The controversy made headline news; there were calls in the House of Commons for George to resign; and the coverage tended to misleadingly imply that he had volunteered the words of the questioner, that 'unemployment in the north is a price worth paying', even though I suspect he would have refrained from expressing it that way himself. His actual words, of course, reluctantly admitted that you could frame monetary policy in that unflattering light, and remarked on it being an undesirable if inevitable feature.

The story was not the first or the last to be blown out of all proportion, in this case because it touched a raw nerve as to the challenges faced by struggling regional economies.

Deception through self-delusion

There is one other form of bullshit for this chapter, which doesn't neatly fit into the mendacity file but has no place elsewhere. This one is dedicated to Tony Blair and the argument he made for the Iraq War in 2003. I call it deception via self-delusion. If someone sincerely believes what they say, they are not lying when they say it, and it's perhaps unfair to say they are trying to deceive us exactly. But we need to recognise that there is a special category of sincerely held beliefs where the assertion being made is not only untrue, but the person sincerely believing it was unreasonable to have done so. They aren't trying to deceive us, but they are trying to convince us of something that is untrue, and the outcome is indistinguishable from instances when they are trying to be mendacious.

Let's look at Tony Blair's case for war, as it was one of the most analysed and misunderstood examples of an important falsehood being propagated to negative effect. The common supposition is that Tony Blair peddled a lie that Saddam Hussein had weapons of mass destruction. But it is important to stress in Mr Blair's defence that this central proposition was sincerely believed by numerous Western intelligence agencies at the time.[30] It simply turned out to be faulty and so in that sense I think it is fairer to say that the war was based on a mistaken premise rather than a lie. We certainly don't want to end up asserting that all those who make controversial or wrong assertions are liars. We have to respect sincere belief as a potential defence against the charge of mendacity.

In terms of the Iraq War, however, there was a second, related falsehood that can less easily be dismissed as a genuine mistake. Tony Blair not only claimed that Saddam had WMD, he claimed that there was indubitable intelligence that this was the case. In fact, there was only *dubitable* intelligence in support of the existence of WMD.[31] Yes, the intelligence services thought that on balance Saddam had them, but they were in no doubt that they had doubts, and they couched their assessments carefully. So where Mr Blair misled the population was in the description of the evidence, certainly according to the report of the Chilcot Inquiry into the war, which set out the facts, both as we understand them in hindsight and as they were understood at the time:

> Mr Blair stated that he believed the 'assessed intelligence' had 'established beyond doubt' that Saddam Hussein had 'continued to produce chemical and biological weapons, that he continues in his efforts to develop nuclear weapons ...'[32]

Now contrary to Mr Blair's assertion, Sir John Chilcot found it was not beyond doubt at all; in his words,

> The judgements about Iraq's capabilities … were presented
> with a certainty that was not justified.[33]

Here, Chilcot is not describing a straight lie; had he been, he probably would have used stronger language. Mr Blair was offering a
personal assessment of the evidence and he is entitled to his own
judgement of what 'beyond doubt' means. But by the sin of merely
exaggerating certainty of evidence he managed to propagate a
widespread belief in the false proposition that there were WMD.

Mr Blair has consistently emphasised that he did not invent
any intelligence. 'The allegation that I or anyone else lied to this
House or deliberately misled the country by falsifying intelligence on WMD is itself the real lie,' he said.[34] That is a fair
point. But the charge he has to defend is that he calculatedly
exaggerated the strength of the intelligence. And on this, Mr
Blair has only one defence: he deployed the all-important get-
out-of-jail-free card that he believed what he was saying at the
time, and was thus not deceiving anyone in saying it.

The Chilcot Inquiry accepted Mr Blair's sincerity ('The
Inquiry is not questioning Mr Blair's belief, which he consistently reiterated in his evidence to the Inquiry, or his legitimate
role in advocating Government policy'), but his mistake did
conveniently – and massively – strengthen the case he was
trying to promote.[35]

Why do so many people consider that Mr Blair's advocacy of
the war was not erroneous but duplicitous? Part of the answer
may lie in the fact that Mr Blair was unreasonable in holding
the beliefs he did. The intelligence services who believed that
Saddam had WMD had reason on their side, but Mr Blair had
no reason to assert that the intelligence case was beyond doubt,
and propagating unreasonable beliefs is a lot worse than propagating reasonable but wrong ones.

However, just as I am reluctant to dump much moral opprobrium on people who are simply mistaken about something, I am loth to do that even if they are unreasonable in their beliefs. Being unreasonable is a sin, but it surely does not in any way imply dishonesty. So I think for a case to be made against Mr Blair, it has to rest upon a third condition: that he was more concerned to promote his point of view than to relate the whole truth. He was a man on a mission to persuade, and whether he believed the case or not he made no attempt to compromise his assertions with inconvenient truths. It is this characteristic of a hard sell that explains why the Blair case for war is regarded by his many opponents as not just misguided or even badly misguided, but wrong to the point of deceitful.

By way of evidence for the assertion that Mr Blair was more interested in *promoting* the case for war than *setting it out* is the fact that he was guilty of being economical with the truth in his presentation of important evidence. As Chilcot summarised it:

> In the House of Commons on 18 March 2003, Mr Blair stated that he judged the possibility of terrorist groups in possession of WMD was 'a real and present danger to Britain and its national security' – and that the threat from Saddam Hussein's arsenal could not be contained and posed a clear danger to British citizens.
>
> Mr Blair had been warned, however, that military action would increase the threat from Al Qaida to the UK and to UK interests. He had also been warned that an invasion might lead to Iraq's weapons and capabilities being transferred into the hands of terrorists.[36]

Those warnings that had been given to Mr Blair might have been a useful contribution to the national debate, to say the least. He was manipulating public opinion to the extent that he was asking us to make up our minds on the case for war while excluding such relevant information, and while exaggerating the evidence he had in front of him.

Mr Blair used more than one of the tricks of modern communicators to persuade us to support a war. For some of his critics, he was deliberately misleading. For others, though, the important feature underpinning his pitch for the war was that he had misled himself and arrived at a false certainty of the case he was making. That account is quite plausible given how common self-deception in its many forms is, in us all. Of course, we can never know what he truly believed as we'll never be able to read his mind.[37]

But this is an important point on which to end this chapter on mendacity. The sad fact is that there is no sharp line between deception and self-deception, and thus no sensible way to restrict the use of the bullshit tag to those who knowingly dissemble. Most deception is not of the form 'I want you to believe x even though I don't believe x'; it is of the form 'Because I want to believe x, I have come to persuade myself that x is true' or 'Because it suits me for you to believe x, I have come to persuade myself that x is true'. We all have a capacity to believe things that are convenient or financially advantageous for us to believe, or which happen to accord with our belief systems more generally. We all also suffer from confirmation bias, the tendency to spot evidence in support of a proposition that we already think is true. So it is not always the case that people start with a belief and then set out to communicate it; much of the bullshit to which we are exposed comes from folks who have a compelling reason to communicate something and then come to believe it. Or to think they believe it.

The author Ian Leslie takes an extreme view of our ability to self-persuade, arguing that self-deception is an evolved feature of an intelligent species; one that helps us compete and survive.[38] Or as Nassim Nicholas Taleb put it, 'Ethical man accords his profession to his beliefs, instead of according his beliefs to his profession. This has been rarer and rarer since the Middle Ages.'[39]

2

Nonsense and Gibberish

When facts are irrelevant

Who needs facts?

In the last chapter, we looked at several different ways in which modern communicators try to persuade us of stuff. A speaker sets out to advance their own interest by attempting to get us to believe something, even when they know (or ought to know) that they are not offering the whole picture. Their deception is proffered in the hope that any false or biased impression will not be detected. Their words or deeds are meant to be taken at face value, and although the facts may be wrong, or presented in a way that is misleading, or are missing completely or are interpreted in an obviously one-sided manner, the purveyors of a particular point of view have the facts at the forefront of their mind.

But somehow the description of these various forms of calculated mendacity fails to capture the full weight of careless nonsense to which we are exposed every day. When one listens to a politician talking obvious rubbish or making inaccurate claims that are easily debunked, one has to concede that there is a lot more going on than simply their desire to persuade us of facts that are not true. In this supposedly post-truth age, the disregard for facts is as much of a concern as the careful misuse of them.

For example, how are we to react when Donald Trump says that US unemployment is far higher than the official figures indicate? 'Don't believe these phoney numbers when you hear 4.9 and 5 per cent unemployment,' he asserted. 'The number's probably 28, 29, as high as 35. In fact, I even heard recently 42 per cent.'[1] Now, this is a case where he was on to something, just not the literal numbers he was quoting. Just over 30 per cent of fifteen- to sixty-four-year-olds in America are not working, and this might be what Mr Trump was referring to. But this number includes students and those looking after a home or who are carers. You would expect that 'non-working rate' to be in the region of 30 per cent (indeed, in no year of the last five decades has it gone below 25 per cent in the US).[2] But the assertion that the unemployment rate – referring to those wanting to work and deprived of a job – is in the thirties not only contradicts expert opinion, but defies even casual observation. Anyone with the slightest interest in understanding unemployment can see this by looking at the data. No one needs to take Donald Trump's word for it as other more reliable sources of information are readily available.

So the point of Donald Trump's comments was not to persuade us of the truth of something in the way that Bill Clinton wanted to persuade us that he did not have sex with Monica Lewinsky, or in the way that George Osborne wanted us to believe the weather had caused the economy to contract. Instead, it is probably right to say that he was intending to make a serious point (that there is a high level of disguised unemployment, which only shows up in the numbers of adults who are not engaging with the labour market) and that he was trying to do so in a theatrical and memorable way. But he made no attempt at all to fit the argument to the available evidence: the facts were irrelevant to him. Yes, there's a debate to be had about jobless-ness, but the figures of 35 to 42 per cent are not where it would take you.

Such assertions are usually designed to achieve two things: first, they aim to create a favourable impression of the speaker, and secondly, they are used to generate a certain reaction from the listeners. A statement might paradoxically create a favourable impression even when ludicrous, by demonstrating a concern with an issue that matters to the target audience. In offering an exaggerated view of the seriousness of the issue of unemployment, Donald Trump could be signalling his sym-pathy with insecure American workers. Similarly, his speech might simply be designed to elicit a response: it could be about attracting attention; or distracting people from another issue; or it could be aimed at stirring up feelings of tribal loyalty among the economically hard-pressed; or it might be trying to inspire the audience into a dislike of others (for example those experts who don't care enough about ordinary people and who want to hide the true scale of unemployment). In these cases, the specific facts on the table are offered as rhetorical devices rather than information to be absorbed.

For those who talk of a post-truth age, this kind of careless-ness with facts is something of a catastrophe, which has recently landed upon the world. But it is interesting to note that, for many listeners, Donald Trump comes across as more honest than tradi-tional politicians – probably because he doesn't mince his words. The CNN 2016 election exit poll suggested that Trump's honesty ratings were almost the same as Hillary Clinton's.[3] He doesn't shy away from his assertions, he hammers them home. The exaggeration (and consequent cavalier approach to the specifics) is part of that delivery that makes it sound that way. For many, the exact numbers are not that important to the argument anyway.[4]

It is also important to note that this kind of non-factual talk goes back much further than 2016, when the term post-truth suddenly became popular. The distinction between deception and nonsense was first brilliantly drawn back in the 1980s by the American philosopher Harry G. Frankfurt, who published an essay which set out to 'begin the development of a theoretical understanding of bullshit'.[5] It turned into a small book, *On Bullshit* (2005), and its central argument was that the bullshitter is different from both the truth-teller and the liar:

> [He] is neither on the side of the truth nor on the side of the false. His eye is not on the facts at all, as the eyes of the honest man and of the liar are, except insofar as they may be pertinent to his interest in getting away with what he says. He does not care whether the things he says describe reality correctly. He just picks them out, or makes them up, to suit his purpose.
>
> [...] By virtue of this, bullshit is a greater enemy of the truth than lies are.[6]

For Frankfurt, the distinguishing feature of bullshit is its absence of relationship to facts, so for him the common household lie is not really bullshit at all. ('For the essence of bullshit is not that it is *false* but that it is *phony*'.) Personally, I think that on this score his definition of the word is too narrow and I prefer to follow everyday usage, which appears to embrace all forms of mendacity and self-deception as well as pure nonsense. For me, the common feature of the different varieties of bullshit illustrated in both this chapter and the last are that a communicator issues a message that does not aim to give the fullest, clearest and most succinct account of their true and reasonable understanding of a situation. But Frankfurt's narrower definition of bullshit is ahead of its time in capturing some of the silliness of twenty-first-century public discourse.[7]

It has to be said, though, that he got there in the twentieth century because non-factual (or post-factual or *a*factual) discourse was even then so common. And it was never just politicians – populist or otherwise – who were in the habit of spouting this kind of stuff. Every day we meet people who try to sound clever by talking as though they are knowledgeable on a topic. Even if they have their facts straight they are being insincere in the way they deploy them. We hear people trying to sound like they're answering a question when they are avoiding doing so. We sit in meetings enduring pointless waffle from people trying to show that they've done their homework, and we go to the pub and listen to stories that are wildly exaggerated; we hear experts proffer forecasts with spurious precision. All these are examples of everyday communication that is designed to create an impression or to ignite a particular reaction rather than to furnish us with information that is to be taken at face value.

This kind of material can be factually misleading and it may stem from some intent to mislead, but mostly in an indirect kind of way. It is perhaps best labelled *guff*. And there is an awful lot of it, not just in the post-truth age, but throughout history. So for the rest of this chapter we will take a look at three of the different forms in which it comes: the empty assertion in which false statements are made, but which are meant to impress rather than to be taken at face value; obfuscation, where true facts are uttered but are irrelevant to the issue at hand; and gibberish, where little of meaning is said at all.

Empty assertion

Donald Trump's 'unemployment is 30-something per cent' is an example of an empty assertion. It is not only untrue, but it bears little relation to the facts and minimal effort has apparently been made to tie it to the facts at all. And crucially, the facts of the matter are readily available to anyone who wants them.[8] Similarly, Russian officials were making empty assertions when they denied that they were taking military action in Ukraine, at a time when the world could see that Russians dressed in (unmarked) combat gear were obviously deployed there. (The head of the self-declared Donetsk People's Republic, Alexander Zakharchenko, reportedly suggested that while there were serving Russian soldiers among his fighters, they were volunteers who were taking a holiday in the region. 'I'll say it openly, we also have current soldiers, who decided to take their holidays not on the beach, but among us.')[9]

Empty assertions do not realistically purport to provide valuable information, and nor would anyone who thinks about it reasonably expect that they do. But while we are apt to focus on the more extreme examples, this kind of afactual talk is all too common – and has a long and distinguished pedigree. We hear phrases such as 'I have full confidence in the secretary of state' from a prime minister who manifestly has anything but;[10] 'I'm two minutes away' from a cab driver who is going to arrive in ten; or 'It's a charming flat' from an estate agent. Few of us would place much importance on these kinds of comments; at any rate, they are so easily exposed as false that they could not have been uttered in the expectation that they would be believed for long.

Or let's focus on a non-political example that is the corporate equivalent of a Trump speech or a Putin denial. This is an extract from Barclays Bank's Annual Report for 2007. It is drawn from a section in the overall business review entitled Corporate Sustainability.[11]

> In all of this, the customer is absolutely central. If we are to make sustainable banking successful, and successful banking sustainable, we must put our customers at the heart of everything we do, and build our services around them. We must earn – and keep – their trust by ensuring that the products we sell are understandable and appropriate.
>
> This may seem like a statement of the obvious, but the banking sector in general has not always had a reputation for doing this. We want to change that. This aspiration covers every aspect of our business and every stage in a customer's relationship with us, from the purchase of a Barclays product for the first time, to the way we assess applications for loans, to the more general aspects of customer service such as complaints-handling, confidentiality, and security. Focusing more on the customer is also an integral part of what we call 'inclusive banking'.[12]

An important piece of context is necessary here. This was written at a time when the bank was selling vast quantities of payment protection insurance (PPI), which would later cost it billions of pounds in compensation pay-outs to misled clients.[13] It was also selling a more complex loan protection product to small businesses, designed to help them in the event that interest rates went up, but which in fact hurt them when interest rates went down.[14] This was found to have been mis-sold too. Finally, individuals within the bank were manipulating their submissions to the organisation compiling data on market interest rates. In short, it was a period in which the bank was involved in several large scandals.[15]

That all said, what are we to make of the passage in the annual report? It is professionally drafted and well written. The clever line 'If we are to make sustainable banking successful, and successful banking sustainable ...' would be one to be proud of if it related to something authentic about the bank. The self-awareness implied by 'This may seem like a statement of the obvious ...' provides emphasis to statements that might otherwise seem clichéd or banal. It too would be admirable if it authentically related to the behaviour of the bank. And the use of the phrase 'what we call inclusive banking' gives the impression that the sentiments being expressed are so deeply rooted in the bank's psyche that they have developed their own language to describe them. Read all this, and you can only think, boy, these guys really take customers seriously.

These words didn't flop on to the page by accident. These are well-crafted phrases that convey a particular impression. But that impression is not rooted in the actual behaviour of the bank. The report was written by a team of professionals who appear to have thought about what the bank ought to say, rather than what it actually did. The *communication* was presumably important to them, not the authenticity of the message being communicated. Those who wrote it would undoubtedly prefer that it was true, but they were not sufficiently concerned to make sure.[16]

Their drafting might have had some relevance to practice at Barclays if, even though the bank miserably failed to meet its own standards of customer service, it had hit on some niche market insight by identifying customers as important. Maybe the bank at least tried to live up to those words and was distinct from other banks in doing so. In that case, the words would tell us *something* about Barclays' outlook and identity. Alas, a quick glance at the Lloyds Bank Annual Report of the same year

undermines any such claim. Lloyds was also involved in various
of the scandals, but expressed values very similar to those at
Barclays, if not quite as well:

> Our customers are critical to our success. Retaining and
> broadening these relationships and adding new customers
> are a key part of our strategy. This will not be achieved unless
> we are providing a high quality service and products that
> our customers want to buy and which provide good value for
> money. Success has been measured through high levels of
> customer satisfaction and customer advocacy and a strong
> sales performance. It is also measured through external rec-
> ognition and I am pleased to report that our businesses have
> won a number of awards throughout 2007.[17]

It is clear that neither Barclays nor Lloyds were special in their
relationships to customers; they were just producing the ritu-
alistic verbiage that banks produce. They knew what the right
message was; they just didn't live up to it. They were making
empty assertions. The banks' words may sound conventional,
but the words are vacuous all the same.[18]

You might suggest that when I use the phrase 'empty assertion'
I am really just describing a particularly egregious form of lie;
that there is no useful distinction to be drawn between the banks'
claims about customers, or the Russians' claims about troops, or
any of Donald Trump's crazier pronouncements and the extreme
lies of Ian Huntley or the (very) near-lies of Bill Clinton. They are
all self-serving and factually incorrect. In every case, they want
you to believe what they are telling you. Harry Frankfurt spoke
of bullshit as being phoney rather than false, but is any sentence
capable of being one without being the other?

Well, any boundary between a falsehood and an empty

assertion is inevitably fuzzy, and we can argue about whether a particular example should sit on one side of the line or the other, but the distinction is still there and it all comes down to whether facts are important in the way the assertion is constructed. Ian Huntley had carefully formulated a story to be consistent with the facts that were known to the police in the unlikely hope of persuading the court that his intentions were innocent. In contrast, the verbiage in the banks' annual reports appears not to have been put together with any care to the facts at all. Nor, indeed, were Donald Trump's claims about unemployment. And in Ian Huntley trying to give an account of events that we could never independently verify (as we were not there and he was), he was trying to exploit his information advantage over us. Barclays and Lloyds didn't really have any privileged information about customer service; we are able to observe their performance ourselves, or to read independent reviews of it. We are entitled to form our own view, whatever they might say. Their efforts are a nudge towards an opinion they might like us to hold, but not a push. There is a certain transparency here that is lacking in most cases of mendacity.

A second difference between the lie and the empty assertion is in the intended effect. Liars really want us to believe the statements they make, and that's why they make them. But the empty asserter is different. It matters less that the statement is believed at face value, than that it is seen to be made. When banks draft their annual reports, is it not clear that the most respectable among them have a section on customer service? For a bank to appear respectable, it had better follow that norm. We, the readers, will have our own views about the reality of their customer service, but it would appear odd, would it not, for them to say nothing about it?

There is one other important difference between some of the

more outlandish empty assertions and good old-fashioned lies: it is in how best to respond to them. You can argue with a liar with the goal of exposing their attempt at deception. But can you seriously argue about facts with someone who shows no interest in adhering to them in the first place? How can you ever persuade Mr Trump that unemployment in the US is *not* 30-something per cent? Apart from politely pointing out that he is wrong, why bother getting involved in the detail of it? Painstakingly explaining the methods used by the Bureau of Labor Statistics, generously conceding that there are problems with unemployment data while suggesting they provide a reasonably good guide to what is going on – it's all wasted breath. If Mr Trump had wanted to know any of that he would have looked it up. All that is achieved by arguing with an exaggerated proposition is a strengthening of the very effect that was the goal of spouting the nonsense in the first place. If Mr Trump says outlandish things in order to draw attention to himself, by arguing with him you simply give him more attention. If in this case he wanted to show that he has a truer understanding of the real economic plight of ordinary Americans than other politicians, then by contradicting him his opponents would simply make it look like they were trying to downplay the insecurity and hardship that some families endure.

It is a real dilemma as to how the fact-conscious person should handle the afactual assertion. To allow wild propositions to stand unchallenged is to acquiesce to the transformation by which untruth becomes conventional wisdom. Of this there is no doubt; the only issue is whether rational argument about the facts is the most effective defence against nonsense.[19] Try arguing with someone who believes in a conspiracy about 9/11: it doesn't get you far. If your goal is to stop people believing things that are plainly silly then your best strategy is to ask why they are disposed to such belief in the first place, and then to attempt to deal with the cause. If people want to believe Donald Trump in his assertion that unemployment is 30 per cent, don't argue with the 30 per cent; ask why they want to believe it. The likely answer is that they think the kind of job insecurity they face has been overlooked and they harbour a hope that more attention will be paid to it.[20] The way to get them to see sense on the literal facts is to have something useful to say about that underlying concern. I will return to this point later on.

Obfuscation

There is a second category of afactual bullshit that is like the first in that it is deployed in order to give an impression, rather than to be taken literally. It is the art of obfuscation. Sometimes you have good reason to say nothing, but you don't want to say that you are keen to say nothing so you say something, but you say something which says nothing. This can be seen as the practice of the crooked and shady, but, like the empty assertion, obfuscation has a perfectly respectable lineage. Quite a few examples come up in diplomacy where countries are keen to park unresolvable issues that linger between them while making progress on other things. They don't want to stress their persisting differences, but nor can they dismiss them.

Here's a notable example: a section of the Shanghai Communiqué of 1972, released by the Chinese and Americans after President Nixon launched his so-called ping-pong diplomacy, and established relations with the communist People's Republic. The stickiest problem, apart from the obvious ideological antipathy, was the status of Taiwan, which had historically been part of China but had been resolutely independent since the revolution on the mainland and showed no inclination to

reunite with its former parent.* Its independence was not recognised by the People's Republic but had enthusiastic support
in the US, which did recognise Taiwan as a sovereign nation. It
was a problem for both nations: China was very upfront about
its concerns while America needed to steer a fine course between
the new, big friend it now wanted to make and the old, small
friend that it still supported. How do you resolve this diplomat-
ically? Here's the key line from the joint communiqué on the
matter:

> The United States acknowledges that all Chinese on either
> side of the Taiwan Strait maintain there is but one China and
> that Taiwan is a part of China. The United States Government
> does not challenge that position. It reaffirms its interest in a
> peaceful settlement of the Taiwan question by the Chinese
> themselves.[21]

It is a beautifully drafted line: *there is but one China and that
Taiwan is a part of China*. Everyone could agree on that, even if
they couldn't agree on which of the two Chinas was the legitimate one. No need to argue about that now ... let's just move on.
If the communiqué had wanted to be more honest, it might have
read, 'This issue remains unresolved, the US can't yield to the
Chinese view just yet, but it doesn't want it to get in the way.'[22]

The careful drafting would not have fooled anyone into
thinking anything other than this, but there was felt to be
advantage to setting it out in a way that was fudged rather than

---

* Taiwan was largely part of Qing dynasty China from the seventeenth century
onwards. It was held by Japan from 1895 to 1945, at which point the Republic of China
took it back. The ROC regime (at the time led by Chiang Kai-shek) fled to Taiwan
in 1949 following the revolution on the mainland, from where it continued to claim
sovereignty over the mainland until democratic reforms led to renunciation in 1992.

explicit. Henry Kissinger, Secretary of State at the time, was said to have coined the phrase 'constructive ambiguity' in relation to the Shanghai Communiqué.[23] Constructive ambiguity is a technique that is used all the time. Take Hillary Clinton's view on the domain of the Israeli state, as expressed in a 2007 pamphlet called *Hillary Clinton – a long history of strong and steadfast leadership for the US-Israel Relationship*.[24] It said, 'Hillary Clinton believes that Israel's right to exist in safety as a Jewish state, with defensible borders and an undivided Jerusalem as its capital, secure from violence and terrorism, must never be questioned.' The 2008 Democratic Party platform had a more ambivalent formulation, but one entirely consistent with Mrs Clinton's earlier version: 'Jerusalem is and will remain the capital of Israel. The parties have agreed that Jerusalem is a matter for final status negotiations. It should remain an undivided city accessible to people of all faiths.'[25] I would not want to argue that these pronouncements are meaningless guff, but they are designed to give an impression of support for Israel while at the same time not taking sides in the long-running dispute between Israel and the Palestinians over the status of East Jerusalem.*

One of the most famous UK examples of obfuscation was a television interview with a Home Secretary, Michael Howard (now Lord Howard of Lympne), who had been accused of threatening to overrule the official in charge of prisons. To have actually overruled him would have been beyond the power of the Home Secretary, and Mr Howard had not done that, but there was still an interesting question as to whether the *threat*

---

* There are plenty of examples of constructive ambiguity in diplomacy. The UN Security Council Resolution 242 omitted a definite article 'the' in requiring Israel to withdraw from 'territories occupied in recent conflict', leaving open the issue as to whether that means all or some territories.

had been made. Mr Howard was obviously reluctant to address this issue. Here is the core of that exchange:

Jeremy Paxman: Did you threaten to overrule him?

Michael Howard: I was not entitled to instruct Derek Lewis and I did not instruct him.

Paxman: Did you threaten to overrule him?

Howard: The truth of the matter is that Mr Marriot was not suspended—

Paxman: Did you threaten to overrule him?

Howard: I did not overrule Derek Lewis—

Paxman: Did you threaten to overrule him?

Howard: —I took advice on what I could or could not do—

Paxman: Did you threaten to overrule him?

Howard: —and acted scrupulously in accordance with that advice. I did not overrule Derek Lewis—

Paxman: Did you threaten to overrule him?

Howard: —Mr Marriot would not suspend him—

Paxman: Did you threaten to overrule him?

Howard: I have accounted for my decision to dismiss Derek Lewis—

Paxman: Did you threaten to overrule him?

Howard: —in great detail before the House of Commons—

Paxman: I note that you're not answering the question whether you threatened to overrule him.

Howard: Well, the important aspect of this which it's very clear to bear in mind—

Paxman: I'm sorry, I'm going to be frightfully rude but – I'm sorry – it's a straight yes-or-no question and a straight yes-or-no answer: did you threaten to overrule him?

Howard: I discussed the matter with Derek Lewis. I gave him the benefit of my opinion. I gave him the benefit of my

opinion in strong language, but I did not instruct him
because I was not entitled to instruct him. I was entitled
to express my opinion and that is what I did.

Paxman: With respect, that is not answering the question of
whether you threatened to overrule him.

Howard: It's dealing with the relevant point which was what
I was entitled to do and what I was not entitled to do,
and I have dealt with this in detail before the House of
Commons and before the select committee.

Paxman: But with respect you haven't answered the question
of whether you threatened to overrule him.

Howard: Well, you see, the question is . . .[26]

Note the contrast to empty assertion: the facts that are stated
are true; it is just that they are irrelevant. The basic feature of
obfuscation is to avoid a question while looking as though you
are answering it, through the technique of saying things that are
on the subject at hand but which have no bearing on the actual
issue. You talk confidently towards the topic but away from the
question.

As with the empty assertion, you can't argue with obfuscation; you can simply do what Jeremy Paxman did on that
occasion and point out that it is occurring. But as that exchange
illustrates, it is sometimes challenging to do even that, because
the obfuscator will generally deny they have not answered the
question and repeat their same line of irrelevant waffle as proof
of how clear they are being.

In the public mind, this is one kind of discourse that has
given politics a bad name – we've all heard the refrain 'they
always refuse to answer the question'. So how harshly should
we judge those who avoid answering? Is it ever reasonable to
decline to answer a question? In my view it can be, and in that

sense obfuscation is sometimes justified. I know that television interviewers are not meant to admit this, but politicians are right to think that sometimes, if they concede a valid point (as the Governor of the Bank of England did in the example in Chapter 1), a disproportionate amount of media hysteria will ensue and so it is better to say nothing. Or, sometimes they might want to make a point and not distract from their own message by answering someone else's question on a different point. To see how things can go wrong if you are too forth-coming and lack the power to bullshit, take the example of the Labour Party leader Jeremy Corbyn in January 2017. He set out to do a series of media interviews about the party's position on Brexit. But in one of them, he was asked by John Humphrys about his views on a different issue: the extraordinarily high salaries of some in finance or business, so-called fat-cat pay. Mr Corbyn had not gone on to the *Today* programme to talk on that subject, but couldn't bring himself to obfuscate, so he gave an honest account of his views:

Humphrys: Would you do anything about their earnings?
Corbyn: I would like there to be some kind of high earnings
    cap quite honestly, because what we're having in Britain . . .
Humphrys: Where?
Corbyn: I can't put a figure on it and I don't want to.
Humphrys: You must have some idea. I mean . . . a million?
Corbyn: No, I don't want to at the moment.
Humphrys: Two million? Three million?
Corbyn: The point . . . the point I'm trying to make and it's
    something you alluded to in your question is that we
    have the worst levels of income disparity of most of the
    OECD countries in this country. It's getting worse and
    corporate taxation is a part of it. If we want to live in a

more egalitarian society and fund our public services
we cannot go on creating worse levels of inequality and
lower levels of . . .

Humphrys: Right, there should be a law to limit income,
quite simply.

Corbyn: I think let's look at it. I am not wedded to—

Humphrys: But you've got a view on it.

Corbyn: I've got a view on it and I'm not wedded—

Humphrys: Well tell us what it is.

Corbyn: I'm not wedded to a figure on it. What I want to see
is—

Humphrys: All right, forget the figure: a law to limit
maximum—

Corbyn: I would like to see a maximum earnings limit, quite
honestly, because I think that would be a fairer thing to
do; because we cannot set ourselves us up as being a sort
of grossly unequal bargain-basement economy on the
shores of Europe.[27]

Now as you read this (or listen to it) it becomes clear that
Mr Corbyn had not fixed his thoughts on the subject of fat-
cat pay. Indeed, he tried to downplay his own views by twice
saying 'I'm not wedded'. It was clear that he was ad-libbing,
rather than announcing a settled party policy, and was only
speaking in answer to questions. But it was also true that what
he was suggesting in his answers was far more interesting than
anything he had come on to talk about. So it was these answers
that made headlines.[28] His vague pronouncement ('I would like
to see a maximum earnings limit, quite honestly') was quickly
elevated to the status of an important policy announcement or
'pledge'.[29] Through the day he had to answer questions on his
new policy (and he was rowing back on it by the afternoon).

Had he wanted this issue to get attention that day, he would
have done better to have worked out his line more clearly in the
first place; having not done that, he should probably have just
avoided talking about it at all. So in this case, his straightforward
answers got in the way of his perfectly legitimate aim to make
a point about Brexit. Obfuscation might have served him well
on this occasion.

But even conceding that it is sometimes reasonable to not
answer a question, there is a subsidiary issue as to how you
should go about that. If you want to say nothing, why not spell
out your reasons for saying nothing rather than trying to pretend
that you are being informative? Why is it so often deemed to be
more attractive to look evasive – in the style of Michael Howard,
above – than to explicitly say, 'It was a private conversation and
I'm not going to answer that question'? Or, even better, a truthful
answer along the lines of 'It was two years ago, and it has been
trawled over extensively; I've chosen my words on this subject
carefully and I don't intend to add to them today.' What would
have been lost by doing that? Any normal person paying attention
to that particular interview would have spotted that Howard was
not going to answer the question, and indeed I think most would
also have surmised that the reason he did not want to answer
it was because he in fact *did* threaten to overrule Mr Lewis.
It is hard to see what was gained by the attempt to divert our
attention.* And in Mr Corbyn's case, he could have avoided the
question from John Humphrys without an obfuscating answer,

* In fairness to Michael Howard, the interview took place at the end of a day in
which he had been campaigning for the leadership of his party. Lord Howard told
me that 'I didn't want to commit myself to anything without clearing my mind,
which was not possible in the context of the interview. It was not as though I was
being interviewed on a subject in the news which I would have thought about and
prepared for.'

by saying 'I'll have more to say on fat-cat pay another day, but right now I want to talk about Brexit.' This kind of honest deflection is far more appealing than opaque obfuscation.

Gibberish and gratuitously complex language

The words used by Michael Howard to obfuscate have a clear meaning. He was making a point, even if it was not relevant to the question asked. But take a look at the following paragraph. This was literally the first entry I obtained on searching the web for the words 'wine review'; it happened to be top of the recent posts on winemag.com. It's describing a Pinot Noir.

> Structured, with years to go to take on added complexity and personality, this wine is also a study in immediate gratification, as it's presently so juicy and easy to enjoy. It comes from an east-facing block, planted to a suitcase clone. Exotic, rich red and black berry and cinnamon form an alliance of balance and mouthwatering seduction. The oak and tannin are fully in sync, while a salty, meaty finish provides additional decadence.[30]

I don't think this a particularly exceptional example of a wine review, but I include it in this survey of different forms of bullshit because I find myself doubting that one can take it too literally. Could anyone really sense the combination of *seven* flavours mentioned: red berry, black berry, cinnamon, oak, tannin, salt and meat – let alone assert that they are in sync?[31] I'm no expert, but I find it hard to know what the words 'structured', 'complexity' and 'personality' really mean in this context (what is an unstructured wine?). And would wine experts be able to distinguish a 'juicy' wine from a 'non-juicy' one in a blind test?

It sounds harsh, but I label this kind of writing gibberish because the value of the review does not lie in the truth or falsity of the assertions contained therein. But I do not use the word gibberish in any disparagement to the writer; this is good gibberish, because I think for the intended readers the material is well-devised. The review does indirectly carry useful information (that the writer clearly likes this wine) and we get the intended message that it is exotic and rich, rather than sharp and light. Perhaps as importantly, we can see that the writer knows a thing or two about wine. A complete novice trying to pass themselves off as a wine writer would struggle to produce a review like that, if only because they would not know what palate of potential flavours was there to be highlighted. However, the review is gibberish in the sense that the subjective propositions it contains lack specific enough meaning to agree or disagree with.

Wine is particularly prone to this kind of prose. The writer Pamela Vandyke Price complained to *Private Eye* that 'Every time I describe a wine as anything other than red or white, dry or wet, I wind up in Pseuds' Corner', referring to the magazine's regular compilation of hilariously pretentious material.[32] But this is not exclusively a wine thing: I could probably have found similar combinations of non-factual material from the world of fashion or reviews of cars. And you'll find plenty of this kind of thing at the average business conference, or the World Economic Forum at Davos (for example, the comment from the then Italian Prime Minister Matteo Renzi, 'I am not here to present a future of tomorrow. For my country, the future is today, not tomorrow').[33] It is common among those who write about business to set out propositions that purport to have practical value, but which on closer examination appear more like tautology or gobbledygook.

The practice of lacing prose with supposed facts that actually lack meaning is but one case of a more general habit of writing text superfluous to the goal of relaying information. I would say that showing off by using complex words – even if they are correctly applied and truthfully used – is a form of bullshit. Hiding a message by diluting it in euphemistic terms is also a form of bullshit. And waffle, the addition of extra text to make it look as though your message is more substantial than it really is – well, that too is bullshit.

Obviously, I wouldn't argue that every time extra words are inserted into a sentence we should automatically deride it. For a start, that would be to dismiss much poetry which uses superfluous or flowery language to good effect; and I would not want to argue that all forms of verbosity are necessarily bad. It is the *intention* of the communicator that often matters in determining the category that applies. Is the communication in any way designed to portray something as less than it is, or more than it is? If so, it is probably bad bullshit rather than good.

The gibberish in this section, and the other two categories of 'beyond factual' material that have been set out in this chapter do not cover all the nonsense that is spoken. There is plenty of ridiculous rhetoric that falls into none of these categories and yet which inspires or hurts or questions without any sort of fact near by (for example, take the line 'who's going to pay for the wall?'[34]). But the three categories I've outlined are all interestingly distinct from the five forms of mendacity in Chapter 1 in that their nature is readily apparent to anyone who cares to notice it. Their transparency gives rise to one of the mysteries of modern communication: why peddle this stuff if we can all see through it? One of our tasks over the next few chapters is to ask what purpose does this kind of material serve. What information content lies therein? How does it have the power to persuade if it is manifestly unconvincing or not to be taken literally? That is for later in the book.

But if the taxonomy in these first two chapters has achieved nothing else, it should have demonstrated that bullshit comes in multiple shapes and sizes; some bad, some ugly, and some even potentially rather good. And that is before we have started on Chapter 3, which now introduces the broadest concept of bullshit of all.

3

Gestures and Phoney Behaviour

Bullshit in the form of action, not words

A message in physical form

Words are very useful. Either spoken or written, they are easy to deploy, so it is no wonder that they are our preferred means of communicating with each other. Unfortunately, the very convenience of language makes it suitable not just for transmitting information, but for transmitting false information as well. When it comes to bullshit, speech and text are the default delivery vehicles and the talk of a post-truth era tends to focus on the things people say and write. However, communication can come in other forms as well: in particular, we are able to take an action in order to send a message. And as with all messages, those actions can sometimes be phoney.

A good old-fashioned legend illustrates the point perfectly: the tale of Dame Carcas and the magnificent southern French city of Carcassonne. Anyone who has been there knows its most important sight is the medieval fortress. But the city had been recognised as strategically important right back in Roman times, sitting as it does on a hill between the Mediterranean Sea and the Atlantic Ocean. The legend of the city goes back to the battles between Muslims and Christians in the eighth century. According to the story, Carcassonne was occupied by Saracen forces and was under siege for five years by the Emperor Charlemagne, who wanted it for the Christian Franks. Charlemagne would never be able to overcome the fortifications, but he could starve the city into submission.

Dame Carcas was a Saracen princess who had ruled since the death of her husband. She tried everything to deter Charlemagne's forces and to give the impression that the siege was failing to have much effect. As things were getting very grim and food was running out, she thought of a clever wheeze. She collected all the food that was left; the sum total was a pig and a sack of wheat, which would clearly not last long. Dame Carcas's idea was to send a signal to Charlemagne that he was wasting his time. So she fed the wheat to the pig and threw it out of the castle.[1]

When Charlemagne saw that the Saracens had so much food they could afford to feed grain to their pigs, he withdrew his forces and gave up the siege. Dame Carcas asked for the bells to be rung in celebration, hence the name Carcassonne (from *sonner*, 'to ring'). She then called on Charlemagne to make peace and they all lived happily ever after. A bust of Dame Carcas sits at one of the gates of Carcassonne, to welcome tourists to the fortified city today.

This is, in every sense, bullshit. The name goes back to the Romans, who called their outpost Julia Carcaso, later Carcasum.[2] And Charlemagne would probably not have besieged the city for five years as his father had already taken it in the 750s, when Charlemagne was a teenager.[3] But don't let the fact the story is apocryphal spoil it for you. What it shows is how actions can be used to send a message without a word being spoken. And in this case, the message being sent was pure bullshit too. There was no food left; the stuffed pig was a bluff.

Let's be clear at the outset as to what I mean when I say actions can be used to send messages: this means *doing something* in order *to say something.* This is not the same as *doing something for some other reason* and in the process incidentally *revealing something.* If I pledge fidelity to my partner but constantly have affairs with other people, my actions in having lots of affairs are not designed to send a message of any sort; they are designed to satisfy my sexual gratification. Those actions do suggest that my words are false and that I'm not a faithful kind of guy, but that revelation is a by-product of my action, not the purpose. In this case my actions speak louder than my words, because my actions reveal my true feelings. We can call my affairs *real* actions.

The Carcassonne legend is quite different, being a case where the action (of throwing a stuffed pig out the castle) was not real, but manufactured precisely to say something. It was not designed to achieve a substantive result other than through its ability to communicate a message to the other side. A parallel example would be to have an affair not for sexual gratification at all, but simply in order to send a message to your other half. Maybe you want to make them jealous, or show that you are still attractive to other people and have other relationship choices. That would be a manufactured affair, not a real one. (And in this case you would have to ensure your action was discovered or it would serve no purpose, unlike with a real affair, where you are simply being unfaithful for the usual reasons.)

Of course, none of this is to deny that you can have more than one motive for your actions. You might be having an affair in part because it suits you, but also in order to send a signal.

Actions can be a mix of the real and the manufactured. For our purposes, though, an action can be thought of as a form of communication if it is at least partially shaped by a desire to send a message of some form.

Manufactured behaviour in practice

You would think that in life we usually do things in order to get them done, but a surprisingly large amount of personal and public time is devoted to message-sending. Everyday examples are not often as extreme or as brazen as stuffing pigs with wheat, but to take a trivial case, when we smile for a photograph we are adopting a certain affectation in order to uphold an impression of our state of mind at the time. The smile is adopted because of what it says about us, rather than because it reflects how we feel. Many smiles are fairly neutral, but we have all seen particularly forced smiles in photos, which definitely qualify as A-grade bullshit. Why do we smile? It is not obvious; it wasn't the convention until Edwardian times; and it isn't the norm in cool photographs of rock stars.[4] But for most of us, it's all smiles. In fact, photographers have even reported that the habit is so well entrenched that they have had to force people in unfortunate circumstances to ditch the smile and pose with a melancholy face.[5]

Smiling is just one small example of keeping up appearances, to which most of us devote a good deal of attention. We are keen to display success; the smile expresses contentment; posting a selfie of you with friends in St Mark's Square, or a photo of your bungee jump, does the same – as indeed does make-up or cosmetic surgery. And as you reflect on it, you'll realise that many things we do are about appearing strong and happy. Just about every bit of ostentatious consumption is aimed that way, from the way we clean the house before guests come round, to the display of Christmas decorations. Status matters to us, and we generally seem to believe that we gain it by projecting confidence and material wealth. Of course, one doesn't want to say that everything we do – from styling our hair to dressing up for a wedding – is bullshit; just because we send a message through our behaviour it does not mean we are being phoney. But a lot of our actions are designed to flatter, if not to lie. And in our own minds, we are often barely aware of what is real and what is contrived.

So much for our personal lives. In public discourse, measures equivalent to stuffing a pig with grain are frequently taken. In fact, if you start looking for them you'll find you never stop. From writers filling their books with endnotes to make them look well-researched[6] to fancy packaging to marble-lined offices. All of these are trying to say something, and may or may not be genuine signals.

Perhaps the most significant areas are in the corporate and political sphere. For example, the reason why companies have corporate social responsibility (CSR) programmes is at least in part to project a certain image to staff and customers. That image may be a genuine reflection of the spirit of the business, but often it is simply bolted on to the company to look good. The Enron Corporation, before it imploded in 2001 and various of its senior management were convicted of fraud or similar offences, had a generous CSR programme and won awards for its good work. It is no wonder that there is a degree of cynicism about the whole notion of CSR.[7]

Similarly, in politics, the need to make a gesture can distort policy. You will hear public officials utter the words that it is 'important to send a signal to the public',[8] which can often imply one of two things. Either that other attempts to justify a bad policy have failed to convince, and this is the last possible reason for adopting it. Or that the politicians want to persuade the public that they care about an issue, but fear that words lack the credibility to express their good intent. The only way to do it is to raise the stakes by being seen to do something, even if it is regarded as useless. This can make the resulting policy bullshit.[9]

Of course, in many cases there is no clear-cut distinction between a policy designed to send a signal and a substantive action. It has been posited that the British government's adherence to the UN's target for rich countries to devote 0.7 per cent of national income to overseas development aid is an expensive form of virtue signalling,[10] but supporters of the aid budget clearly see it as a good thing, regardless of any supplementary PR benefits. You would have to know the sincere intention of those responsible for the policy to really understand the motivation. However, there are cases that are more straightforward, and where an action is taken for what can only be described as communications purposes. Let's take a couple of UK examples.

A fashionable method of sending a signal is to enshrine a policy target in legislation on the grounds that this makes the target look serious. The goal of cutting greenhouse gas emissions was put into the Climate Change Act 2008;[11] the ambition of eradicating child poverty was put into the Child Poverty Act 2010.[12] Numerous acts have also been passed to provide for budget responsibility, with specific borrowing limits written into them.

But does the passing of a law to express a target really allow the voter to distinguish between a government that genuinely cares about child poverty or climate change and one that does not? If the government can simply change the law when it looks like the target will not be met, then surely the law tells us nothing. The government can pass a law committing itself to motherhood and apple pie, and then repeal it when the apple pie and the mother become inconvenient. And in practice, of course, laws enshrining targets have been repealed without much ado when the targets have become difficult to hit. A target to reduce 'fuel poverty' was put into the Warm Homes and Energy Conservation Act 2000. The Act required the Secretary of State to have a strategy to ensure that 'as far as reasonably practicable persons do not live in fuel poverty'. By law, the plan had to be produced within one year, and had to 'specify a target date for achieving the objective'; '[the] target date specified ... must be not more than fifteen years after the date on which the strategy is published'. So, after the law was passed, a strategy was duly produced, with a target to eradicate fuel poverty by 2016.[13]

Unfortunately, the number in fuel poverty rose between 2004 and 2010 (mainly as a result of high energy prices) and the target began to look hopeless. So what was the outcome? Did the government take extreme measures to make sure the target was met? Did it throw money at the poor or subsidise their fuel bills – both measures that were quite practical, had anyone been minded to adopt them? No, of course not. Under a new government, there was a review of the old approach and there then emerged a new fuel poverty definition, and a new target for 2030.[14] The fact that the new target could be seen as representing a failure of the old one was overlooked; it was instead an opportunity to rejoice in the government's dedication to dealing with fuel poverty. The Department of Energy and Climate Change press release spelt it out in positive terms:

> Future governments will be required by law to help fight fuel poverty by making the coldest, leakiest homes in England more energy efficient. Tackling this problem is a priority for government.[15]

Yes, the law will compel government to insulate homes and deal with fuel poverty. Even though the same law had just failed to require past governments to sort the problem out. So the law as originally conceived turned out not to be a genuine signal of commitment. The target might as well have been pursued without a law at all.[16]

Equally, I could offer the sorry history of the reduced income tax band as an example of phoney message-sending. For the vast bulk of UK taxpayers, income tax is normally marvellously simple. You pay no tax on the first few thousand pounds of annual income, then you pay the basic rate of tax on the rest. Governments know that, all things being equal, people generally prefer taxes to be lower rather than higher. Unfortunately, cutting the basic rate of tax is expensive and the vagaries of economic life imply that some governments are unable to demonstrate their tax-cutting instincts by actually cutting taxes in a very significant way. So on various occasions a reduced-rate band has been the chosen device to demonstrate tax-cutting intent.

The reduced rate complicates an otherwise simple system: as before, you pay no tax on the first slice of your income, but then you pay the reduced rate for the next portion, before the basic rate kicks in as normal. So there are two tax rates rather than one. There is only one problem with the policy: there is no advantage whatsoever in adding a new lower rate of tax that would not be achieved by simply extending the tax-free slice of income. The vast bulk of taxpayers will still be paying the basic rate of tax on most of their income. For example, a government wanting to make a small income-tax cut could introduce a reduced rate by halving the basic rate of tax on, say, £2000 of income. But that is an identical giveaway to imposing a zero rate of tax on an extra £1000 of income. All that has been achieved with the reduced rate is an extra complication in the tax system. As the reputable independent think tank the Institute for Fiscal Studies summarised it,

> An alternative policy to achieve such a tax cut – increasing tax allowances – produces similar, though slightly more progressive, distributional results and avoids any administrative problems.[17]

So why would any government introduce a reduced rate? The answer is that, in return for undermining the simplicity and transparency of the tax system, there are some notable presentational advantages. The reduced rate focuses public attention on the number attached to the lower rate. If the basic rate is 23 per cent, being able to stand and talk about a 10 per cent rate is especially impressive. It can sound like the government is really making tax-cutting progress, without actually damaging the revenue base. You can also exploit people's confusion about tax by convincing them it is aimed at the low-paid, when it in fact helps everybody on basic rate tax in exactly the same way.

The stunt is so seductive it has been tried several times. It was first introduced in 1978 as a reduced 25 per cent band, only to be abolished in 1980. The Conservative Chancellor at the time said,

> The case for the lower rate band was never at all clear ... For those on lower incomes an increase in the personal allowances would always have been more valuable than the lower rate band, and the existence of this lower rate band added significantly to the complexity of the tax system.[18]

But a new 20 per cent lower rate was introduced by the same party in 1992, and that was then reinvented by Labour in 1999 as a new 10 per cent band. The then Chancellor Gordon Brown said of the idea's third incarnation:

> The 10p rate is very important because it's a signal about the importance we attach about getting people into work and it's of most importance to the low paid. This is not about gimmicks; this is about tax reform that encourages work and families.[19]

He announced the abolition of the 10p rate in 2007.[20] It had always been designed to skew the impression of the burden of taxes in the country – it was in that sense, pure gesture. During the era of the 10p tax rate it was pointed out that political spin had been taken to a whole new level: in the good old days, it was said, politicians used to try to put a good spin on their bad policies. In this new era, politicians would introduce bad policies simply because they lent themselves to good spin.

Once you have clocked the tendency for politicians to do things, sometimes simply in order to be seen to be doing something rather than to be actually doing it, you notice that bullshit behaviour is everywhere. In fact, we can often explain behaviour that looks dysfunctional by reference to the sending of signals, phoney or otherwise. Competing supermarkets know that many of us are inclined to compare the prices we have to pay at different outlets by only looking at the charges on a handful of frequently purchased items; that explains why they are more likely to trim their margin on milk than they are on canned rice pudding.[21] Hidden charges are another form of the same thing: we judge the cost of a product on the headline price, so the headline price will be kept low while extra charges push the actual price up (for example, in buying cars there is often an extra price of several hundred pounds for metallic paint, with only one choice of non-metallic paint colour at the quoted price). And then there are the up-front prices versus the ongoing charges. Teaser mortgage rates that become expensive later, cheap printers with expensive cartridges and cheap razors with expensive blades are all examples of the same thing: behaviour distorted by a desire to send a message.[22]

The ubiquity of bullshit behaviour

All these phoney signals work in the same way. The manufactured action is designed to imitate a real action, in the hope that we will interpret it as meaningful. By keeping a headline price low, the hope is that we assume that the overall price is low. By passing a law expressing concern about fuel poverty, the hope is that we assume this is more than an empty gesture. But this blurring of the perceived boundary between real and contrived behaviour relies on us, the ones being fooled by it, to be foolish in the way we judge what is real and what is contrived. And as it happens, we are pretty easy to manipulate in this regard. We tend to make important judgements on the basis of a few key indicators, and so by manoeuvring those indicators our perception can be controlled. We tend to assume certain things go together, so we allow ourselves to assume that when we see one of those things the other is attached. We think that good magazines have good covers, so when we observe a good cover we infer that the magazine underneath will be worth buying. As long as editors understand this rule of thumb, then you can expect inordinate effort to go into the design of the cover, even to the possible detriment of the rest of the magazine. As long as we come to a judgement based on only a selection of the available evidence, canny communicators will have a disproportionate impact on our thinking by being selective in the evidence they put forward. They spot where our eyes are disposed to look, and then they put their efforts into making those bits look particularly attractive.

Another way of expressing this is to say that most of us make broad judgements on the basis of narrow signals, thus encouraging those who want to impress us to invest in polishing up the things that are noticed. This explains a lot of what we see and hear around us, including phenomena that one might not even recognise as direct attempts to communicate or persuade. In design, it explains why hotel lobbies are often more lavishly decorated than the rooms upstairs. The signal sent out by the lobby is more cognitively accessible than the information about the rooms, and so more weight is put on it by passing customers. In accountancy, it explains why companies might strive to put certain items (for example, the cost of the management's stock options) into the footnotes of their accounts; it allows them to say they have disclosed everything, while hoping that some readers of the accounts will focus on the main published profit number to the exclusion of the detail in the footnotes. And in showbiz, it explains why celebrities get free invitations to premieres and red-carpet events: their presence attracts the attention that event organisers crave.

It even explains why a propaganda-obsessed nation like the old German Democratic Republic made such a large and grotesque effort to win medals in Olympic sports. The country could not compete in economic terms with West Germany because it didn't have an economic system that worked very well, but it knew that in framing judgements about the overall success of nations, we tend to pay disproportionate attention to sporting success.[23]

It also explains why you probably know more about the Spanish city of Bilbao, with its famous showpiece, the Frank

Gehry-designed Guggenheim Museum, than you do about the bigger city of Valencia; or why you probably have a clearer image of St Louis, with its famous arch, than you do of Kansas City, 250 miles away. Those of us who know very little about these cities tend to create a mental picture based not on a view of their urban environment, but on the architectural icons within them.

It's worth saying that a decision to focus effort on features that are noticed rather than ones that really matter can be seen as a kind of flashiness; the effort is all about the show rather than reality. The company that puts its effort into marketing rather than product quality, or the individual on a low income who tries to impress the neighbours with an unaffordably smart car, are part of this phenomenon. You might also see a call for a more honest and less bullshit-ridden public discourse as similar to a quest for a society less superficial, less ostentatious and somehow more solid.

But this discussion poses a question. These messages work because the audiences to whom they are directed use a limited amount of data to draw their conclusions. You might say we get what we deserve: if we judge products by the quality of their packaging, we shouldn't be surprised if companies make the packaging lovely but leave the products grotty; if we always choose large red strawberries on the supermarket shelf, we shouldn't be surprised if the strawberries are bred to look large and red even if they have no flavour. The information we are fed is largely based on the information we choose to consume. So the key question is, why do we allow ourselves to be fooled by this kind of thing? Are we suckers or what?

We will look at some of the reasons that bullshit survives in an age of relative enlightenment shortly, but before we do, we should think more about the nature of all the mendacity, insincerity and fakery set out in these first three chapters, and work out when an action is a genuine signal rather than a phoney one. And to enlighten us, we turn now to the masters of bullshit: academic economists.

Bullshit: The Theory

Cheap talk versus expensive signals

The role of economics

Having looked at practical examples of the kind of nonsense that is often generated, in this chapter we'll move on to some theory. It turns out that there is a huge corpus of academic literature on when something should be believed and when it should immediately be disregarded. It has even been modelled mathematically. This literature sets out what it is that characterises much of the bullshit we've been talking about.

In fact, you may be surprised to hear that communication and the information it conveys has been at the centre of a revolution in the thinking of economists over the past fifty years. They have come to understand that information and ignorance play a bigger part in the workings of our economic system than anyone realised. This study of the 'economics of information' has led to big changes in the subject, and yet non-economists have rarely heard much about it. The new thinking has allowed economists to explain many observed phenomena in the real world that had previously been a mystery to them. You may think economists are a group who produce copious amounts of bullshit, but in fact they are the ones who have done as much as anyone to understand it.

Economists are never coarse in their theoretical academic musings so, unsurprisingly, the word bullshit is not one that crops up in academic journals, even though bullshit is at the very centre of this field. The economists' concern is perhaps not bullshit itself, but the precise opposite. What their literature does is delineate the conditions under which a message communicated to me by a stranger is worth paying attention to. If it is not worth paying attention to, well then it is probably bullshit or it is at least worth assuming that it is bullshit. What the economists have done, therefore, is think about the features common to the bullshit that comes in the form of either speech or action, and what it is that distinguishes a credible message from an incredible one.

Economists are not the only ones to have grappled with this: similar models have been used in the study of evolution and sexual selection. Animals are not capable of bullshit in human terms, but they do sometimes want to deceive. And they have often evolved ways to send credible and believable messages to their potential mates. So, to aid our understanding of bullshit, for the next nineteen pages we'll enter a theoretical world where it doesn't exist.

The accidental revolution

Most revolutions spawn a revolutionary leader, or a team of them. Think the Bolsheviks, or Iran. Or Charles Darwin. There have been revolutions in economics too, led by characters with charisma and zeal: John Maynard Keynes, or Milton Friedman.

Each has made an enormous contribution to the subject, and each has received massive public recognition.

But for some reason Michael Spence has never gained the same prominence, despite being right at the helm of the information revolution in economics. His contribution was recognised with the Nobel Prize in 2001. Professor Spence perhaps doesn't have the character of a revolutionary; he's a mild-mannered man, not prone to overstatement or self-aggrandisement. As a teenager, he knew he wanted to be a scholar, but he didn't really know which subject that would be in. He majored in philosophy at Princeton in the 1960s, but chose economics for postgraduate study because it seemed to be a nice combination of theory and practicality. When I spoke to him in researching this book, he was quite matter-of-fact about his achievements and the haphazard way he stumbled into them. 'My attitude, to be honest, was I'm going to give this a try. This is really fun but if it doesn't work out, I'll do something else. I'll go to McKinsey or something like that.'[1]

It was good that he stuck to it. In 1972, he produced the PhD thesis that would later earn him his Nobel Prize. It was called 'Market Signaling'. In the timeline he compiled for his biography on the Nobel Foundation website, he records that it 'seemed quite well received'.[2] There was no eureka moment, he said: 'When you're doing theory, you just spend a lot of time fiddling around; it's leaving out the stuff that's not so important for this purpose and putting in the stuff that is. There's not a rule book for that. So I probably spent quite a lot of time just knocking around before I stumbled on what I thought was the model that had the pieces that I really wanted in it and didn't have a lot of extraneous baggage as well. I don't remember exactly, but that doesn't happen instantly. The fiddling around part some people find frustrating. I find it fun, but I suppose it would have got frustrating if it never produced anything.'

So what was in this thesis, and what was the information revolution in which it played such an important part? First, note that this was nothing to do with information technology. It is true that the IT revolution was just getting going, and very significant it turned to be too, but that was nothing to do with economists. Spence's revolution concerned an insight into the way information – or the lack thereof – could affect economic behaviour, and could do so more dramatically than anyone had hitherto imagined. He had applied his mind to one specific problem that turned out to be typical of many others. His preoccupation was the jobs market. To caricature it in the most simple way, we all know there are clever people and less clever people, and most of us know whether we are clever or not, but prospective employers don't. Their challenge is to find the clever people for the clever jobs, but how can they tell them apart from the less clever?

Now they could try to obtain the information they need by asking us – maybe inserting the question 'are you clever?' into the job interview. But they know that would simply be an invitation for us to peddle bullshit. Of course we'll all say we're clever as long as the clever jobs pay better than the less clever ones. The words of the clever and the non-clever employees will not allow for a distinction to be made between them – the words thus carry no information. The clever candidates may tell the truth, but no one will be able to tell that apart from the bullshit of their less clever counterparts. What Michael Spence wanted to do, therefore, was ask what it would take for the clever candidates to communicate their cleverness and distinguish themselves from the less clever.

Before answering, observe just how ubiquitous this kind of

situation is. Although it is a very stylised account of the challenges of candidate selection, in essence we have two players (the employer and the prospective employee) in an economic game. They don't know each other and may never meet again, but one has information that the other needs and which requires some kind of communication between the two. We also have misaligned interests (the less clever employees want a good job, but the employers don't want them to have it). So there is an incentive for mendacity on the part of some potential employees. The problem is one of asymmetric information. Notice this is not just a problem for the employer. It is also a problem for the clever employees, who have to find a way of showing employers how clever they are, rather than merely asserting it.

It turns out that asymmetries of information permeate everything we do. George Akerlof, who won the Nobel Prize along with Michael Spence, has written about the market for second-hand cars. If I'm selling my car, I know whether or not it is one of those duds that have endless problems, but you, the prospective buyer, have no idea at all. You can ask me, but why bother? I'm likely to say the car runs very well.[3] Joseph Stiglitz, the third Nobel winner in 2001, had analysed the same problem in the insurance market.[4] I know whether I'm a safe driver or not, but the insurance company doesn't. It can ask me lots of questions to try to ascertain the truth, and it can expect honest answers on specific questions concerning verifiable facts. But the one thing the insurance company can't do is expect me to give an honest answer on the important subjective fact as to whether I am safe or not.*

---

* The problem is especially severe in areas where insurance is not compulsory, such as private health insurance, because in these cases it is precisely the people who are the worst risk that will most want to take out the insurance. Sick people want medical cover more than healthy people. This is known as adverse selection.

It is fair to say that economists were not the first to realise how important bullshit is in everyday economic life, but they were the first to think carefully about its enormous effect on the workings or failings of markets.[5] Cases like the jobs market, second-hand cars and insurance soon multiplied.[6] It became obvious that masses of difficult problems come down to this kind of information and communication problem: one person knows, the other needs to know; but the one who knows has no reason to give an honest answer to the one who needs to know. Think about patients: they want to know whether the advice they get from the doctor is good or has been tainted by a conflict of interest. Consumers more generally want to know about the quality of the products they are thinking about buying, while the manufacturers will always want to say quality is high. Shareholders want to know how well their company is performing; the chief executive will have an incentive to say it is performing very well. Voters want to know whether the candidates standing for office are corrupt or incompetent; the politicians will tend to argue they are neither, whatever the truth of the matter. And so it goes on. Life is one great struggle in which we try to make decisions on the basis of incomplete information, with the people who know the truth having an incentive to peddle bullshit rather than disseminate valuable information.

In the real world, of course, there are ways in which the ignorant can become informed. Consumers can read product reviews; shareholders can analyse the actual results of the company to make up their own mind about it; voters can look at the record of the politicians seeking their votes. But the argument goes that there is always a problem of some residual asymmetric information. The world – the free market – doesn't work as well as it might because ignorance gets in the way.

Michael Spence thought hard about this problem in the jobs market and ultimately developed an interesting theory about how clever students can distinguish themselves from the rest: college. His insight was that because clever people find it easier to get into university than less clever people, clever people can use a college degree as a badge of intelligence to proffer to prospective employers, thus distinguishing themselves from the less clever.

Now, I will concede at this point that, as a Nobel Prize-winning revelation, this sounds rather underwhelming. But a lot of the best economics seems obvious once it has been explained. In this case, it's just that no one had explained it as carefully as Michael Spence. I suggested to Professor Spence that summarising his work in two sentences does make it sound rather less than profound. 'To be honest with you,' he said, 'if you randomly selected somebody in the street and said, "Can you explain the principle that you're implicitly using every day to distinguish bullshit from credible utterances or other things that are supposed to carry information?" most people wouldn't be able to answer that question until you told them the answer, in which case they'd say it's obvious.' That is frequently the plight of economists.

Obvious or not, the Spence formulation has some big implications that are useful in thinking about credible and incredible messages. The most important is that it gives clever people an incentive to go to university to prove they are clever, *even if they and prospective employers expect them to learn nothing when they are there*. College is simply useful as one of those actions we take to say something about ourselves, regardless of any substantive benefit it may bestow.

But what Spence did was to formulate in precise mathematical terms the conditions that need to hold if college is to be a reliable indicator of brainpower, as opposed to a piece of bullshit. Spence's maths imposed a certain clarity of thinking about the specifics of the problem, which is that for college not to be bullshit, the clever people must want to go and the less clever ones must not. Only if that is the case do you know that college separates the sheep from the goats. The model demonstrated that there has to be some differential burden of going to college for the bright and the less bright. Maybe the less bright can't get a place; or maybe it's just that it is particularly dull going to university if you aren't clever and don't like sitting in libraries. Whatever the cause, the differential burden of getting into college helps segment the bright and the less bright. And then, on top of that, it is important that the benefits of looking clever must more than compensate the clever for the cost *to them* of going to university. Meanwhile, the less clever people must shun university, because even though it would be nice to look clever and to get a clever job, the costs of college *to them* are simply too high.

In this model, university will stop being a reliable indicator of intelligence in two cases. First, if the benefits of looking clever are so great that even the dim will choose to go to college; and second, if the benefits of looking clever are so small that even the bright won't bother going. In these cases, admission to university will lose its meaning. But otherwise, if university does differentiate between the clever and the less clever – and the value of looking clever is in that sweet spot between being too high or too low – then you have a useful signal.

In somewhat theoretical terms, Spence had explained the existence of a curious real-world phenomenon: colleges teaching people things that are of no inherent use to them at the time, or later in their eventual occupation. The teaching may be useless, but the college education is economically useful as a device to promote the honest communication of talents. In the abstract world of economic theory Spence had formulated in precise terms the solution to the problem that no one would be believed if they were simply asked how clever they were.

Since formulating his account of why we go to college – not to learn but to impress – Spence has had a career teaching at eminent and expensive universities, an irony not entirely lost on him: 'The people in the University of Chicago, which was the home of human capital theory [the branch of economics looking at the costs and benefits of investing in education], went bananas.' He had to carefully explain that his signalling model left out the motivation of going to college to actually learn things, in order to keep the maths manageable. 'I only produced it to keep it simple because if you put the two together you have to know something about differential equations.' But Professor Spence certainly acknowledges that, in practice, we can go to college for both learning and impressing.

From costly signals to cheap talk

None of us like differential equations, so you might well ask what is so interesting about Spence's account of college outside the abstract world of economic theory. Well, the central insight is that an important feature of many a useful signal is that it has to be costly, and differentially costly to the various types of communicator between whom we wish to distinguish. As no clever person would be believed if they simply said they were clever, they have to prove it by spending tens of thousands of pounds on demonstrating it, knowing that less clever people will not find it worthwhile. And if useful signals tend to be expensive, then by contrast bullshit as a phenomenon is characterised by its cheapness. Words cost nothing to say and so have limited power in helping us distinguish between the genuine and the

fake. Even actions can be cheap: the phoney gesture that pos-
tures as expensive, but which says little. You'll remember Dame
Carcas from the previous chapter; that pig stuffed with wheat
gave the impression of being a costly signal, but was not at all
useful in distinguishing between a fortress that had a lot of food
and one that was bluffing. It was silly of Charlemagne to have
believed the pig told him anything at all. Likewise, it would be
silly to believe a government is saying much by enshrining a fuel
poverty target in law, given that it in no way binds their hands
if the target is missed.

From Spence's paper, signalling theory was born, and suddenly in economics signals came to be seen everywhere. Once
we realised that honest communication can be a costly business,
wherever there was some mysterious costly behaviour it could
now be looked on as a possible signal. An expensive engagement
ring? A costly signal from the man to prove to the woman that
he is serious about marrying her, because words would never
prove anything. Why do companies pay dividends to shareholders when it is inefficient in tax terms to do so? Must be some
kind of signalling mechanism by the corporate insiders to tell
shareholders how successful the company is. It is not much of
an exaggeration to say that wherever there was an unexplained
phenomenon, the default explanation became that it was a signal
of some kind.

While Spence was thinking about college and what it
is really there for, some parallel work was going on in the
field of evolutionary science. Ever since Charles Darwin, an
enormous effort had been expended in trying to explain the
peacock's tail. The problem is simple: the tail looks like more
of a burden to the bird than a help. So how did it survive, in
an evolutionary process run along the lines of survival of the
fittest? We can see how giraffes' necks might get longer, as

the long-necked giraffes had an advantage over the shorter-necked ones in reaching the foliage on taller trees. But there was no such account to explain the process generating longer and more flamboyant tails on peacocks. Darwin himself had written, 'The sight of a feather in a peacock's tail, whenever I gaze at it, makes me sick!'[7] It appeared to be a counter-example to the theory of natural selection. Even today, some creationist websites will tell you that the peacock is evidence that Darwin was wrong.[8]

Darwin spent some years thinking about the problem, and twelve years after *On the Origin of Species* he published *The Descent of Man, and Selection in Relation to Sex*, setting out his own account of sexual selection.[9] Although never given as much attention as natural selection, his came to be the dominant view as to why species might adapt to have features that are functionally disadvantageous. But in the 1970s, along came a piece of analysis that independently of Michael Spence explained the peacock's tail in the language of costly signals. As long as that tail is easier for a fit peacock to carry than an unfit one, and as long as there is some benefit to being seen as fit, the fit peacock has some incentive to invest in extra tail as a sign of fitness, notwithstanding the burden of having to carry the thing around.[10]

The information revolution and signalling theory gave economics a new lease of life, making possible a new understanding of markets and their inhibitions and failures. It gave economists licence to look at all sorts of social institutions that might be analysed as signals rather than as curiosities. And interestingly for our purposes, Spence's work also gave life to a stream of papers looking at what economists call 'cheap talk'.[11]

The clue as to what this work is about is in the title. It was concerned with trying to find the precise conditions that allow words – that cost nothing to utter – to be credible. When can we ever assume that simply asking people things will elicit the truth? Obviously, if I ask you whether you want a ginger biscuit or a digestive with your tea, you will very likely tell me the truth as it is in your interest to do so. But whenever our interests are not fully aligned, you will have some incentive to deviate from giving me the fullest, frankest and most straightforward version of the truth. Suppose we are sitting at home together, trying to work out whether to go bowling or to the movies. I'd rather go bowling; you'd rather see a film. In this case, even though we enjoy each other's company and want to be together, our interests are not entirely aligned; you might choose to concoct a story about having a sore elbow in order to nudge me to give in to your desire to see a film. In that case (in the world of economists, where couples behave in a curiously selfish way), I should probably assume that you are talking bullshit so as to prevail in the choice of outing.

The overall finding of these models is that cheap talk has more value the closer the alignment of interests between the parties communicating. Costly signalling is what you need when the interests are not aligned, and the more out of line interests are, the less useful is cheap talk.*[12]

So, according to the theory, we have two things that underlie a lot of bullshit: a form of communication that is, loosely speaking, too cheap to properly distinguish between a genuine and a fake message; and some misalignment of interests that gives

---

* Economists study this using the framework of game theory; in most of this analysis, each encounter is highly stylised, and each player knows precisely what they want and what the other player wants. This helps in working out what each player should say or do in each circumstance, and thus helps calculate what the outcome of each game is. In practice, it is possible that the players don't know which game they are playing or what they themselves really want. In this case, cheap talk may have more value than the simpler models suggest.

reason for someone to be a fake in the first place. All communication is about the transfer of information from one person to another, but in order for communication to genuinely be useful, I either need you to want to tell me the truth, or I need you to face some cost in lying. If neither of those conditions holds, then expect bullshit to follow.

It was hard to foresee that such a rich seam of study would come out of Professor Spence's early work, and that of other economists who worked on similar problems. 'What I did know at the time was that these structures were common in economic and social interactions,' he told me. 'I knew it was very general. That's basically what I was seeing.' But, somehow, the public have not clocked bullshit detection as a specialist subject for economists: 'They know about it based on experience. They don't know anything about it based on contact with either literature or commentaries on it. And in a way that's understandable.'

The theory is, in its own way, rather intuitive, but it helps us frame the questions we should ask of any message we receive: does the communicator have an interest in directly deceiving, or in trying to impress? And does the way that they have tried to persuade us they are honest and genuine really show that they mean what they say? What is particularly interesting about this body of theory is that it is not just useful in defining those underlying preconditions of bullshit; it can also absolve the innocent by helping us tell when things that look like bullshit might not actually be bullshit after all. In any case of apparent bullshit, we have to ask if there is a costly signal underneath the cheap talk, and whether that costly signal offers any useful information. On reflection, we might find that there is more information in a statement or action than it first seems. And let's take a closer look at one important example of that.

The example of advertising

Persuasive advertising can be seen as a bit of a mystery. It surely has to be mad for us to buy a particular soap powder just because a man in a white coat pops up on TV to tell us that laboratory tests show this powder washes whiter than the main competitor. After all, we know the man is paid by the washing-powder manufacturer to say that, and the company paying him has a direct interest in you believing it, so why should we trust the man in the white coat?

But there is one thing we know about advertising: a lot of it is quite expensive, particularly the more artsy kinds you get on prime-time TV and in cinemas. Why would any company hire Ridley Scott to make a television advert, as Apple did in 1984? Why would any company have an ad without words? Why would any company pay more than four million dollars for one thirty-second slot during the Super Bowl?[13] None of this could be said to be cheap talk – it is the most expensive talk on the planet. But how on earth could any of this advertising be furnishing us with useful information? And if ads don't furnish us with useful information, why on earth would we pay heed to them? And if we don't pay heed to them, why would anyone bother to advertise?

Well, signalling theory can provide a logical rationale for at least some advertising. The central point is that the informative content of expensive commercials is simply the fact that the company paying for them is willing to spend so much doing so. Now on its own, this is not very helpful. For signalling theory to explain advertising properly, it must show that commercials send useful information to those at whom they are aimed. And that means the ads somehow have to help consumers distinguish between good and bad products. Those washing-powder ads have to tell the consumer which washing powder is the best one to buy. And for that to be the case the expensive advertising must not just be costly to the makers of washing powder, it also has to be less costly or more beneficial to the makers of good washing powders than to the makers of bad ones. If quality suppliers have more incentive to advertise than the bad, they will presumably advertise more, and then – hey presto – we have a justification for advertising: it furnishes consumers with useful information about quality, so they will pay attention to the ads, and the advertisers will thus advertise. For this bullshit-free explanation of the whole institution of expensive ads, signalling theory relies on there being some mechanism by which the makers of products that are worth buying have more reason to advertise than the makers of products that are not, just as the signalling theory of college relied on there being some mechanism by which brighter students would be more likely to go to college.

As it happens, there are reasons to suspect that advertising makes more sense for companies that truly believe their product is good. Let me take you through one argument, even though you may not be persuaded by it at the outset. The crucial assumption is that if we use the same washing powder for a few months, we will be able to tell for ourselves whether or not it works well. If we come to the view that it is good, then we'll likely carry on buying it. If we decide for ourselves that it is ineffective, we will avoid it next time we buy washing powder. That simple (and reasonable) premise means that the producer of a good washing powder has more to gain from securing a sale than the producer of a bad washing powder: from one sale, the good powder is more likely to be purchased again and again. The bad powder will be used only a few times. Now let us assume that producers know whether their powder is good or not; the good producers have more incentive to throw money at advertising than the bad producers because they will get more repeat purchases as a result. Now, if good producers are more anxious to secure sales than bad producers, and are thus more likely to advertise, then as a consumer it is quite rational for me to respond to adverts on the assumption that the products advertised are good.[14]

There are other similar arguments,[15] but in this account the active ingredient of an advert is not what is said in the ad (we ignore that as the advertiser has an incentive to lie). The useful feature is that the ad tells me the company has some confidence in their product and they expect it to be around for a while, otherwise it wouldn't be worth them spending all this money on advertising. You might think that advertising is bullshit, but it works as a genuine signal of quality because it is reassuringly expensive, and by benefiting good products more than bad ones it allows us to discriminate one from the other.[16]

I find people are initially a bit sceptical of this argument, and I would never suggest that it accounts for all advertising, or even most. But I have no doubt that there is more than a germ of truth in it. Take an example. In 2002, T-Mobile paid Catherine Zeta-Jones to serve as a brand ambassador, and in particular to promote their new mobile phone service in the US. I don't know how much she was paid, but I would assume that cheaper and lesser-known potential brand ambassadors were available. So what was the point of employing Catherine Zeta-Jones? When the appointment was made, T-Mobile announced it with a quote from Kai Uwe Ricke, chief executive of T-Mobile International: 'Catherine's hard work, dedication, and engaging personality have given her strong international appeal as a respected actress who lives life to the fullest – on her own terms – and make her the perfect choice to represent T-Mobile.'[17] But does that really explain the market appeal of a Zeta-Jones when it comes to selecting a mobile phone? What was the active ingredient of her role in those ads? And what are the alternatives to signalling theory in explaining it?

The most obvious and naive theory is that the ads worked because consumers are not very worldly and thought, Catherine Zeta-Jones likes T-Mobile, we like Catherine Zeta-Jones, so we should like T-Mobile too. Could that really explain buyer motivation? Sure, consumers can be dim, but they must have been aware that she didn't do the ads for free; they know she picked T-Mobile because they were paying her, in which case her presence tells us little about her genuine views of the different mobile phone providers.

A second, alternative theory is that the ads didn't work at all; that sparky consumers spotted the wheeze and said to themselves, 'She only did it for the money. She doesn't really believe in T-Mobile, so let's disregard her role in the advertising when thinking about how good T-Mobile's service is.' On this account, it is T-Mobile that is dim: they could have got someone almost as attractive, and much cheaper, than Catherine Zeta-Jones to read the script of the ads. But that flies in the face of the evidence that these ads do work.

And then there is signalling theory, according to which consumers looked at the high-quality celeb endorsement, had a subliminal sense that this was quite an expensive investment in the US market and made the judgement that T-Mobile was a reasonably serious player. Neither the consumer, nor indeed T-Mobile, need necessarily be consciously aware that the signal was in the money spent on the ad, not in the appearance of Catherine Zeta-Jones per se.[18]

Of course there are other hypotheses that can explain why celebrity endorsement might work,[19] and why signalling theory could not possibly explain all advertising. Clearly, a lot of ads are very cheap and they do not work this way; clearly, a lot of products (such as Coca-Cola) are heavily advertised for decades, even though most consumers have had ample time to ascertain whether they are good or not; and clearly a lot of products are simply sold on the basis of emotional attachment and costly signalling can't explain that. But for all its limitations, evidence has been found that wastefully expensive advertising is taken as a subtle sign of reassurance by consumers. Companies with money to spend like that probably see themselves as in business for the long term and think that their product is solid. These companies are unlikely to poison you, or run off with your money, or let your plane crash.

Many people prefer to think that persuasive advertising is wasteful and uninformative. They think that advertisements work by duping gullible consumers with self-interested, unreliable messages. I would never say there isn't some element of that in advertising, but this account is belied by the fact that so much advertising is aimed at the top end of the income spectrum. Understandably, advertisers obsess over the rich and well educated – *Financial Times* readers are far more interesting to them than tabloid readers – and it doesn't seem plausible to assume without evidence that they are all credulous.

If you are still not convinced, perform a little thought experiment. You've probably seen cheap ads for a local restaurant and expensive ads for a national bank. Now transpose the two, and ask yourself how you would feel about the bank if it advertised in the same way as the local restaurant.

I first encountered this argument in the late 1980s and found it transformational; suddenly ads made more sense. Flamboyance, extravagance, a lack of any direct information – all these slotted into place. They are not the vehicle for carrying a message; they are the message itself. What looks like one of the most obvious examples of bullshit is not in that category at all.

The mystery of bullshit that economics cannot explain

Notice that, in the Michael Spence world, nothing is as it seems. I don't go to university to learn; I go to show how clever I am. And I don't buy a particular brand of washing powder because a man in an advert tells me it is good; I buy it because the ad is expensive and no company would be likely to justify the investment if they knew their product was rubbish. What Spence had done was to describe a world in which no amount of bullshit will ever persuade anyone of anything, and in doing so he explained a lot of what we see, and he told us that, sometimes, what you think is bullshit is actually a costly signal delivering useful information.

But there is one huge piece of the modern world that the theory struggles to explain. This kind of economics does not give us an account for the most basic fact of all: just why there is still so much bullshit in the world. It's worth explaining why economics has this gap, for in many ways it defines the great mystery of bullshit.

The economic account of information and communication is based on what might be called the rational model of the world. I won't get into the detail of what that means or how plausible an assumption it is, but it is a very useful simplifying device for pinning down the maths and making it manageable. Loosely speaking, it implies that we all act in a way that advances our self-interest. But for economists, this assumption has the important implication that if we hear cheap talk from someone who we think would say that anyway, or if we spot a phoney signal, we should and would disregard it completely. We would be mad to take it seriously, as it furnishes us with no useful information, and is likely to be bullshit. In the world of abstract theory, if someone has reason to lie we'd be irrational to pay heed to what they say (unless they have sent a message with some costly signal that indicates they are telling the truth). And it follows that if I am not going to believe what you say, there is no point in your saying it. Why waste your breath?

Economists describe this kind of impeccable logic using the word *equilibrium*. An equilibrium basically describes a situation in which everybody behaves in a way that is rationally consistent with everybody else's behaviour. There is something stable and consistent about a world in which I believe nothing and you say nothing. But there is something illogical about a world in which I don't believe you, but you say it anyway. That would surely imply you are irrational. There is also nothing logical and consistent about a world where I believe you when you say you are good, even if bad people would also say they are good. That would imply I am irrational.

This is where the rational model – in all its simplicity – comes up against the observations we make of the real world. For one thing, we observe people telling the truth when it may be in their tactical interest to deceive. Is that rational? More importantly for our discussion of bullshit, we observe people saying things that are implausible and untrue, and we observe people believing them; and we even observe people saying things that are untrue, and which are likely to be detected. In short, rationality has its insights, but it leaves us with a lot to explain.

In fairness to the rational model, there is one colourful exception to the rule that words which are not credible serve no purpose and thus can be assumed away. The mathematical models come up with the possibility of what they call a 'babbling equilibrium'.[20] This is a situation in which talk is so cheap everybody talks the whole time, but nothing anybody says is believed. Everybody just babbles for the sake of it. So I tell you how clever I am and you ignore me. I tell you how stupid I am, you ignore me too. Your distrust of me is reinforced by my tendency to talk rubbish, and your distrust makes it as reasonable for me to talk rubbish as to speak the truth. We are all happy. This only occurs, though, when there is no cost to wasting your breath.

You might argue that this babbling does not just exist in mathematical models of stylised encounters. It also exists in a lot of pubs after about half-past ten, in some infant-school playgrounds, and more than a few parliaments. I'm sure that some of Donald Trump's critics would say that his tendency to change his mind about things renders many of his assertions a kind of occasional babbling in this strict economic sense. But the babbling equilibrium is not a very interesting one. As soon as you assume that spewing bullshit has a cost, even just the cost of printing a press release or writing a speech, then it no longer pays to babble. You might as well shut up. And anyway, what we observe in the real world is that, contrary to the babbling equilibrium, bullshit sometimes works in actually persuading or influencing other people.

So the economists' rational model of the world offers a theoretical account of many things, but it can't really solve the central paradox: that much of the bullshit we observe should not exist. Rationally, it should be ignored; and if it is ignored, there should be no point in the futile task of producing it. So what is going on? Either the world is mad and people are irrational, or there are other things that explain why bullshit is prevalent. I think both of those explanations have some truth in them, so we leave the world of economics, and it is to Planet Earth that we now go, as we start to consider some of the reasons why bullshit is produced in such vast quantities.

SECTION TWO

WHY

Some explanations as to why
bullshit is so pervasive

5

Hidden Messages

How the untruthful and unclear can still be revealing

The importance of context

As we start our journey into understanding why bullshit has an enduring appeal, let me devote a few pages to a man called Steve Nesbitt. Although you won't have heard *of* him, you have probably *heard* him, because in one brief moment of tragedy he ended up coining one of the most prominent euphemisms of the second half of the twentieth century. At a first hearing, you might think that in selecting the words he did, Steve was not being straightforward. But the story of the two-word phrase that Steve uttered tells us a lot about why we shouldn't always just blurt out the simplest and most direct words to describe our thoughts. Our language is shaped by the context in which we are communicating: we select the words that fit our function. Steve was not obfuscating or being misleading in any way, but it was certainly not plain speaking either. And it makes the point that plain speaking is not always the best policy. It all depends on the circumstances.

Steve, who is now retired, worked for many years in the Public Affairs Office at NASA, and during that career he was one of several people who served as the so-called Voice of Mission Control. That particular job is to sit in the main mission-control room and provide the official commentary during NASA launches. As fate would have it, Steve was a senior member of the team and scheduled himself to commentate on the launch of the *Challenger* space shuttle on 28 January 1986. This was to be a particularly historic event as Christa McAuliffe was on board, and she was set to become the first teacher in space.[1] Schools across the US had been following the build-up to her flight, and it's estimated that 17 per cent of all Americans – and almost half the country's nine- to thirteen-year-olds – were watching live.[2] Which meant that they were listening to Steve's commentary. Steve himself was sitting in Houston, a thousand miles away from the launch site at Cape Canaveral, but he was comfortable with the task at hand. 'I never used a script,' Steve told me when I spoke to him about his recollections of that day. 'Some people did have a script to remind them of what was coming up next, but with enough practice you don't need that.'[3]

Steve was not paid to sit watching the event on television. 'At the time we had two small black and white monitors in front of me. They were probably twelve-inch monitors with a lot of little white numbers on them scrolling by very fast, that were giving me things like the velocity, the altitude, the arranged distance, the performance of the fuel cells, the auxiliary power units, the throttle percentage of the engines, a lot of other information. You have a tremendous amount of things going on and you have to watch those numbers. It's like a juggle and you've got to not drop anything. You've got to be ready when a gap comes and you can throw something in there. You don't ever have the luxury to watch television,' he said.

It may have felt like a familiar assignment at first, but the *Challenger* launch turned into a national catastrophe. 'So you hear the call, "Go at throttle up",' Steve recounts. 'Dick Scobee, the Commander, responded, "Roger, go at throttle up." Then just a second or two after that the space craft came apart.'

The strange thing is that Steve didn't see what everyone else saw, as he was sitting looking at his two monitors full of numbers. 'I'm still looking at the numbers – velocity, altitude – so I'm going on for another fifteen seconds maybe as I don't see it. But as I'm studying that, there was a young Navy captain, a medical doctor, sitting on the medical console position right to my left and she was looking at the screen because she didn't have any particular thing to do at that moment. I heard her say "What was that?" She didn't have much experience in watching space flights, otherwise she would have said something a lot more disturbing, I'm sure. So I finished my set of velocity, altitude, down range distance things that I say and I look over at the screen, and as I do, the only thing I see is two solid rocket boosters going off on their own. I thought, Oh man, that's bad. And at that point things just sort of froze for several seconds. Nobody in the room was really saying anything ... Everybody was kind of stuck for a moment because most of them are not seeing any television as well, but they did see that the data coming on their screens had frozen. We had lost our communication link, so we were not getting data from the space craft.'

The first thing Steve did was to pause. For thirty seconds. And then, as the world gazed in puzzlement and some horror at *Challenger*'s ominous Y-shaped vapour trail, he said what he could:

Flight controllers here are looking very carefully at the situation. Obviously a major malfunction.

He went on to say:

> We have no downlink. [Thirty-nine-second pause.] We
> have a report from the flight dynamics officer that the
> vehicle has exploded. The flight director confirms that. We
> are looking at checking with the recovery forces to see what
> can be done at this point. [Pause.] Contingency procedures
> are in effect.[4]

'I felt like a house had fallen on me,' Steve says of that moment.
'The floor goes out from under you, you feel like, how could this
possibly be happening? But you have to do something.'

And what you have to do in that situation is act like the
professional that you are paid by NASA to be. 'I knew something terrible happened but I didn't know what. I felt the need
to provide some statement that we're still here, we're still
watching this. So I said, flight control was "watching the situation very carefully, obviously a major malfunction" because
I certainly was in no position to say "Oh my God, the space
craft exploded. They're all dead." You can't say that. I mean,
it would be irresponsible ... I just always wanted to do what
was right and my journalistic instincts said, "Okay, I'm on air.
Something's happening. People are getting a video or image of
something happening." Unfortunately, I didn't see it. I know
less than the people who are watching television, but basically
everything in the room was a wave of shock as people began
to say "Something terrible has gone on." But nobody else in
the room knew what had happened either because they were
all watching the data. And in the absence of data, we are just
basically thirty people in a big concrete box with no windows.
So I put that out there and then I began to hear on the communication loop little things that I would then repeat. "We have

no down link," was what the Communications Officer said. So I repeated that.'

Steve has no regrets about following his professional instincts and giving lines that were generic and restrained. 'It said something is terribly wrong, but it didn't come out with details that I didn't have . . . I did not want to be saying things that I couldn't confirm and, obviously, things that would be wrong.'

There was something else that weighed upon Steve as he tried to find the right words for the disaster unfolding in real time a thousand miles away. 'Among the other thoughts that went through my mind was I knew the families of the astronauts were at the launch site, watching . . . They were hearing my voice as well as the voices of the people on the space craft and mission control. I knew they were listening and they would be in a moment of horror watching their loved ones crash into the sea. I tried to be as sensitive to that as I could, so my commentary was mostly limited to here's what we know, here's what appears to have happened, here's what we're doing now, and to try and keep it as apparently unemotional as possible. I certainly felt for the families who I knew were watching their sons and daughters and their husbands and fathers, mothers, dying before their eyes.'

As for those two memorable words, major malfunction, which sounded like some ghastly attempt to play down the horror, it turns out it was not a well-worn professional euphemism. 'That just came into my head at the moment,' Steve says. The phrase was quickly picked up, however, as striking language so often is; it went on to be used in the film *Full Metal Jacket* ('What is your major malfunction, numbnuts?'[5]) and then became an ironic descriptor of bad happenings generally (and surely had some part in the birth of the phrase 'wardrobe malfunction'[6]).

*

It is interesting to contrast Steve Nesbitt's controlled commentary on the *Challenger* disaster with the uncontrolled description of another twentieth-century disaster, the crash of the *Hindenburg* in 1937. Reporter Herbert Morrison had been assigned by his Chicago radio station to describe the airship's arrival in New Jersey and was an eyewitness to it exploding and being incinerated in a matter of seconds as it came to dock. His emotional reaction provides one of the most dramatic pieces of live event coverage ever recorded. Here are some extracts:

> They've dropped ropes out of the nose of the ship; and they've been taken ahold of down on the field by a number of men. It's starting to rain again; it's ... the rain had slacked up a little bit. The back motors of the ship are just holding it, just enough to keep it from— It burst into flames! It burst into flames, and it's falling, it's crashing! Watch it! Watch it, folks! Get out of the way! Get out of the way! Get this, Charlie! [Charlie Nehlsen was the radio engineer at Morrison's side] Get this, Charlie! It's fire – and it's crashing! It's crashing terrible! Oh, my, get out of the way, please! It's burning and bursting into flames ... it's a terrific crash, ladies and gentlemen. It's smoke, and it's flames now ... and the frame is crashing to the ground, not quite to the mooring-mast. Oh, the humanity ... Honest, it's just laying there, a mass of smoking wreckage. Ah! And everybody can hardly breathe and talk, and the screaming ... Honest: I – I can hardly breathe. I – I'm going to step inside where I cannot see it. Charlie, that's terrible. Ah, ah – I can't. I, listen, folks, I – I'm gonna have to stop for a minute because I've lost my voice. This is the worst thing I've ever witnessed.

It was raw and as descriptive as any commentary could be, devoid of any euphemism in any form. And the phrase 'oh the humanity' has been picked up in popular culture, taking on an active life as a tongue-in-cheek stock phrase in film and television.[7]

It is tempting to compare the two commentaries and think that because Morrison gave the audience a more emotional and less controlled reaction, his was somehow a more communicative description than Steve's carefully chosen words. But for me, this is wrong-headed. Yes, Morrison's description was more vivid in alerting listeners to the magnitude of what had occurred, but that is not the only information conveyed by a commentary. Imagine that Nesbitt, a NASA official, had succumbed to his emotions. It would have been more honest as to the awfulness of the event, but it would have given the impression of NASA taking leave of its senses, rather than trying to fathom what had happened. And it would have been a misleading signal to the public, giving a false impression that emotion was taking over mission control. It wasn't. Nesbitt was not obfuscating by using the phrase major malfunction, he was just doing his job well by talking in dispassionate terms that suited the occasion. There would be a time for emotion, but not as the shards of the destroyed shuttle and its rocket boosters were still falling. Morrison and Nesbitt were trying to achieve different things and their styles accurately conveyed that information to us. Both are human reactions to an appalling event, but in different forms.

Steve is painfully aware of the magnitude of that disaster, with seven lives lost and a nation left in shock. He was simply a messenger, in a low-profile role that happened to put him in the spotlight, yet it was a career-defining moment. 'I did feel shaken. I felt the energy had all been drained out of me. I went back to my building, went in through the back door because the front of my building was the news centre and there were reporters everywhere. I knew that I would be mobbed and my management recognised that as well. So they kept me out of sight until the next day … but yes I was shaken. I felt like I had just been through a very traumatic experience. I think when I got off duty at the end of the day I went home briefly and then I went over to the shopping mall and got an ice-cream cone and just walked around. That was pretty much it.'

The fact that Steve's two-word phrase, 'major malfunction', subsequently came to enjoy a certain comic value could be seen as a sign that it was inadequate as a description of a space shuttle blowing up. For me, though, the words fitted the occasion perfectly and make the point that context matters. The words that are chosen, however obscure they may seem, communicate something useful about the situation. So in this chapter I want to show how much of the apparent bullshit we encounter contains enlightening information of this kind. The precise choice of bullshit reveals something about the communicator, and thus it is not always easy to dismiss it as mendacious or nonsensical. Only once we have explained why it sometimes makes sense to speak indirectly might we understand why that habit sometimes goes too far.

Reading the subtitles

Words have literal meaning, of course, but it is also useful to think of them as having extra meaning embedded within them. You might remember the famous balcony scene in *Annie Hall*, where Woody Allen uses subtitles to unmask the actual thoughts of Alvy and Annie as they engage in stilted conversation trying to impress each other. Alvy says, 'Photography is interesting because, you know, it's a new art form and a set of aesthetic criteria have not emerged yet.' The subtitle says, 'I wonder what she looks like naked.'[8] Those subtitles could appear beneath much of the language we encounter in public discourse, and in our everyday interactions.

Let's take a more prosaic example than the commentary on a major disaster. You go to a friend's for dinner; the host serves up a perfectly nice first course with a respectable bottle of white to accompany it. Then follows a gooseberry tart that he has prepared. It comes out the oven and – oh no! – it's burnt. Not burnt to a cinder, but more than a little overcooked. 'Oops,' he says as he brings it from the kitchen. 'I'm so sorry, I've managed to burn it. How annoying. I do hope it's edible. Be honest – do leave it if it's too charred for you.'

Now let us suppose you are there, gazing upon the scorched pudding. How do you respond? My guess is, notwithstanding the fact you are an honest person, you say words to the effect that 'Oh don't worry, it looks fine.' You then proceed to eat as much as you can, perhaps leaving the blackest pieces of pastry. At some point while eating, you go out of your way to reassure your friend that it's actually rather nice. And if you leave a little, the reassurance will be repeated. The reason for leaving some is not that it's burnt, but that you have eaten a feast already.

Most of us would not regard this as dishonesty, but as good manners. And you can be sure that your host will interpret it that way. He will be happy that you have not made a scene, but he will know that his guests' protestations that the gooseberry tart is fine provide no reassurance at all; he will rightly understand they are mere protocol, and at the end of the evening he will still be annoyed with himself for bungling the baking.

So, the first point to note is that this is a case not of socially acceptable lying, but of socially mandated lying. In our society, which tends to put a strong weight on authenticity, something complicated is going on here. There is no loss of sincerity merely because the words stated are untrue. No one rails against your post-truth comments on the gooseberry tart. The second point is that the encouraging words spoken by the dinner-party guests are devoid of any information content about the quality of the food. Whatever words they used were not meant to be taken literally, and nor would they be.

But the third and most important point is this: just because the words can be categorised as cheap talk, and carry no information as to what the guests think of the pudding, it does not mean they have no information content at all. Those gracious words say a lot about you, and your attitude to your host. When you say 'the pudding is fine', here are some examples of the many things you might really mean, and indeed you would probably be interpreted as meaning:

- The gooseberry tart is not good, but at least it's not actually toxic.
- Don't worry about the pudding, the evening is very pleasant.
- I don't want to blemish the evening by making a big deal of something relatively inconsequential.
- I like you and I want you to know that I'm not judging you on the quality of the food.
- I'm concerned for your feelings.
- I'm well brought up and know how to behave in polite company.

Obviously, these propositions (bar the first) are potentially more significant than any expression of support for the pudding. You may not have an exact idea as to which of the above propositions you are trying to express – maybe it is all of them. Your communication is indirect and imprecise. But it is nevertheless clear.

What might you be saying if you did choose to state your sincere feelings about the pudding? You would be giving far more honest feedback; your host would be in no doubt at all that the pudding was disappointing. And you could also be saying something about yourself. You might be indicating that you are very intimate with the host, and are thus not afraid of saying what you think; or you might not be intimate, and be demonstrating a certain directness of personality. But in this case the host would find it harder to ascertain, should he not know you well, whether you are someone who cares for his feelings or is well brought up.

What this simple example illustrates is the complex relationship between language and message. Words are intricate enough, but the way they are said adds a whole extra dimension to the problem of interpretation. Quite why some messages are expressed literally (like 'pass the butter') while others ('I care for your feelings') are sometimes communicated in a more oblique fashion is an interesting question, but it is an undeniable feature of human expression that a high proportion of what we say falls into the 'the pudding is lovely' category. We have to recognise that while using words to convey a message indirectly can be thought of as bullshit, it is not a form of obfuscation or deceit. Rather, it is part of our language; it is every bit as human as laughing at a joke, frowning when puzzled or nodding in agreement.

Recognising the subtle message

Words that look like drivel often carry a subtle (or not so subtle) hidden message, and there is a simple test to ascertain what that message is: ask yourself, what is being said here that would not be said if it was expressed in the bluntest of terms? When you apply that test to what is spoken, you quickly see that the choice of language tells you a lot about the context in which the speaker is delivering the words.

Take these two phrases: 'brutal terrorist murder' and 'regrettable historical event'. These could both be describing the same thing, but the formulation used may tell us a lot about the speaker's views. The more direct account tells us that the speaker is likely not a supporter of the cause supported by the perpetrators. The more indirect phrase suggests that the speaker does not want to have an argument about which side is right.

Something close to this example came up in the Queen's visit to the Republic of Ireland in May 2011, the first time a British monarch had gone there in a hundred years. It was a journey of reconciliation, with enormous symbolic importance. It was a moment to both mark and deepen the improved relations between Britain and Ireland following the 1998 Good Friday Agreement. The most memorable moment came at the dinner at Dublin Castle on the second day, when the Queen made a speech to the attending dignitaries about relations between the two countries. The speech was masterful, with words carefully chosen to suit the occasion: the language was English, but the style was diplomatic understatement. Referring to the fraught Anglo-Irish history of cruelty and terrorism that spans the callous British attitude to the Irish during the famine of the nineteenth century, the struggle for independence, and the Troubles, as well as the murder of the Queen's cousin, Lord Mountbatten, by the IRA, she said:

Of course, the relationship has not always been straightforward; nor has the record over the centuries been entirely benign ... With the benefit of historical hindsight we can all see things which we would wish had been done differently or not at all.[9]

At a different time and place, you could imagine those words being criticised for inappropriately minimising the magnitude of past crimes. But understatement has a place, and this was certainly one. The Queen, I suspect, was not trying to say that history was inconsequential by using language that downplayed it; she was trying to say that she (and by extension the British state) thought it was unhelpful to dwell on it. She could have given a vivid and frank description of some of the brutality committed by both sides, inevitably stirring up passions among her listeners, but that would not have achieved the same thing at all. As she said, 'Indeed, so much of this visit reminds us of the complexity of our history, its many layers and traditions, but also the importance of forbearance and conciliation. Of being able to bow to the past, but not be bound by it.'

It was not just the Queen's diplomatic expression that made that Dublin speech so successful. With a select few words at the start of her remarks, she made history: '*A hUachtaráin agus a chairde.*' It was Irish Gaelic for 'President and friends'. Never has there been an occasion when the words uttered mattered less than the language they were uttered in. It was an important gesture.

But a successful gesture requires not just a gesturer to send a message, but also a gesturee to receive it. Many who watched the speech on television will remember the reaction of the Irish President on that night. Mary McAleese mouthed the word 'wow' at the fact the Queen had briefly departed from English. That 'wow' was itself an important moment. By saying 'wow', the President had in a single word told us what she thought of the Queen's comment. Her exclamation said, 'What the Queen has just done is no mild pleasantry. This is an immense offer of respect to the Irish people, and more than we expected.' The 'wow' gave the cue to everyone else: the reaction of the Irish nation matched that of President McAleese, and the success of the Queen's trip was sealed.[10]

A little bit of Irish went a long way on that occasion, as did the Irish President's exclamation and the Queen's euphemistic tone. The Queen's speech had a clear answer to the question, what is being said here that would be not be said if the bluntest of terms were adopted?

We don't want people to use complicated or indirect language for no reason at all. But if someone is making a point by selecting convoluted English as their medium, the effort required is not necessarily wasted. Sometimes, spades are best not referred to as such. By embellishing plain English, we can often clarify the context, and the context usually matters. You might think of linguistic styles as analogous to fonts in printing. There are better fonts and worse fonts, attractive fonts and ugly fonts, useful fonts and ones you can barely read. But just as with language, the right font in any particular instance depends on the context. There are fonts that might look right for a wedding invitation, but would not be right as an invitation to a stag night, a children's birthday party, or a summons to court. If there was one ultimate, all-purpose font, people would quickly invent variations upon it to enrich their expression: to show how important their event is, or how subversive, or how informal. In each case, the choice of font gives you information about the kind of invitation it is. If you are a student of fonts, you might ask, what is the choice of font expressing here that would not be said if Helvetica or Times New Roman had been used instead?

In the case of fonts, as long as the same letters can mean different things in different contexts, the font can carry some information about what the context is. And so it is with words.

How you say it can carry relevant information, just as much as *what* you say.[11]

Now, the Queen's Dublin speech is an exceptional case, but think of all the types of language you might encounter: diplomacy, courtesy, euphemism, formality, calculated informality, jargon, legalese or journalese; not to mention modesty, sympathy and condolence, encouragement, romance, forced apology, and loyalty. None of them will ever win a plain-speaking award: each is stilted in its own way, but all are appealing in the right context, and annoying (or worse) in the wrong one. They mostly need to be taught to people, just as Irish phrases had to be taught to the Queen. But the language has a purpose, and often tells you what that is.

Once you know to look for subtle information buried in prose, you can't help but spot examples of language that appears artificial, but which has a justifiable purpose. Who cares if it comes across as pretentious or insincere if it is in the service of a greater good? Take the convention in the House of Commons, by which MPs refer to each other as 'my honourable friend' or the 'honourable member'. It sometimes sounds comically hypocritical to preface an insult with those deferential words, but doing so implies respect for a rule that 'guards against all appearance of personality in debate', as *Erskine May: Parliamentary Practice* puts it.[12] In that case, by demanding stilted language, the rule imposes a certain restraint upon the arguments that occur in the chamber. Few would argue that our parliament would be improved if it instead encouraged insults, on the grounds that members could then say what they really thought about each other in the most direct of terms.

The message is that the virtues of plain speaking are exaggerated. Language says more than can be expressed in the starkest way. Indeed, this simple insight explains why words can be so contentious: it isn't the words, it is the values buried in the message. Let's consider the example of politically correct language. The phrase 'People of colour' says something very different from the words 'coloureds' or 'blacks'. Words like 'negro', 'cripple' or even 'handicapped', which were once deemed acceptable in polite society, have become unacceptable. Some anti-PC crusaders would argue that this is because we have succumbed to the demands of bossy lefties who are obsessed with policing our language rather than improving real things. On that account, it could be argued there was never anything wrong with the word 'handicapped', except that it had a negative association with disability, and so in a futile bid to pretend that disability isn't a problem, the silly PC brigade rebadged the condition in the hope that would make the condition sound better.[13]

That is one view, but our choice of words expresses far more than the colour of a person's skin or use of a wheelchair. It is not that 'negro', 'cripple' or 'handicapped' were ever unclear as descriptive words; it is that they were associated with an age in which attitudes were generally rather narrow-minded. People who wanted to signal a fresh and more positive view of minorities found they could communicate that by adopting a fresh word to describe them. The choice of politically correct language offers an answer to the test question, what is actually being said here that would not be said if it was expressed in the bluntest of terms? The answer is that the information being conveyed is about the speaker's attitude. As time passed, of course, most people wanted to be associated with the progressive attitude so general usage evolved, the old words were replaced by the new and the old words came to signify an avowedly non-progressive attitude, which is why the politically correct are so intent on condemning those who persist in using them.

So we can defend politically correct language on the grounds it carries a message broader than the simple words might imply. And this, incidentally, gives us a guide as to how far we should police it or impose it on people. It all comes back to the message that you think people are trying to send by not using PC language. If someone is not trying to say something in code, then it is not worth getting obsessed by the language they use. If someone refers to 'coloured actors' instead of 'actors of colour',[14] you have to look at the context, the likely intention and the record of the person speaking to see if this was revealing some animosity to people of colour or whether it was just a slip of the tongue. Or if a pleasant ninety-eight-year-old uses the word 'negro' in a non-insulting way, you might guess they'd simply failed to cotton on to the change in usage from the 1960s, in which case there is little point in berating them for getting it wrong as they probably mean no harm. On the other hand, if someone in his forties uses the word 'negro' in a perfectly knowing way, we can use our ordinary experience to spot that they are trying to tell us that they don't want to conform to twenty-first-century norms; that is their right, but the rest of us are entitled to judge them accordingly. Not on the word they are using, but on the attitude they are trying to display by using it.

Whether it is a NASA Voice of Mission Control, a polite dinner-party guest, a beacon of political correctness or a queen promoting reconciliation, what drives the choice of language is the communicator's desire to make a point. It is not insincere or dishonest; it is just right for the particular occasion. When you see a sign that tells you where to 'purchase a ticket' or 'alight' from a bus, you might reflect on the fact the people who produce these signs do not go home and talk of purchasing bacon at the supermarket and nor do they tell their six-year-old to alight from the car, but they do evidently take the view that a little formality in a sign is fitting, and thus adopt that idiom in that aspect of their professional life. Perhaps a sign telling you where to purchase a ticket says 'we are a professional outfit' or 'in our culture, we like formal procedures and rules'. Perhaps using the word 'alight' conveys a sliver of stiffness that reminds you to pay attention as you get off the bus. Or perhaps those words are used precisely because there is a danger that more everyday words might convey an individual personality inappropriate in a sign; the formality could be seen as a means of taking away the subtitles. But the point remains: the real message is not always explicit.

Bullshit: the unfair criticism?

This argument blunts much everyday criticism of bullshit. If linguistic contortions are, contrary to first impressions, subtly informative, then one should not criticise the language but only the objectionable thoughts that may underlie it. My colleague, the broadcaster John Humphrys, has written two books on language, and has become a prominent supporter of saying what you mean. In his book *Lost for Words*, he says:

> Poor language is more than pointless and ugly: it can be dangerous. Journalists are always interested in power. The first sign that it is being abused may be the misuse of language. If a politician, a business leader, a pressure group or the PR spokesman for any number of public organisations is not using straightforward language that most of us can understand, we should smell a rat.[15]

He cites very many examples of annoying English, some of which demonstrate his point that language can be used to impose a controversial worldview: one is the phrase 'delivering care to the patients'. John Humphrys says, 'Language of that sort puts a barrier between doctor and patient. What's wrong with simply "caring"?'[16] Another of his examples is the mission statement of the Department for Education and Skills: 'creating opportunity, releasing potential, achieving excellence'. The verdict is that 'This is worse than management-speak. This is insidious.'[17] Similarly, he rails against the London borough whose parking tickets were administered by Camden Parking Solutions.[18] And so on and so on.

I think we all know what John is getting at in these examples; they are pretty awful pieces of public-sector English, and you can certainly laugh at the Parking Solutions one. But annoyingly, if we apply the hidden meaning test question to them, I think we do get an answer: in all three cases the people in charge of the relevant activity are trying to convey the sense that theirs is a business as much as a traditional public service. You may not agree with that way of looking at it, but that is different from criticising the choice of words. Using a phrase like 'delivering patient services' is, as John Humphrys would probably agree, a way of talking about health care that says, 'Let's forget that this is human welfare at stake, and think about it as though we're providing stationery.' And in a conversation about hospital efficiency, that might signal a certain, appropriate dispassion. I accept that it may be that dispassion is always wrong, but the point is that whatever the merit in applying the corporate managerial ethos to health care, by aping the language of business (or what they think is the language of business), public-sector managers are making a statement that a business ethos is useful – that they think there's a useful connection to be drawn between, say, paper clips and hospital patients. By using the annoying formulation 'delivering care to patients', they are perhaps trying to look businesslike. Or, equally likely, they are persuading themselves that they are businesslike.

There is another prominent critic of obtuse expression. In 'Politics and the English Language', George Orwell attacked what he saw as the debasement of language through stale metaphors, and meaningless and pretentious words and indirectness. Orwell, like John Humphrys many years later, saw awful prose as not just ugly but politically dangerous: 'if thought corrupts language, language can also corrupt thought'.[19] He saw the politics of his age – just after the Second World War – as captured by bad linguistic habits that reflected rotten values, believing that 'political speech and writing are largely the defence of the indefensible'. Abstract words and euphemism try to disguise the true horror of what is being written. For example, he writes 'Millions of peasants are robbed of their farms and sent trudging along the roads with no more than they can carry; this is called *transfer of population* or *rectification of frontiers*.' But his most interesting contention of all is that 'The great enemy of clear language is insincerity. When there is a gap between one's real and one's declared aims, one turns as it were instinctively to long words and exhausted idioms, like a cuttlefish spurting out ink.'

His essay has attracted enormous attention, being reprinted as recently as 2013. And in many respects Orwell's argument stands up well. He is surely right that insincerity leads to poor English. To his credit, he is not a pedant, nor someone who thinks, in the style of the Académie française, that there is correct and incorrect usage. His aim is not to grumble about declining standards of grammar, like a cantankerous letter-writer to a newspaper. And if everybody strived to obey Orwell's much-quoted (but unrealistically demanding) six rules for clear writing,[20] we would have a far more constructive public discussion. He was ahead of his time in identifying some egregious forms of unclear language. But the heart of his argument is a criticism of indirect language, illustrated with choice examples all drawn from cases where the indirectness appears objectionable. He fails to address the obvious occasions, such as the Queen's visit to Dublin, where it serves a noble purpose.

For me, Orwell's tract demonstrates how easy it is to overlook the richness of expression offered through prose that appears redundant or pretentious. This is not to say all redundant or pretentious prose can be called richly expressive, but some of it can be. The failure to recognise that thus led Orwell to overstate the degree to which English was in decline. For one thing, if we think of language as a hard-wired human facility (Steven Pinker in *The Language Instinct* compares it to the ability of spiders to weave webs) then it is unlikely to degrade in just a generation or two.[21] And in addition, Orwell fails to take account of the vibrancy of language: he criticises all sorts of expressions that may have been irritating then, but which are now part of ordinary English, such as *cul de sac* and *status quo*. (According to Orwell, these are 'used to give an air of culture and elegance'.) He mocks 'pretentious diction' and meaningless abstraction, but it surely arises and persists for a reason. There's often a message buried in unsightly words, and it is that which makes those wishing to convey a certain image of themselves use them.

Who am I and which side am I on?

I have hammered home the general point that indirect language can carry a message if you care to notice it. But there is often one specific piece of information that is conveyed by the choice of language adopted. It can tell us the kind of person the communicator is, or the category of people to which they see themselves belonging. By your choice of bullshit, you tell me a lot about who you are, or aspire to be.

Remember the gooseberry tart: the polite comment tells the host nothing about the pudding, but a lot about his guest.

Well, I could select example after example of apparently awkward statements that do this. Academic jargon may not be the most elegant way of expressing a point, but it is a badge of membership of a community. Or listen to a politician painfully arguing a point that they don't believe, out of loyalty to their party. Their message is not 'the party position on this is right'; the message is 'I am loyal to my party's position on this, even if I think it is wrong'.

You might see the choice of words as akin to a young man opting to wear a suit to visit the bank manager or while in the dock of a magistrate's court. It is dressing for the occasion. It is not misleading as such – the bank manager or magistrate knows that just because he has a suit on, it doesn't mean he is the sort of person to wear a suit all the time. The suit simply says, 'I'm smart enough and socially engaged enough to know that this is the kind of occasion where I'm meant to dress up.' The same is true of many forms of idiom. We all see ourselves conforming to some role whether we are a diplomat, a banker or a waiter. And we adopt language that tells people which role we are trying to conform to. Often, that language will have elements of bullshit about it, either in the form of superfluous complexity or waffle, or adherence to formality or ritual, or faux deference. We simply can't help ourselves, and nor should we.

If our language provides subtle cues as to who we are, it is also revealing as to whose side we are on. Or, to put it another way, it is often by our bullshit that we reveal our allegiance. Our words convey a sense of belonging to a particular club. And because it is a subtle form of communication, it is harder to fake than an explicit statement of loyalty. To take an everyday example: the loud music blaring out in shops selling youthful fashions. It is not functionally useful to the shop assistants or to the customers in transacting their business, but it is an honest form of communication designed to signal that this is a shop for youthful and fashionable people, not one for old fogeys.[22] You could put up a sign saying 'No old fogeys here: this shop is for cool young people', but it wouldn't have the same power.

None of this will be much of a surprise to anyone working in advertising, where it goes without saying that the design of any message starts with the thought of who it is aimed at. In the last chapter I suggested that a lot of ads signal the confidence of the advertiser in their product through their willingness to invest in expensive advertising. Now we have an additional reason for apparently uninformative advertising: it indirectly tells you who the product is for. Stressed housewives, young clubbers, the confused elderly, men who are handy round the house, aspirant young professional women, the super-rich and stupid rich, teens and tweens – it is not hard to think of ads you've seen that are aimed at these tribes. The ad does not spell it out literally, but demonstrates a connection to the target by the choice of content. The pictures, the humour, the storyline (if there is one), the language and tone will all make clear who should buy (and perhaps who should not buy) a particular product.

Take the example of the famous Dambusters ad for Carling Black Label lager. Created by WCRS, the well-executed commercial re-created the celebrated Second World War bouncing-bomb raid on a German dam, but had a German guard sharp-wittedly taking on the role of a goalkeeper and deflecting the bombs. 'I bet he drinks Carling Black Label' was the slogan.[23] By mashing up two subjects that disproportionately preoccupy young men – war films and football – the intended market is clear. You could call these signals dog whistles: subtle (or in this case not so subtle) cues that are especially likely to be appreciated by the intended audience. The lack of hard content in the Dambusters ad, in the form of useful information about the lager itself, is irrelevant. The ad is in some sense bullshit, but the only information a prospective buyer needs, apart from the reassuringly expensive quality of the ad, is that the beer is something young men might see fit to buy; and that it is cool enough in laddish twenty-something male circles that you can consume it without fear of looking stupid.

You might ask why the advertiser needs to go to such lengths to target a market of young men. Why did we have to invent the institution of advertising to come up with such an elaborate means of communicating basic information, when the brewer could just tell people who the drink is for? The answer is that by adopting the favoured bullshit of the target market, you demonstrate an intimacy with that market which proves you mean business in serving it. The use of subtle cues is an expression of sincerity.

The case of politics

And that brings us to politics, where the question of whose side you are on is often the main determinant of who voters support. To what degree is political bullshit explained by the presence of subtle cues aimed at demonstrating the speaker's allegiance?

The first point to make is that politicians have always used *unsubtle* cues in an attempt to be all things to all people. They face an inevitable vote-limiting quandary in that by increasing their appeal to one group they often decrease their appeal to another, so the solution – if they can get away with it – is to say different things to different groups.[24] But this is what I would call bullshit in the form of classic mendacity, stemming from a traditional desire to have a cake and eat it. It is not a new phenomenon, and if anything, it has become harder to sustain because national and social media has become more aggressive in exposing these kinds of contradictions. Two-faced politics can only get you so far.

However, the more significant recent phenomenon is the use of a different kind of bullshit to show 'whose side I am on'. This is in some ways far more transparent than old-fashioned mendacity as it is not about saying one thing to one group and trying to hide it from everyone else, it is about openly tailoring a pitch to a selected segment of the population by entertaining its members with fantasies or myths that have a particular appeal to them. Think of Donald Trump and his connection to Wrestlemania and appearances at World Wrestling Entertainment (WWE) events. Mr Trump featured in several storylines, including the Battle of the Billionaires in 2007, in which he was pitched against Vince McMahon, the chairman of WWE.[25] At one point Trump bodyslams McMahon and beats him to the ground; the main contest is conducted by professional wrestlers, selected to fight on behalf of the billionaires, and as Mr Trump's wins the fight, Mr Trump gets to shave Mr McMahon's head, to the obvious delight of the crowd. The video of the event is highly entertaining.[26] Now, not only do I imagine that the rivalry between the two was choreographed, I imagine that the fans have always understood (or at least suspected) that WWE has elements of stagecraft about it because that has more or less been admitted in public.[27] It is perfectly possible to enjoy WWE while believing the participants to be playing out scripts and roles, but could there be any better way for Mr Trump to demonstrate a connection to a certain segment of the US population than by participation in WWE stunts, even though he was not a presidential candidate at the time he appeared? It is worth mentioning that he looked very comfortable in the WWE environment. He was not awkwardly engaging in a gimmick to court popularity; he revelled in it in a way that most other business leaders or politicians could not.

The point here is that Trump's supporters know where he is coming from, without necessarily taking everything he says or does at face value. Consider this passage from Kathy Cramer, a professor of political science who spent the best part of a decade interviewing rural voters from Wisconsin.[28] Speaking to the *Washington Post* about the appeal of Donald Trump, she said:

> I really resist this characterization of Trump supporters as ignorant.
>
> There's just more and more of a recognition that politics for people is not – and this is going to sound awful, but – it's not about facts and policies. It's so much about identities, people forming ideas about the kind of person they are and the kind of people others are. *Who am I for, and who am I against?*
>
> Policy is part of that, but policy is not the driver of these judgments. There are assessments of, *is this someone like me? Is this someone who gets someone like me?*
>
> I think all too often, we put our energies into figuring out where people stand on particular policies. I think putting energy into trying to understand the way they view the world and their place in it – that gets us so much further toward understanding how they're going to vote, or which candidates are going to be appealing to them.
>
> All of us, even well-educated, politically sophisticated people interpret facts through our own perspectives, our sense of what [and] who we are, our own identities.
>
> I don't think that what you do is give people more information. Because they are going to interpret it through the perspectives they already have. People are only going to absorb facts when they're communicated from a source that

they respect, from a source who they perceive has respect for people like them.

And so whenever a liberal calls out Trump supporters as ignorant or fooled or misinformed, that does absolutely nothing to convey the facts that the liberal is trying to convey.[29]

This is surely the best way to understand much of the afactual category of empty assertion discussed in Chapter 2, and the appeal of Donald Trump in the election campaign of 2016 in particular. He makes an assertion exaggerating the level of unemployment, not because it is true but because it sends a signal to the particular segment of the population he is targeting for votes. Similarly, his contentions about spiralling crime in inner cities or claims about foreign rapists all confirm that Donald Trump is not part of the old liberal establishment (who would never say such things) and that he is on the side of angry non-metropolitan white voters who feel their concerns have been overlooked, and who would like to believe that the world of metropolitan liberals is all going wrong. If you (rightly or wrongly) fear change, or feel your economic and social status has been undermined by progressive values, multiculturalism and international trade, it really doesn't matter to you whether Donald Trump tells the strict truth about these issues; it does, however, matter that he conveys his adherence to your values. If he says the NAFTA trade deal 'has destroyed our country', it matters not a jot whether that is correct if you are simply interested in understanding where he is coming from.[30] When he says a state that has seen a high level of Somali immigration has 'suffered enough', he is saying things that many believe, even if liberal social convention looks down on those who spell these things out.[31] By entertaining that proposition, fantasy or not, Trump is showing how well he understands his target audience.

You didn't need to be taken in by any of these assertions to still want to support him. That is why Salena Zito's article in the *Atlantic*, 'the press takes him literally, but not seriously; his supporters take him seriously, but not literally' is quoted as often as it is.[32] You can't even call it dog-whistle politics, as that implies it is heard only or mainly by the target audience. In Trump's case, it was far too blatant for anyone to miss.

In all these cases, Donald Trump chose to show his support for a particular portion of the electorate by making bold, questionable, and sometimes plainly untrue claims. It was a more powerful way of showing his allegiance than simply saying 'I am on your side', which anyone might choose to say in order to win votes.

Using bullshit to convey an allegiance does carry a risk. A candidate asserting verifiably false propositions may be discredited among potential supporters who put a high value on integrity, competence or a grasp of the facts. But there are fraught times in the life of a nation when these attributes for a president are generally seen as secondary to knowing the candidate supports the right team. And in practice, for Donald Trump in 2016 the benefits of demonstrating an emotional connection with that big pool of voters outweighed the cost in terms of lost credibility.

Odd as it may seem to compare Donald Trump's election rhetoric to Steve Nesbitt's 'major malfunction' or the Queen's speech in Ireland, they are all examples of dressing up language with unnatural superfluity, or infusing it with other kinds of bullshit, in order to signal a particular context or our conformity to a type. For Trump supporters, the truth value of any proposition offered in this regard is about as relevant as the truth value of a claim about the pleasantness of a friend's burnt gooseberry tart. It's not about the fact of the matter as such, it is about the sentiment beneath. You can apply all the usual fact-checking tools to the literal claim, but the real point is always buried in the subtitles, and no amount of correction will belie that.

This signalling of tribal allegiance through a particular selection of anecdotes, lines, metaphors, jokes and occasional myths is one ingredient of the politician's appeal. This is not a very profound point, but it has been surprisingly hard for opponents of the likes of Donald Trump to grasp. They have found it all too easy to condemn as stupid anyone who supports populist politicians or appears unperturbed by their falsehoods.[33] Undoubtedly, some supporters are gullible, but many probably know exactly what is true and what is not and simply decide that it's better to support someone who is on their side rather than someone who has a grasp of the facts. If I feel my segment of the population has been sidelined for decades, why would I not consider it in my interest to support the person who makes clear they are thinking my way?

The way to counter that sentiment is not to assert the primacy of the facts in increasingly exasperated tones, or to question the intelligence of those seduced by the 'lies'. It is perhaps the precise opposite. If you want to make friends with or influence people who begrudge the fact they have been neglected, you usually do it by showing more love and respect for them, not less. It is the willingness of the authoritarian opportunist to do precisely that which often accounts for their appeal.

It is also important to say that if the era of post-truth politics is characterised by a willingness on the part of politicians to peddle reassuring myths, it is also marked by a readiness on the part of many voters to rise to those myths. That disposition to accept bullshit probably derives from a sense of tribalism fuelled by feelings of grievance. The bullshit becomes more than just a signal of tribal allegiance; it becomes a way of strengthening a sense of membership of the tribe.

It is no coincidence that fears of an increased level of bullshit in public discourse have coincided with the era of so-called identity politics, with voters primarily thinking of themselves as belonging to a group and putting more weight on a potential leader's respect for their identity than attributes such as good sense, intelligence or decency. The message of this chapter is that because tribal bullshit contains real information as to who supports which tribe, to counter its appeal you need to think about the causes of the tribalism rather than simply try to debunk the myths that are spread around.

If the arguments I have laid out in this chapter are right, we can immediately see why the real world is so much more complicated than the bare rational model implies. A proposition may be informative even if it is a lie, because the choice of lie (or more generally, the choice of euphemism, embellishment, exaggeration or language) is itself informative. However, this is merely one explanation of some of the less-than-straightforward material we encounter. It is also the case that even if bullshit is not informative, it sometimes has the power to convince us of things. We are not rational beings: we are open to persuasion and even manipulation, good or bad, by friends and foes. We have psychological foibles that affect our disposition to accept a message and believe it. And it is those that are the subject of the next chapter.

Being Human

The importance of irrationality in perception and belief

Psychological pricing

In the economy section of its 2005 manifesto, the Monster Raving Loony Party had a pledge to introduce a 99p coin in order to 'save on change'.[1] Given the prevalence of 99p prices in our shops, it was by no means the silliest policy in their manifesto (or probably those of the other parties either). But it raises a good question: why do we have so many prices that end in 99p?

It is certainly not down to chance. According to a huge survey of product advertisements in American newspapers, no fewer than 30 per cent of the quoted prices ended in the digit nine – a higher proportion than those ending in zero and more than those ending in one, two, three, four, six, seven and eight combined.[2] The attraction of the digit nine is sometimes explained by a theory that shopkeepers like to prevent staff theft, and thus force transactions through the till by ensuring that customers require change. But while this is plausible, it can't explain why the price of the cheapest Ford Fiesta is, at the time of writing,

£9995, or why seventeen of the twenty-five prominently advertised products on the front page of the DFS furniture store
website have a price ending in £99. In these cases, the pricing
strategy is clearly not driven by staff theft, cash transactions or
tills.

Another theory says that by trimming a penny off the round-
number price of something, vendors signal to price-conscious
consumers that the item is aimed at them. A price with a 99 at
the end screams out 'Buy me! I'm the cheap and cheerful one,
not the expensive posh one.' It is just vendors' shorthand for the
kind of appeal they want their product to have. On this theory,
vendors of quality items will use round numbers. But while I
think there is something in this, a forty-five-second perusal of
the Harrods website shows Vivienne Westwood, Hugo Boss and
Paul Smith items mostly priced in numbers ending in nine, and
I assume that they are not attempting to appeal to low-budget
shoppers. So there has to be more to the 99p prices, and the best
clue as to what motivates it surely lies in the name often given to
it: psychological pricing. It is pricing that cleverly plays on certain of our mental habits, which give us a tendency sometimes
to treat almost identical numbers as significantly different from
each other. When we gaze upon the prices £9995 and £10,000,
the former looks a lot less than the latter; certainly it seems like
there's more than £5 to separate them. If you want to present
your car as better value, it is obvious which of those two prices
you should select.

Psychological pricing is of relevance to this book because
£9995 is best seen as a form of spin. It is a technique for dressing
up a price of £10,000 to make it appear less than £10,000, when
in fact it is materially the same. The question as to whether it
works in getting us to buy things is absolutely central to the
more general understanding of bullshit. If it does work then yes,

you can fool at least some of the people at least some of the time, and bullshit generally can work too.

Now, you will remember when we looked at the economics of information in Chapter 4, we said that in the rational model of information and communication it was hard to explain the prevalence of bullshit because the model assumes that sensible people would never fall for it. Surely we can see that 9.99 and 10.00 are more or less the same number, so we would not let the difference influence our purchasing decisions. And, more generally, we would never trust cheap talk from anyone who had an incentive to mislead us. For the economists, the mystery is why so much bullshit is peddled, given that it is futile and no one should be responding to it. In the last chapter we gave one answer as to why it may persist: bullshit contains subtle information and people respond to that. In this chapter, we entertain the idea that certain forms of bullshit really can hoodwink us.

There is no better test of that proposition than to look at the effect of psychological pricing. Does it succeed in securing extra sales? To help us answer that we must meet Robert Schindler, Professor of Marketing at Rutgers School of Business in Camden, New Jersey. He's a psychologist by training and first became interested in this question when he was working for AT&T, the telecommunications company, in the US. He was in market research, and the Economics Research Department gave him the task of estimating how much a price promotion would affect sales. The economists had evidence that the price sensitivity of long-distance calling was very low, implying a promotion would have little effect. But everything that Schindler had seen indicated that a sales promotion would prompt a bigger consumer response than the ordinary price sensitivity suggested. That was back in the late 1970s. 'I got interested in pricing from my work there,' he told me, 'and one of the things I discovered when I started to get interested in pricing is that this phenomenon that we see everywhere around us, this nine-ending pricing, has barely ever been investigated. You would sort of think that something like that was really well figured out, but it wasn't. So I started doing research on it and now I've done over a dozen studies on it.'[3]

It's all too rare for social scientists to be able to carry out real-world controlled experiments. They can look at real-world data or carry out rigorously controlled trials, but not often at the same time. But Schindler was lucky, and through a contact at the University of Chicago he found a mail-order retailer who was interested in helping him. The company sold women's clothing and agreed to send out three versions of a catalogue consisting of 169 items, identical except that in one version the prices ended in 00, in the second the prices all ended in the digits 99 and in the third, in 88. The average price of the items in the catalogue was $31, so it's safe to say the differences in prices between the three catalogues were trivial. In substantive terms, $30.00 is the same price as $29.99 or $29.88; it's just the *look* of the price that differs. Each catalogue was sent to thirty thousand names on the company's mailing list and a tally kept of how many orders were then forthcoming.

We'll come back to the result of Professor Schindler's experiment shortly, but before we do it is worth asking yourself what you expect. Would you think there would be an uplift in sales from the catalogue with nine-ending prices? Or the slightly cheaper eight-ending prices? And what would constitute a significant uplift? One per cent, 10 per cent, or 30 per cent? It is only one test, but for me it is the ultimate one of whether the public are susceptible to these kinds of mental games.

The belief that psychological mechanisms can have a significant effect explains the existence of a lot of the modern communications industry – and the bullshit it produces. The industry survives and thrives, it could be argued, because human beings have many quirks, and clever communicators can exploit these to get our attention or to persuade us of things. For supporters of the industry, communication can demonstrably have an effect on us through these psychological channels, independent of any rational logic, and that justifies the salaries of those working in communications. For sceptics, the fact that human beings might be taken in by 9.99 pricing is a sign that we can be manipulated or brainwashed by the ruthless and disreputable; that clever propaganda can turn us into monsters. We live in a post-truth age because significant numbers of gullible people are taken in by fake news and false narratives that are put about by those who play to our disposition to believe.

The contrast between what one might rationally expect to happen and what actually happens brings to mind the observation of a mathematical friend during the swimming relays at the last Olympics. He pointed out that as addition is a commutative operation (i.e., A + B = B + A), it was surprising how much attention appeared to be devoted to the order in which the members of the relay teams were selected to swim. Logic was on my friend's side: the same four swimmers should have the same overall time, whatever sequence they swim in. But as swim teams are made up of human beings, team managers know psychology makes the order significant. *It may not be rational, but it works*, a phrase that could be a slogan for the PR industry. It is true that the order of the swimmers is, at best, of secondary importance. The relay teams who spend all their time finessing the order in which they swim will probably perform less well than the ones who train to swim fast. But clearly psychology explains a bunch of human reactions that defy the world of rational economics, so let us look in more detail at what might be going on.

The importance of psychology

The power of human psychology to interfere with the assumptions of the rational model of human behaviour has become more recognised in the last decade than ever before. For one thing, psychology has become very fashionable in higher education. In the twenty years from 1995/96, the number studying the subject in UK universities has risen more than threefold.[4] It has become one of the country's most popular subjects, with nearly four times as many students starting undergraduate courses in it as in physics, for example.[5] But it wasn't just students who caught the psychology bug. The economics profession came round too, having spent most of its existence studying human behaviour with simple models that, in effect, took as a starting point the idea that psychology doesn't exist. Life for economists was much simpler that way, as it allowed them to imagine that everyone pursues simple objectives (minimising effort, maximising profit or utility). The models built on that assumption generated clear results of the kind we derived in earlier chapters, telling you when people may or may not believe things, for example. The only small problem was that the clarity of those models came at the expense of usefulness. There is an old gag (one of many at the expense of the economists) that has a physicist, a chemist and an economist stranded on a desert island, pondering on how to open a tin of soup. The punchline has the economist suggesting, 'Let's assume we have a can opener.' It encapsulates a fair critique of economic method, and through the 2000s the limits of the old approach were becoming more and more obvious; this weakness was recognised in that one of the winners of the 2002 Nobel Prize in economics – the psychologist Daniel Kahneman – wasn't really an economist at all.[6] Five years later, with the onset of a full-scale financial crash, it was apparent that much of the interesting action in the global economy was driven by the very human factors that had been previously been assumed away. At that point, behavioural economics emerged as one of the hottest topics around.[7]

In 2009, Stefano DellaVigna, an economist at the University of California, Berkeley, wrote a review of the evidence that psychology can have an effect in the kinds of ways economists had generally ignored.[8] He covered a host of areas, sweeping up the available evidence in each, and demonstrated just how powerful and varied the human factors are in explaining behaviour, rather than narrow economic self-interest: people responding to low, temporary teaser rates on credit cards rather than the permanent standard rate when deciding how much to borrow; people deciding pension contributions simply on the basis of the default set by their employer; people paying too little attention to postage and packing costs when ordering online; people tipping more in sunny weather; people working more or less hard depending on how nice their employer is to them; and so on and so on. He has myriad examples, none of which conform to the standard economic models. In the same vein, the popular book *Nudge* by Richard Thaler and Cass Sunstein described the ways that policymakers could exploit these quirks to improve behaviour without resorting to the illiberal steps of banning different actions or making them compulsory.[9] If you want people to put litter in bins rather than on the ground, then introduce litter bins that make a nice noise when rubbish is deposited in them. Want people to eat less? Then encourage the use of smaller plates, as our perception of how much we've eaten is shaped by how full the plate in front of us is. The trendiness of this approach became apparent in 2010 with the arrival in Downing Street of the Behavioural Insights Team, whose job was to find practical ways of using psychological 'tricks' to improve public behaviour.[10]

My favourite example of the kind of subconscious psychological bias that might affect some of our decisions is the so-called
name-letter effect. It is the tendency we apparently exhibit to
favour things that start with the same letters as our first or last
names. For example, it has been found that a disproportionate
number of people called Jack live in Jacksonville, and more
Lauras gravitate to careers in law than you would expect from
the numbers of Lauras in the population. It was first set out in
1985 by the Belgian social psychologist Jozef M. Nuttin, Jr in
an article with the fabulous title 'Narcissism beyond Gestalt
and awareness: The name letter effect'.[11] It prompted quite a
debate in the psychology literature, with more and more evidence accumulating in its favour, based around a theory called
implicit egotism. I mention this particular effect because I can
remember supporting Everton as a child (rather half-heartedly,
I should admit, as football wasn't my thing) on the basis that it
sounded a bit like Evan. If you believe all the evidence proffered
in its favour and think the name-letter effect is strong, then you
surely believe that psychology can drive anything.

As it happens, most of the evidence for the name-letter effect
has been questioned, if not completely demolished. (You can
read a complex statistical paper with lines like 'Study 6 here
shows that Dennises are just as overrepresented (compared
with Walters and Jerrys) among lawyers as they are among den-
tists' and 'These results suggest that, if anything, Georges and
Geoffreys are slightly less likely to be geoscientists rather than
any other kind of scientist'.)[12] But even if name-letter effects do
turn out to be a figment of the psychologists' imaginations, there
are still all our other perceptual biases.

All in all, the study of behaviour that appears irrational, or is
rational in subtle ways, has added useful insights to the models
that had been kicking around hitherto. It must have been a

bit annoying for psychologists, who had been looking at these issues for decades, to suddenly find economists taking the credit for discovering them. But even if economists were a little late to the party, they did start getting a fuller understanding of human decision-making once they arrived. When it comes to most issues, traditional economics, behavioural economics and psychology all have something to offer.

If the study of psychology tells us that human factors are important in most areas of life, then they must be relevant to communication and persuasion, offering us an appreciation of how far and for how long the use of sophisticated presentational techniques can convince us to believe things we might not otherwise believe. The excellent book *Yes! 50 Secrets from the Science of Persuasion* opens with the words 'If all the world's a stage, then small changes in your lines can have dramatic effects.'[13] It suggests that it's not just the substance of a message that matters, it's the way you get it across. At issue is the degree to which subliminal mental processes can affect our behaviour, and whether those processes can then be exploited or abused. Are we more likely to buy a house if it is tidy when we view it, or if there is a pot of coffee brewing in the kitchen, even though these are factors that should be irrelevant to our assessment of the property?

The orthodox view is that these mechanisms do operate. I asked one estate agent for his view, and he was clear: 'Presentation is ninety per cent of the battle,' he said. 'It makes an enormous difference to experience a clean, uncluttered, fresh-smelling (or of coffee/flowers if you like) property and we often strongly advise our clients on what is the best way to enable us to show their properties in the best light ... First impressions are *crucial* ... The little touches matter a great deal.' He quite reasonably draws an important distinction between good presentation and deception (by painting over a damp patch, for example). For him, it is just common sense and I trust his judgement as he has made a good living selling houses. For my purposes, the important thing is that if trivial aspects of presentation matter we do not appear to conform to the rational model, and we have some kind of psychological case for bullshit, such as putting the coffee on when prospective buyers visit. And, importantly, you don't need to fool everyone to justify the use of these tactics; you just need to fool enough people to cover the minimal cost of the coffee.

The belief that an understanding of psychology can help communicators frame a message in more or less convincing ways is based on the premise that we have certain mental habits that can be exploited: rules of thumb, preconceptions and biases that we deploy when making a judgement. Understand those cognitive short cuts and you stand a good chance of influencing us. But all this presupposes that human beings are influenced by the way things are presented to them. That bullshit works. But is that true? Well, that brings us back to Professor Schindler's experiment with the friendly mail-order retailer.

The experiment proceeded well. The company did all the work and handed over the raw data to Professor Schindler and his colleague Thomas Kibarian to see what effect the different pricing schemes had. And the answer came back. Yes, the 99 version of the catalogue *did* generate more sales: $78,317 compared with the $72,529 earned by its round-number equivalent. Its sales were 8 per cent higher. The 88 prices came in third, with $71,699 of sales. The experiment was a victory for psychological pricing. 'It was pretty substantial – I was impressed,' Professor Schindler told me. Or, as the academic write-up in the *Journal of Retailing* put it, 'Managerially, an 8 per cent increase in sales revenue at a cost of a one-cent per item decrease in price is undeniably attractive.'[14]

In fact, it was so attractive to the management of the

mail-order company that the collaboration ended. Professor Schindler told me what happened: 'We had another meeting, again very jovial, and that's where I asked them. I said, "This is really interesting, shall we do another one?" But from their point of view they didn't want to do it again because they lost so much money in the zero-ending condition. They said, "We can't afford to do another study like this. We need to have it all nine-endings next time." But they were very gracious about it.'

Why does psychology matter?

It seems psychological pricing does work, which is an important finding because it implies that we can be hoodwinked. This, in turn, tells us that the rational model of communication – which would suggest that it is the price, not the way it looks, that matters – is wrong.

It raises the question why. In the case of Professor Schindler's experiment, it must be something to do with the way our brain assesses the price, and the prominence we assign to certain features of it. The most obvious theory to explain the effectiveness of a price ending in a nine, which is known as left-hand truncation, suggests that we generally pay most attention to the left-hand digits in a number as these are the most significant. As busy people we've adapted not to waste time studying all three digits to spot that 25.3 is bigger than 15.7, so in this case we only compare the leading digits – two and one – and ignore the rest. If we get locked into the habit of doing that, then we will also habitually overlook the 99 pence at the end of a price and only focus on the number of pounds ahead of the decimal point. On this theory, we see both £7.99 and £7.01 as £7. It thus makes sense for vendors to price as high as they can without triggering a rise in the perceived price.

Robert Schindler describes consumers, in this case, as judging the book by its cover. And to substantiate the proposition that round numbers have psychological power, he cites evidence that the finish times for runners in the New York Marathon cluster just under the round hours (maybe people find a little extra push to finish just under four hours, for example); people are more likely to retake SATs tests when they were just under a round number score; and baseball players' batting averages disproportionately cluster just above a round number too. Should we be surprised? Robert Schindler thinks not: 'It's a powerful emotional effect and the thing that makes it mysterious is because our society is so rationalised. We say, "Well, if it's not rational, it's not fair," and I think there should really be more respect for the emotional side of ourselves, which is very real. In emotional terms having that left digit lower feels better, seems better, and therefore is better.'

Left-hand truncation is not the only theory to explain psychological pricing, and for me it matters little which particular account is true. What is important is that it is typical of many psychological explanations for 'irrational' behaviour: it posits that we put disproportionate weight on a chosen piece of the information available simply because it is more cognitively accessible. You can understand why the brain has developed as it has, but it means that even though the full information is there for those who want it, vendors know that we don't tend to use it.

This is just one example of us taking a mental short cut and leaving ourselves vulnerable to mistakes. There is a long list of cognitive biases that result from these mental short cuts, from the 'endowment effect' (our tendency to want more compensation to give up something that we already have, than we would be willing to pay for it if we didn't have it) to the 'availability bias' (our tendency to attach too high a probability to an event with a vivid outcome, such as winning the lottery or being in a plane crash). That a huge number of such biases exist is indisputable. And they are difficult to resist.

Psychologists have explained them by reference to two different systems of thought, rather drearily labelled System One and System Two. System One is our capacity for quick and intuitive thinking; and System Two is our more conscious cognition, slow and calculating. As human beings we have evolved to have both, and each has a place in helping us survive and thrive. System One gets us through most of the basics of life without wasting time thinking too hard about things, but from time to time it calls on System Two to ponder an issue more carefully. In *Thinking Fast and Slow*, Daniel Kahneman lists examples of the two: System One detects hostility in a voice, understands simple sentences, completes the phrase 'bread and ...', and allows us to drive a car on an empty road. System Two is used when we fill out a tax return, maintain a faster walking speed than is natural, or count the occurrences of the letter 'a' on a page, and it helps us park in a narrow space.[15] Humans are blessed in comparison to other animals by having System Two thinking, but it would be mad to think that most of what we do is conscious and deliberate. The important suggestion for our purpose is that although System One is clever and quick and gets most things right, it inevitably makes mistakes, and those mistakes fit certain patterns. It is System One that responds to the instruction 'Don't think of an elephant' by thinking of an elephant. And System One tends to believe things: show someone a cigarette and a fit-looking model, and System One immediately logs an association between the two. It is System Two that reflects on the association and then works out whether there is a connection. And System Two is more likely to make a conscious effort to *un*believe what it has been shown.

Faced with a decision as to whether to believe something,

System One does its best to come up with a verdict, but it is subject to a huge number of biases in everyday mental processing. They can be overcome by inviting System Two to examine the options, but that takes quite a mental effort. If the System One result is in some sense gratifying, it may be rather difficult to overturn it: our desire to believe something makes it harder to resist System One telling us it is true.

Successful communicators can use well constructed messages to appeal to our System One brains and influence our thinking or behaviour. That is what psychological pricing does. Crisply and honestly setting out the facts is not the way to succeed in a System One world. Those who fail to realise this, and who eschew bullshit to tell it straight, do so at their peril. For example, in the late 1990s Coca-Cola faced a brief flurry of negative articles over the idea of programming vending machines to charge higher prices in hot weather. The then chief executive Douglas Ivester said in an interview with a Brazilian news magazine that as the demand for a cold drink rises when the outside temperature is hot, 'it is fair that it should be more expensive. The machine will simply make this process automatic.'[16] To most people, this does not sound like progress at all, and arch-rival Pepsi was clever enough to spot the own goal and responded by saying, 'We believe that machines that raise prices in hot weather exploit consumers who live in warm climates.'

Had Mr Ivester understood how people react instinctively to things, he could have expressed exactly the same policy as a price reduction on cold days without it sounding like exploitation at all. Any Coke drinker applying their mind to this issue – their conscious, calculating, System Two mind, that is – would quickly see a similarity between a winter price discount and a summer price surcharge; but it is not the kind of issue to which Coke drinkers tend to apply their mind. They jump to a view of the policy on the basis of one or two salient features. They can't process the idea of a high summer price without thinking about high prices. It's a textbook case of how psychology really matters, and how by framing the same thing in different ways you get a very different reaction. Mr Ivester, incidentally, was gone from Coke within a few months (to be replaced by a Mr Daft).[17]

For those who have an instinctive sense of how to exploit our psychological vulnerabilities, the rewards are great, even if mendacity or nonsense flow. So let us take a brief tour of five techniques of clever communication that can sell or persuade, using facts, misusing facts or sidelining the facts. All five take advantage of our cognitive filing systems to encourage us to put a core piece of information into a positive mental file rather than a negative one.

Emotion

More than any other System One thinking, emotions motivate us to respond to things very quickly. Canny communicators can thus sell us their messages by couching them in ways that induce suitable emotional reactions. If you want to persuade people to wear car seat belts, you may not elicit much reaction by just presenting the statistical evidence that it's a good idea to do so; better to publicise grisly pictures of people who weren't wearing seat belts and who have had accidents. This can be expected to arouse fear in your target audience and provoke the desired reaction. This example tells you why emotional appeals are strong, and also why we should be nervous about them. You can make a pretty effective emotional pitch that is quite detached from any objective evidence. In responding to such a pitch, we simply characterise a situation as worthy of a particular emotion, but we don't really think the whole issue through (that's the whole point of the brain having a rapid-response mechanism). This invites anyone trying to sell us a product or a cause – particularly those with the weakest arguments in their favour – to overstate their case by dressing it up in a form specifically designed to stop us thinking too hard about it.

When our emotions are assailed by this sort of friendly fire, we don't complain. We even choose to make ourselves cry by clicking links to stories with headlines like 'Walnut the whippet has gone for his final walk and there wasn't a dry eye on the beach'.[18] We expose ourselves to a piece of writing or video in the sure knowledge of an involuntary physical reaction.

The joy we evidently derive from being emotionally exploited gives us yet another explanation for seemingly uninformative commercial advertising.

Large numbers of people in Britain anticipate and love the John Lewis Christmas ads, looking out to see if this year's is more or less of a tearjerker than the previous one. Whether it be little kids wanting to buy presents for their parents, animals bouncing on trampolines, the joy of a lonely man on the moon receiving a gift, and so on, the ads have become a national institution, attracting headlines such as 'Did the new John Lewis advert make you cry?'[19] In fact, on social media there are grumbles if the ad fails to pack a powerful enough emotional punch. The primary effect of the ads is presumably to arouse a pleasing emotional reaction, which we then associate with John Lewis. Of course, this link between emotion and product is entirely constructed by the advertiser. It is an invitation not to think about the retailer using our System Two brain, but to enjoy it using System One.

While the comforting arousal of gentle, warm-hearted feelings by John Lewis could hardly be said to be threatening – at worst, it causes us to shop at John Lewis – when emotional manipulation is in the hands of those with malign intent it can be a dangerous tool, and no more so than when the emotion is anger. Because emotional appeals invite us not to think, the literal truth of anything underlying them is never at the forefront of the mental appraisal we give them, which means rage can be incited by lies or half-truths and few will stop to engage their System Two brain to work out how things might look in a more objective light. No wonder that opportunist politicians through the ages have tried to foster emotional reactions in their target voters, and at times have particularly flourished when they've succeeded in stirring up anger. They offer vivid accounts of how other groups (elites or immigrants, for example) have conspired to make life difficult. Their rhetoric suggests the problems of the target voter are not just the unfortunate outcome of a set of difficult circumstances; they are the deliberate work of an enemy. In an era in which politics has become more tribal, and identity (class, race, religion or nationality) is more of an issue than usual, it is no surprise that anger is the emotion that has come to the fore as a political tool.

In fairness to those who are accused of stirring up anger, the grievances of the angry may be perfectly justified and you would want a political system to give voice to those who have cause to complain: that is what is meant to happen in a flourishing democracy. But if demagogues come along and succeed in *creating* anger rather than merely giving voice to it, it is perhaps less healthy. When looking at the political phenomenon of so-called populism, this is the question that ultimately divides opinion. For supporters, the populists are at last allowing decent, ordinary people to have their say.* For opponents, the populists have

---

* Nigel Farage, then leader of the UK Independence Party, asserted that the Brexit referendum result was 'a victory for real people, a victory for ordinary people, a victory for decent people'.

managed to win support by whipping up anger and spreading hate that is neither justified nor helpful.

The use of story

At the very least, everybody recognises an emotional appeal when they see one, and the technique is both well understood and not particularly clever. But there is another strand of communication theory that thinks of our mental filing system in a rather different – and more sophisticated – way. It was developed in the 1980s by Professor Walter Fisher, who sees humans as innate story-tellers.[20] According to Fisher's account, when we are given a message we don't appraise it in a straightforwardly rational or emotional way; instead, we slot the message into a story of some kind and think about how convincing that story is overall. In this account, stories are the human way of making sense of things. Narrative structures are a device the human being uses to slot information into a meaningful form.

What is a story? It involves heroes and villains, or other characters whose actions are guided by values and history, with events and consequences following from them. According to Fisher's 'narrative paradigm', we have evolved to structure our thoughts around these narratives rather than organise them in logical folders. Certainly, if you try to remember a sequence of fifteen facts, you will be able to do so more easily if they form a story than if they are random, or presented in alphabetical order. And story-telling is a very democratic form of public discourse, in that anybody can spot a good story when they hear one, including people who would not find it easy to read a think-tank report on some policy or other. That is, incidentally, why the writers of books like this one tend to follow the master of exposition, Malcolm Gladwell, in using stories to explain abstract points.

For an example of how a story can be used to sell a commercial product, look no further than Innocent Drinks, a successful purveyor of smoothies, fruit juices and other products. It was founded in 1999 by three Cambridge graduates who were working in advertising and management consulting at the time, and who created one of the best-communicated brands of the last couple of decades. The founders always stress that the quality of their product underpinned the company's rapid success; their smoothies were made from fresh fruit rather than concentrate; they were sourced from Rainforest Alliance and other ethically credited sources; they were sold in bottles made only from recycled plastic; and they gave some of the profits to charity. All that may have been important to customers, but for me Innocent's success was less about the product and more about the *narrative* behind it, which was strikingly distinct. The desirable product features seemed important in that they buttressed the story. With that tale, aided of course by the general competence of the management, the founders managed to squeeze themselves into a very crowded market. The company has now been sold to Coca-Cola, and has been valued at hundreds of millions of pounds.

So how did Innocent do it? It starts with a story, told many times by the company founders:

We started Innocent in 1999 after selling our smoothies at a music festival. We put up a big sign asking people if they thought we should give up our jobs to make smoothies, and put a bin saying 'Yes' and a bin saying 'No' in front of the stall. Then we got people to vote with their empties. At the end of the weekend, the 'Yes' bin was full, so we resigned from our jobs the next day and got cracking.[21]

The story is memorable, and according to the founders of the company has the advantage of being true. And it helps the company get our attention. We want to buy the product and give the lads a hand to help the story end well (that's the way stories draw us in).

But that story, although well known to the company's devotees, is just one tale in a far bigger account of the product range which governs our view of the company. This is a business set up by enthusiastic youngsters who took a chance to pursue their passion and who want to show that business does not have to be corporate. The name, the logo, the website, the promotion of ethical business principles, the use of a silly car covered in artificial turf, the address ('Fruit Towers'), the contact details ('Call the bananaphone . . .') – these all invite us to think of Innocent as innocent, a bunch of clever, quirky lads having a good time, and most definitely *not* as a corporation trying to sell us fruit juices. Once you've bought into the Innocent legend, price is no longer the main factor in determining a choice. And detailed questions get ignored, such as, is Innocent fruit really any different from that which is bought on the global market by any other juicing company?

The Innocent story permeates every piece of the company's communication. Take the cooking instructions for one of their old range of products, a vegetable pot. Bear in mind that this product was basically a microwave ready-meal in a plastic container, the kind of convenience food that can be bought anywhere and which is generally despised by true foodies.[22] The directions for the Innocent Veg Pot are basically the same as for all the other products in this category, except that is not how they sound on the Innocent pack:

Cooking Instructions

Our veg needs a bit of cooking so follow the instructions below to make your tasty little meal ready for eating.

1. **In the microwave (for best results):** Remove card sleeve and lid. Replace lid loosely before heating on full power (Cat E – 850kW) for 2 minutes. Stir and cover again. Heat on full power for a further 1 minute 30 seconds until piping hot throughout. Be careful – the pot gets hot too.
2. **On the hob:** Pour contents into a small saucepan. Add 2 tbsp of water. Cook over a low-medium heat for 6–8 minutes, stirring occasionally until it's thoroughly hot.
3. **On the campfire:** Pour contents into cooking pot. Sing campfire songs until bubbling nicely.

We are all aware that the campfire instructions are there as a joke, but you can just about picture yourself 'cooking' your veg pot over a fire at Glastonbury with a fun-loving crowd larking around beside you. However, it is much more likely you'll be following the first of the three instructions, and zapping your pot in the office microwave. But what these instructions do is demonstrate how the whole Innocent story has clarity, consistency and appeal, and thus why it works so brilliantly. It's a kind of bullshit, but it makes a plain microwave meal into a premium one. Each individual message that Innocent wants to get across – the details on the label, the launch of a new product, a piece of news – is all presented within the overall narrative. Indeed, that is what a narrative is about: it unites the use of a variety of good communication tools in an overarching message that achieves widespread acceptance.

When it comes to politics, the master of the art of using story to present his case was Ronald Reagan, president at the time Walter Fisher outlined his theory. Reagan didn't just sprinkle his speeches with the odd yarn as a technique of enlivening them; stories framed his whole approach to the presidency. At its simplest, he made many of his points by telling anecdotes (he sold his tax reform plan by arguing that it would 'simplify a code so complex even Albert Einstein reportedly needed help on his 1040 form'),[23] but he also sustained a much bigger narrative about the US. According to William Lewis, a professor of rhetoric at Drake University in Des Moines, his story was of a nation 'driven inevitably forward by its heroic working people toward a world of freedom and economic progress unless blocked by moral or military weakness'. Lewis writes that it is 'a simple and familiar story that is widely taught and widely believed. It is not exactly a true story in the sense that academic historians would want their descriptions and explanations to be true, but it is not exactly fiction either'.[24] Within that grand narrative, Reagan had a tale for every occasion. For example, in his second inaugural address he related the following history:

Two of our Founding Fathers, a Boston lawyer named Adams and a Virginia planter named Jefferson, members of that remarkable group who met in Independence Hall and dared to think they could start the world over again, left us an important lesson. They had become political rivals in the presidential election of 1800. Then years later, when both were retired, and age had softened their anger, they began to speak to each other again through letters. A bond was re-established between those two who had helped create this government of ours.

In 1826, the fiftieth anniversary of the Declaration of Independence, they both died. They died on the same day, within a few hours of each other, and that day was the Fourth of July.

In one of those letters exchanged in the sunset of their lives, Jefferson wrote: 'It carries me back to the times when, beset with difficulties and dangers, we were fellow laborers in the same cause, struggling for what is most valuable to man, his right to self-government. Laboring always at the same oar, with some wave ever ahead threatening to overwhelm us, and yet passing harmless ... we rode through the storm with heart and hand.'

Well, with heart and hand, let us stand as one today: One people under God determined that our future shall be worthy of our past.[25]

You'll either think it brilliant rhetoric, or possibly you'll ask someone to pass the sick bag, but I lean to the former. It is more than an appeal to emotion (although it is clearly emotive) because what President Reagan's story does is give sense and historical place to his policies while diverting eyes away from detailed scrutiny of their effectiveness. You are invited to support him not on the basis of the particulars, but because you like the overall story and can assume that his polices are designed to fit into the sequel. By offering a little detail of the account of Jefferson and Adams, describing the poignant coincidence of the timing of their deaths and the emotional appeal of 'the bond re-established', Reagan makes the story vivid, memorable, touching and powerful enough to inspire as a symbol of a bigger message.

A lot of political stories are of course exaggerated or embellished.[26] But that does not mean they don't have a purpose. The useful attribute of a good story is that if it has certain truth in it, people are not too worried about whether it is all strictly true or how it is being used. It kind of misses the point to pick holes in a great yarn, and those who try to do so end up looking as though they are attacking the insight or moral lesson of the story, rather than the reliability of the story-teller.* Reagan understood how people think and judge, and knew which buttons to push in order to be persuasive. He may not have scored points in a contest based on reason, but when it came to *narrative* reason no one could beat him. His communication defied close rational scrutiny, just as pure emotional appeals often do. It is that which makes them powerful and, on occasion, dangerous.

The bandwagon

When we're not choosing what to buy or who to vote for on the basis of emotional reactions and well-told stories, we're often making decisions on the basis of what we think others are doing. Our minds have a strong tendency to rush to judgement on the basis of 'I'll think what she's thinking'. We're happy to take advice from the right sort of person, be it the Nobel Prize-winning scientist, the affable and down-to-earth politician, or the lung-cancer victim deployed in an anti-smoking ad. A message can mean more if it comes from one kind of messenger than another. *Source credibility* is the term used in communications literature for the important attribute of a particular message, that it carries more weight if it is conveyed by someone who is authoritative, likeable, or with whom the listener can identify.

---

* The best treatment of this point is to be found in 'Lisa the Iconoclast', episode 144 of *The Simpsons*, in which Lisa stumbles upon some unpleasant truths about the town founder and hero Jebediah Springfield. She ultimately chooses not to reveal the secrets that she has uncovered, because to do so would shatter a myth the town shares, and all the good things that come with the myth.

Perhaps as important, or more so, is having a person of the right quality to sell a message, it can be useful to show there is a quantity of opinion behind it. We are a species with a herd instinct, and thus we tend to follow the crowd. After all, we can't always trust our own judgements so we'd better learn from what others say and do; and we don't want to be socially isolated so we'd better get with the programme. Clever communicators can exploit this tendency by trying to show us – truthfully or not – where the crowd is going. The first two of the secrets in *Yes! 50 Secrets from the Science of Persuasion* concern this bandwagon effect. Infomercials successfully increased sales-call volumes by brilliantly changing their advice from 'Operators are waiting, please call now' (implying that a couple of lonely operators are sitting patiently waiting for the odd request) to 'If operators are busy, please call again'.[27] A hotel's experiment on the best way to persuade people to re-use their towels rather than leave them on the floor to be laundered found a 26 per cent increase in re-use when the wording of the card inviting guests to do so pointed out that most other guests do.

The technique of selling things by showing how momentum is moving in a particular direction is ubiquitous, and it tempts those trying to sell things to lie about how much support they have. Shops trying to flog their leftover stock offer a reason why it's left over (other than that it didn't sell);* nightclubs hold queues outside to give the impression that people are desperate to get in;[28] politicians suggest that data from their private polling shows them doing better than the published polls.[29] These are all ways to give a subconscious reassurance that the rest of the world has signed up to the message, so it makes sense for you

---

* They may reframe items as 'overstock' (rather than 'under bought'), or use a particular holiday or anniversary as a reason for the sale.

to do so too. Social proof is particularly useful when people are not quite sure as to how to behave – who to vote for, how much to contribute, whether to clap.

A neat demonstration of the bandwagon effect can be found in the appreciation of comedy with and without audience laughter. It turns out – not altogether surprisingly – that most of us laugh more when we are in the presence of other people who are laughing. Academics who have studied these things have measured what they sometimes call 'mirth reactions', and it's fair to say it has been robustly demonstrated in the psychology literature.[30] Comedians do not need to have read the journals to know it to be true. A person wandering into a comedy club is more likely to stay around for a bad act with an audience in fits of laughter than a good act playing to a quiet group of fidgeting spectators. Two theories might explain why laughter begets laughter. One is based around social conformity: we like to fit in with others, so when they laugh we do too. The other theory focuses on the information we derive from other people laughing. It suggests that we are not entirely sure which bits of a comedy to find funny, and use the laughter of others to highlight the presence of a joke; once alerted, we make a split-second special effort to appraise it and then laugh if it is funny. Either way, comedy is more fun as a social activity than as an individual one.[31]

For decades, the people who make recorded comedy programmes have spotted a way to exploit the fact that laughter is contagious to make their shows seem funnier: if too little live audience laughter is available at the time a show is recorded, you can enhance the quality of a product by grafting false laughter on to it afterwards. In American television, the master was a man called Charles Douglass, a broadcast engineer at CBS who from the 1950s was adding canned laughter to many comedies, and who invented a device called the laff box to do so. Historically, most comedy was filmed in front of a live audience, but recorded sound was useful for those programmes or segments shot in locations where an audience could not be accommodated, or where the noise of the live audience needed editing or enhancing. The first programme to use pre-recorded laughter was a short-lived sitcom called the *Hank McCune Show* in 1950.[32] *Variety* magazine reviewed *Hank McCune*, and said: 'Although the show is lensed on film without a studio audience, there are chuckles and yocks dubbed in. Whether this induces a jovial mood in home viewers is still to be determined, but the practice may have unlimited possibilities if it's spread to include canned peals of hilarity, thunderous ovations and gasps of sympathy.'[33] Needless to say, it did spread, and it became the conventional wisdom that laughter had to be included with comedy. A useful history of the practice has been written by Jacob Smith, who points out that the one or two shows which hadn't used artificial laughter found they rated better when the sponsors got their way and forced them to do so. But, of course, there was no reason to restrict the artifice to those situations where no real audience was available or the audience sound needed a bit of editing. Smith refers to a 1959 article about the comedian Sid Caesar, who evidently liked to have canned laughter available for those occasions on which the live spectators were not quite good enough: 'If the weather were poor; if the audience were unsophisticated, morose or from Missouri – the degree of laughter on the air might be anywhere from debilitated to disastrous.'[34] You can't risk an expensive TV production on the whims of the crowd. The skills of those who added (and sometimes removed) laughter were highly valued. Smith quotes one account of the art: 'The trick of the Laff Boy's trade is timing ... To manufacture a natural-sounding laugh, the Laff Boy must let a few "people" in his box anticipate a joke. This is called "giving it a little tickle". Then he might punch in a "sharpie" just before the main laugh ... Gags frequently build, each capping the last, so the Laff Boy must likewise build and hold his biggest laugh for the pay-off.'[35]

Canned laughter designed to make a comedy seem funnier than it otherwise would, and crafted in such an elegant way, can reasonably be viewed as a construct similar to the inauthentic paragraphs of a company annual report or the overstated claims of a sales pitch. All use a device built on insincerity to improve the appearance of a product. The recorded laughter, however, is more potent in shaping our reactions than most other forms of pretence, as it directly appeals to our instinct for empathy in amusement. Yet in being so effective, canned laughter is also more of a betrayal than the usual sales hype. Laughter is meant to be a natural reaction – carefree, spontaneous and open. With the possible exception of a faked orgasm, nothing could more offend our sense of shared pleasure than recording it and using it out of place. It is thus not surprising that many people in the industry have always viewed canned laughter as something of an embarrassment, even back in the early days. In the late 1950s, the president of CBS, Frank Stanton, became worried about it being seen as a form of deception and he inaugurated a policy of informing viewers when the laff box had been used, with lines displayed in the closing credits to the effect that 'Audience reaction technically produced' or 'Audience reaction technically augmented', but the comedians didn't like it at all and the policy was dropped after a few months.[36] The use of laugh tracks was not. It tells a simple truth about the bandwagon effect: if it is there to be exploited, it's hard to resist.

Canned laughter reminds us how social we are as creatures, but it is worth remembering that not only do we take subliminal cues from other people, we also use those cues to bond with other people. Laughing, nodding or clapping along with others can give us a satisfying sense of togetherness. Or if we click 'like' on someone else's post on social media, that very act not only reinforces our mutual belief in the thing that was posted, but it can also make us feel closer to each other. Sharing a belief is a way of expressing friendship, and deviation from the beliefs of your circle can come across as anti-social.

This groupthink can underpin a sense of tribalism. For good reason, people have worried recently that too many of us live in social media echo chambers in which we only mix with people who share our views, so that all social reinforcement works in favour of our existing prejudices.[37] For me, it is equally worrying that it is by the very act of sharing our views that we cement our relationship with our social circle. It implies that we lose our faculty for critically appraising the evidence; we simply believe what our gang subscribes to. And as I have already said, it is no coincidence that concerns about a post-truth era have emerged at the same time as deep political division and a strong sense that identities have to be asserted. Nothing does more to block sensible questions about the truthfulness of a proposition than a desire to fit in with a group by believing in it. This is a very significant point, and I shall return to it later on when looking at ways in which we might counter some of the falsehoods that creep into public discourse.

Managed expectations

It is one of the oldest and most widely understood communications techniques in the world: to make people think something is big, get them to expect something that is small. For example, on 15 July 2002, the then Chancellor of the Exchequer Gordon Brown set out one of his regular spending reviews in parliament, allocating budgets to government departments for the three years to 2005/06. Education was meant to be the centrepiece. At noon, just before the announcement, the *Daily Telegraph* told us that 'Schools will be presented as the big winners, with the education budget rising by about £10 billion from 2003/04 to 2005/06'. When the news came a few hours later, education spending was in fact budgeted to rise by £12.8 billion. What a surprise – who could have predicted the number would turn out to be higher than the spin had suggested?

Gordon Brown and his team did not invent that technique; we all instinctively recognise and use the device of managing expectations. While at school, we tell our parents we think we have done badly in exams so there is an upside surprise when the results come in; at home, we tell our loved ones that we have only got them a small gift when we have bought a large one; at work we tell colleagues a task is going to be more difficult than it is, in order to generate more recognition when it is completed.

The cognitive basis of this effect is *anchoring*. It's becoming widely understood that human beings find it hard to judge magnitudes in absolute terms; is a building tall, a temperature hot or a price high? We yearn for some point of comparison to help us come to a conclusion, and most amazingly, we hanker for that comparison even when we know it to be entirely arbitrary. We just need some number or other to prompt us to come up with a view. There are many studies on the way in which assessments of magnitude can be influenced by sense and nonsense. One involved asking people to estimate the average temperature in San Francisco. But in the test some of the participants were first asked whether that temperature was higher or lower than 558 degrees. Because the average temperature in San Francisco is obviously below 558 degrees, you might thus assume the presence of that question would have no bearing on anyone's estimate of the actual number.[38] But it did: those who had been asked the irrelevant question came up with higher average results when producing their own figure. And findings like this have been replicated time after time – the age at which Mahatma Gandhi died,[39] the percentage of African countries in the UN,[40] the price of a book.[41] In each case, the guesses of these magnitudes have been analysed in experiments and shown to be far more malleable than you would imagine, and affected by irrelevant numbers thrown at people beforehand.

Because we have this need to anchor our estimates against something – *anything* – communicators who are good at dropping carefully chosen anchors into a conversation can affect our judgements. Project a high number into our minds and suddenly everything else appears low. Anchoring, like the other techniques catalogued here, gives communicators a reason to manage expectations, and in doing that gives us a good psychological reason to allow our public utterances to deviate from our private views. So long as unrealistic propositions can materially affect perceptions, it can pay for us to assert unrealistic things.

One area where we all tend to engage in bluff and bullshit is negotiation, and given that we all intuitively understand anchoring it is commonly exploited here. It turns out that an opening bid in a negotiation can have a disproportionate influence over the final result through its effect on the expectations of both parties as to the range within which the outcome will fall. An unreasonable demand for a second-hand car, as long as it does not alienate the buyer, makes any price below that feel like a concession. And in pricing more generally, you can make an option appear more acceptable by pitching it up against a really bad alternative: having some expensive bottles of wine on a menu might be useful even if you never expect to sell any, simply because they reduce the customers' perception of the prices of the other bottles.

Framing

The last on my list of five psychologically powerful communication techniques is framing. Here are some examples. Those in favour of gay marriage prefer to expunge the word gay from any discussion of the subject, instead referring to equal marriage. They presumably think that most people are in favour of equality, and so by using language that suggests the argument is not about gayness but about equality they are more likely to win it. Similarly, in the debate over abortion, both sides try to win the argument by focusing it on an attribute of abortion that suits their side of the argument. No one is pro- or anti-abortion, they are pro-life or pro-choice. Each side is trying to frame the debate by taking the argument to a terrain that favours them.

The cognitive point here is that we generally make sense of confusing things by judging them against various preconceptions. When confronted with a new proposition we don't start thinking about it with a blank sheet of paper in front of us; instead, we place the proposition somewhere in relation to our pre-existing structure of beliefs and attitudes. This makes life much easier, because we can reduce even a complicated judgement to a simple binary one – does it conform to my existing views or not? What the clever communicator does is prompt us to use the most favourable of those preconceptions to view the issue. If I'm in favour of choice, when a complex issue like abortion comes along I decide what it implies for choice. How else would I ever find the time to come to an opinion?

George Lakoff, a liberal-minded American cognitive linguist, has written extensively on the power of language and metaphor to persuade us of things by appealing to a particular worldview. Subtle choices of language can help communicators do this. In his book *Don't Think of an Elephant! Know your Values and*

Frame the Debate he looks at examples that the political right has used to advance its cause.[42] The use of the words *tax relief* to describe a tax cut supports a notion of tax as a negative thing from which we need relief (like pain). But tax does not have to be viewed this way; it can be seen as an investment in the social good, or as the membership fee of a flourishing society. If we take Lakoff's analysis, can we think of other ways of talking about a tax cut that would make it sound less like an aspirin? We could call it a form of *corporate welfare* or a *selective* tax cut, and immediately its appeal diminishes. Or, more emotively, we could think of it as a *bribe*.

Lakoff's main point is that getting the frame right is far more important than getting the facts right. If you can ignite the desired values in people when they come to a view, you have won them over. He also thinks that most political debates involve a subliminal competition between two overall value systems. One is the 'strict father model', personified by Arnold Schwarzenegger, and the other is the 'nurturant parent model', as exemplified by Bill Cosby's television persona. (He was writing before Bill Cosby hit the headlines for all the wrong reasons.) The strict father is obviously more appealing to the right wing, but Lakoff shows how most of us come to a view about an issue with reference to a choice between those two. He suggests that a third or more of the population are firmly in one camp or the other and their views will follow a reasonably consistent pattern based on their outlook, but there is a big chunk of the population in the middle and the folks stationed there can see issues from either side. The task, as stated by Lakoff, is to 'activate *your* model in the people in the middle'.

But don't assume that framing is just a technique for politicians. If I am trying to sell a brand of washing-up liquid that is soft on the hands, my task is not just to promote the washing-up liquid; I must also promote the idea that softness on hands is the most important feature of a washing-up liquid. If I can frame the contest between washing-up liquids as a competition about hand softness, then I win because when people come to judge the rival washing-up liquid they don't ask the many other potential questions that can be asked about washing-up liquid – does it work, how nice does it smell, is it environmentally friendly, how much does it cost per wash? No, they ask the question I want – how soft is it on the hands? I have planted the seed of what a good washing-up liquid is about, and it grows into an idea of what washing-up liquids should be in a way that favours mine. This is surely the way that James Dyson managed to conquer the market for vacuum cleaners: by successfully framing the decision facing consumers as essentially a choice between bagged or bagless products, which drew attention away from the purchase price. As he was selling an expensive item that happened to be the first and best bagless product at the time, this was the right way for him to get consumers to think about vacuum cleaners. My impression is that we've been paying more for vacuum cleaners ever since.[43]

Most often, framing works because our preconceptions play a large part in helping us jump to conclusions about things. It is simply a way of connecting a message to a favourable existing belief. Our minds are full of prejudices – values, attitudes, views – through which incoming information is processed. In fact, we all know that our preconceptions are so important that once we have one lodged in our head it is hard to displace. They are the way we make sense of the world. But like the psychological underpinnings to the other four communication techniques we have discussed, that sense can become nonsense in the hands of those able to manipulate our thinking.

Insidious or benign?

It won't have escaped your notice that the five techniques described interact and overlap, and the best way to make a case powerfully is to use all of them: you want to make a pitch, then embed it in a story of some kind, preferably one with positive emotional appeal, and one which frames your argument in a favourable way and distracts attention from opposite points of view. This process involves deliberately shaping the argument rather than offering an intellectually robust case. And if you get some way in this direction, success breeds success. If your story can just get a foot in the door with your target audience, your case becomes self-reinforcing. First, thanks to our herd instincts, the more people who accept it, the more people will come to accept it. And secondly, once people believe it, thanks to our wonderful ability to look for evidence in favour of hypotheses that we already believe, we will come to accept it even more strongly.

But what is common to all communication that plays to our System One self is that it induces us to drop rational thought when working out how to respond. It literally appeals to our instincts, and sometimes our baser instincts at that. It has become prominent in the recent era of identity politics and grievance in the form of lies and afactual bullshit. For those who think that public discourse should be built around evidence, this is an intensely frustrating development.

So how malign is it for professional communicators to exploit our psychological foibles to get us to see things their way? Well, let's start with the simplest everyday case: the mental exploitation that we endure when shopping and gauging prices. Robert Schindler takes a gently dim view of psychological pricing. 'It's not evil, it's just part of life,' he says. But he wouldn't do it if he were a retailer. 'I do think it's a little bit distasteful to do that and I would not do business that way.'

He has carried out quite a few studies now, including one on the comparative cost of goods priced psychologically or otherwise. 'I found that, if anything, the prices that ended in nines were actually higher than competing prices for the same things. The reality wasn't that they are lower, which is a further suggestion that there is manipulation involved,' he told me. This suggests that we are not just being persuaded to buy more, but that sellers enjoy some of the fruits of their manipulation by putting prices up.

Schindler may not be alone in finding it a mildly cynical way of carrying out business. He cited a study that compared second-hand cars sold online by professional dealers and those sold by individuals. The ordinary folk tended to price in straightforward round numbers; it was the dealers whose prices ended in nine.[44] For Schindler, it is clear: 'Individuals would be ashamed to do it ... you're going to be dealing with the person who's buying it, it's embarrassing. But if you're a company you can say, "Oh, that's the policy here. So and so told me to do this." There is something a little bit shameful about doing this.'

A long way from charging £9.99 for something, what about the rhetoric of politicians, populists or demagogues? The best of them instinctively exploit multiple techniques for reaching into our System One minds. The worst make successful appeals to anger and fear, frame all problems in terms of one group versus another and wrap their worldview up in appealing stories that have a distorted plausibility. Sometimes, their techniques work best in large rallies where they can exploit the bandwagon effect by whipping up an enthusiastic and angry crowd. The techniques of propagandists have been well studied and it is hard to be comfortable with them. Jason Stanley, a philosophy tutor at

Yale (and author of *How Propaganda Works*), takes a very dark view of the presidential campaign of Donald Trump.[45] Writing in the *New York Times* he suggested that Trump was far worse than any normal peddler of myths; it was not just that in his 2016 election campaign he was insensitive to facts, it was that he was never carelessly so; his was a calculated campaign to describe a society gripped by problems to which he was the solution:

> The simple picture Trump is trying to convey is that there is wild disorder, because of American citizens of African-American descent, and immigrants. He is doing it as a display of strength, showing he is able to define reality and lead others to accept his authoritarian value system.[46]

For Stanley, it is unhelpful to even write about someone like Donald Trump in a chapter that also looks at the ingenious messaging of a company like Innocent Drinks.

> To lump Trump's rhetoric into a category that includes advertising is strange. It is *prima facie* bizarre to be satisfied with a description of the rhetoric of a dictator like Idi Amin's as 'insensitive to truth and falsity'. Why have we been satisfied with such descriptions of Trump? Perhaps our media, as well as our academic class, assumes that we are [a] healthy liberal democracy, and not susceptible to authoritarian rhetoric. We now know this assumption is false.[47]

For Stanley, authoritarian rhetoric is in a category of its own.

But there is one similarity between it and the milder version of psychological exploitation that we all observe in prices that end in nines. It is that being aware of it can make us more resilient to it. As Robert Schindler put it to me, 'The thing that needs to

be fixed is for people to be more in touch with their feelings . . .
If you're in touch with your feelings you're better able to handle
people trying to influence you by those feelings. You know
what's happening and you can decide whether to act on it or not.'

That supposes that we don't want our feelings to be manipulated; of course, we are often willing accomplices to bullshit
peddlers, seeking out tear-jerking Christmas ads and revelling
in the heady excitement of mob anger. If people are happy to
respond so favourably to manipulation, we should not be surprised that manipulators come along.

7

Short-Termism

The link between dishonesty and short time horizons

The butterfly effect

As we've seen, it can sometimes be effective not to be wholly straightforward in the way one communicates. In this chapter, we need to introduce the element of time. It matters because while deception may be effective, it will probably not work for ever. At some point, the truth will emerge. So the question for a communicator is: which time period matters more? The here and now, or the long-term future?

We start by taking a visit to the Aegean Sea, and the beautiful district of Petaloudes on the Greek island of Rhodes. Here you will find a lush wooded valley climbing around a river with rock pools and small waterfalls. It is Europe's only natural forest of *Liquidambar orientalis*, a species of sweetgum tree with a strong-scented resin. But this site is not renowned for its flora; it is better known in English as the Valley of the Butterflies because each summer millions of gentle beautiful-winged insects arrive there, attracted by the scent of the sweetgums. Everywhere you look you see them, covering every tree, top to bottom. They mate in the valley in the last weeks of the summer, and then the females fly away to lay their eggs and die. The next year, when the new generation is fully grown, the smell of the valley draws them home, ready to repeat the cycle all over again. The Valley of the Butterflies is, not surprisingly, one of the island's great tourist sites; it's extensively publicised and well organised, with a small museum and refreshment facilities.[1]

There is just one thing you should know before you make your excursion to the Valley of the Butterflies. The specific breed that gathers there is a subspecies of *Euplagia quadripunctaria*, which is not a butterfly at all: it's a moth. It's fair to say that, as moths go, this one is at the more colourful end of the spectrum, and it's certainly more interesting than the plain brown ones that fly out of the wardrobe from time to time. And it is also true that in some languages, the distinction between moths and butterflies is not made. But in English, it's a moth, albeit one with some butterfly characteristics.

I visited the valley and was impressed by the sight, the lack of butterflies notwithstanding. I'd expected it to be one of those typical beach-holiday excursions designed to break the monotony of the vacation routine with a visit to a second-rate cultural or nature destination, but in fact the sight of millions of moths made it a truly remarkable spot. And the branding is interesting too. The good folk of Rhodes obviously decided at some point that the b-word was preferable to the more scientifically accurate one. You can see why: butterflies have always enjoyed much better PR than moths. So is this a case where it was sensible for the community to label itself in a flattering light? If they'd said it was about moths, maybe we would have stayed at the villa and missed one of the best moments of the trip. There is no moral problem with the mendacious name. If it has the effect of making the valley enticing to visitors, I doubt many people show up and feel cheated, so it's not a criminal case of false labelling.

But even if the name had been deliberately designed to dupe foreigners into visiting a valley of moths, by a cynical tourist authority hell-bent on cheating us, it's worth observing why this might have worked. Tourists probably only visit the site once. Its promoters don't need us to be impressed with our visit; just interested enough to buy a ticket while we spend a few days in Rhodes. They appeal to our passing trade. This is an example of a business that doesn't need to fool people all of the time; it only needs to fool some of us for a single day, because by the time we've paid our five-euro entry fee it no longer much matters what we think about it; we've been ensnared, and it's too late to do anything about it. At first sight, this can be said to be a perfect example of a business where long-term repu-tation matters not a jot; all that is important is making that quick buck. Each season brings a crop of new tourists, and the Rhodes authorities' only worry is to get them to spend money the once. Most will be on holiday elsewhere next year, so you get them now or you don't get them at all. If a business is based on passing trade, the tactic of deploying any amount of bullshit is perhaps understandable.

That is not true of most businesses, which have reason to main-tain a long-term reputation even if it is costly to nurture one in the short term. But I put the example of the Valley of the Butterflies here because even though the name in this case is not really a problem, the purpose of this chapter is to show that short time horizons and bullshit are inextricably linked. Spouting exaggerations or lies can make sense right here, right now (in the short term) if I don't care about being caught out later on (in the long term). Speaking non-sense to a roaring crowd of adoring supporters has an irresistible satisfaction if you don't need to worry about reality imposing itself at some point. In a world where the future doesn't matter, the case for honesty diminishes. This implies that the prevalence of bullshit could to some extent reflect short time horizons. In fact, I'd suggest that much of the bullshit of those in business and politics is best viewed *not* as a result of them being innately less straightforward than ordinary folk, but as more short-term. If they think that their future career depends on their performance in the next interview rather than on their long-term standing, don't be surprised if they say whatever helps them get through that next interview.

There is a tale from some years back – apocryphal or not – of a meeting of UK Treasury ministers and advisors to discuss the latest headline-grabbing announcements when one says, reflectively, 'This is ridiculous – we are far too obsessed with the stories in tomorrow's newspapers. It's the *Sunday* papers we should be focusing on.' If, like those in politics, you start with an outlook that deems a week a long time, you're never going to be forthright because you will always rate success by looking at the immediate impact of your message rather than the full and final effect. You'll look at the coverage you've garnered in this Sunday's papers without taking into account the fact that what you say now also has an effect on next year's Sunday papers. You can get away with nonsense today, but if it is exposed as nonsense in twelve months' time it won't have improved things for you. If you are marketing the Valley of the Butterflies to this year's crop of potential customers, you may not care about a year's time, but if you are a Treasury minister you should – though that doesn't mean you will. To understand bullshit, you have to understand those short-term pressures.[2] So let us focus on the link between time horizon and honesty.

Opportunism versus long-term reputation

When it comes to communication, there is a high road and a low road. The high road – or long-termist approach – is to tell the truth; to adopt a policy of consistently telling the truth; to stick at it for a lengthy enough period that people can spot the pattern in your behaviour; and to reap the benefits at the point at which they realise they can trust you. In the long term that trust – based on your reputation – will bring all sorts of attendant benefits, from credibility to credit. In contrast, the low road – or short-termist approach – is to be dishonest when there is an immediate benefit to being so, taking the benefit and ignoring the problems that might follow once your lies have been detected. Over time, if you stay on this road you will not be trusted as people will spot the pattern of dishonesty in your behaviour.

If we want to understand why there is so much bullshit around, we have to come to a view as to why it is tempting to follow the low road, despite its disadvantages, rather than the high road. If you expect to die soon, are genetically programmed only to have concern for the present, or are just plain desperate, you'll probably set out on the low road and try to reap the immediate benefits of dishonesty before the world catches up with you. Perhaps the most socially important example of short-termism in this form is the phoney election-campaign promise. 'I will not raise taxes' may be a helpful thing to say before polling day, but if you do need to raise taxes your false promise will be quickly exposed after the vote.*[3] But as you have

---

* The case of George H. W. Bush at the 1988 Republican Convention obviously comes to mind: 'My opponent won't rule out raising taxes, but I will, and the Congress will push me to raise taxes, and I'll say no, and they'll push, and I'll say no, and they'll push again, and I'll say to them, "Read my lips: no new taxes."' President Bush consented to a budget that raised taxes in 1990, under pressure from Congress. He lost the subsequent election. The British Conservative government was similarly re-elected in 1992 after a campaign lambasting the opposition's plans to raise taxes, but it went on to impose big tax rises of its own once in office. It too lost the next election, although other factors were involved.

won the election, you will probably think you were right to have made the promise you did. Another good example of a lie told for short-term impact is found in boasting on a first date. It's done to help secure a second date. If it fails, no harm is done by the exaggeration; if it succeeds and a relationship develops later on, the truth will probably become apparent, but by then you'll be in love and laugh together at the silly things you each said to impress the other when you first met. Another small example is the taxi telling you he is two minutes away in order to stop you cancelling the booking and hiring a different one. By the time you realise he was actually twelve minutes away, it is too late to do anything about it.

Occasionally, there is a noble reason for focusing on the short term and allowing some bullshit to creep into your words. This could be when there is a need for some useful obfuscation. In diplomacy, where there's a hope that fudging on a difficult issue now will allow nations to move on and unlock a host of problems down the road, then maybe fudge is the right approach. The classic example was the US–China talks in the early 1970s referred to earlier. The phrase 'we'll cross that bridge when we get to it' is a useful one, implying that we can't worry about everything all the time, and so sometimes we need to park a problem for consideration later. In these cases, bullshitting our way round a short-term obstruction may yield long-term results. But these are probably the exception.

More generally, to understand short-termism, think of the time that elapses between the making of an assertion ('the cheque is in the post') and the point at which external evidence confirms or denies that assertion (the post arrives with or without the aforementioned cheque). This interregnum between assertion and verification exists because while it is right to say that, in most areas of life, the truth will out, it can take a while to do so. The lags between assertion and verification are long and variable: promises are offered and thereafter kept or broken; fake news is propagated and (hopefully) at some point exposed; swindles are perpetrated and later uncovered; predictions are made and outcomes corroborate or contradict them. These intervals give rise to a potential short-term benefit from not being honest. Often, a decision to lie simply suggests that your number one concern is the immediate result, with little weight put on the long-term impact of the lie's detection.

But while the low road may have its benefits, it ultimately leads nowhere. Over the longer term, a pattern of behaviour can be observed, and a reputation for dishonesty will develop. By scooping up any short-term benefits from lying, I forgo the long-term benefit of being trusted. If each week I tell you the cheque is in the post and it arrives time after time, then the next occasion that I buy something from you, you'll send it over and accept payment afterwards by cheque. If, on the other hand, the cheque fails to arrive time after time, then you will probably start demanding that I pay cash up front.

You can also apply the concept of the high and low roads to brands and the qualities they stand for. A corporate brand that has longevity will inevitably be associated with certain product attributes. That means companies can follow the high-road by pursuing quality and integrity, or follow the low road and try to palm off a rotten product on unwitting consumers. But in either case they must expect consumers will eventually notice. Imagine a company on the high road that manufactures cars; over the years, its vehicles perform well. When the company releases a new model customers can use the performance of the earlier models to help judge the likely performance of the new one. If the company has been in the business of selling reliable cars for many years, buyers are right to trust the brand's good standing in determining whether the new car is reliable. That is the value of a reputation, and it is only in the long term that the company can acquire one. The reputation is an asset and, having built it up, the company has no incentive to destroy it by producing rubbish cars. In contrast, a car manufacturer on the low road produces unreliable cars; it enjoys a short-term benefit by dispensing with the annoying hassles of having to engineer cars to a high standard, but in the long term it is likely to sell fewer cars as it will not have a good name.

I use the analogy of the high road and low road here because I suggest that whichever route you choose, you tend to stick on it rather than flip between. For those on the high road, once your reputation has been earned you've done the hard work and you'd be mad to throw it away, so you should remain honest. Just one silly lapse could destroy it all.* But those who choose not to invest in a long-term reputation will probably end up being forever mendacious. Having started on that route, they have nowhere else to go. The politician who breaks their promise not to put up taxes will probably also choose to lie in the next election; why wouldn't they? They have no reputation to lose by so doing. They'll try saying, 'This time I really mean it when I say I won't put up taxes,' but will rightly not be trusted. They may kick themselves for not having invested in their reputation earlier, but they can't take the short-term benefits of deception and then enjoy the benefits of a good name in the long term as well. It is one or the other.

Does it ever make sense to follow the low road? To think about this in line with the economists' rational model of human behaviour one can perform a cost–benefit appraisal of the high-or-low decision, to which there are two main components. First,

---

* Hence Warren Buffett's line, 'It takes twenty years to build a reputation and five minutes to ruin it. If you think about that, you'll do things differently.'

you have to ask yourself if there is a benefit to lying in the short term (and how often you can get that benefit if you stick to lying). Secondly, you have to weigh that up against the benefit that would accrue from building a long-term reputation. Looking at it like this, the low road is short-termist in two distinct ways: it puts a big weight on the immediate benefits of lying; and it puts a low weight on the long-term benefit of reputation. If you are not going to be around for the long term, the short term is all that matters. Or if you know you will get away with your lie, you might decide not to be truthful because there will be no long-term cost to lying at all. Or if your reputation for integrity is unlikely to be recognised it makes less sense to be honest, as there is no long-term reward to compensate for the short-term cost. (That explains why tourists sometimes have to be wary of taxi drivers, because until mobile apps allowed drivers to be rated individually, no client could ever expect to look at the reputation of the driver they happened to hire.)

There is another way to think about the choice between the high road and low road. The dishonest approach has more logic in relation to single encounters with strangers: the benefit of a reputation is likely to be small as you don't expect to meet again and so there is no long term to worry about. Whereas the high road makes more sense in a relationship in which there are repeated encounters in which we learn about the other and prove ourselves. What one would expect is that in a world of brief or anonymous encounters we would behave in less trustworthy ways as there would be little chance of any comeback for being dishonest. This is the world of the Valley of the Butterflies, which we likely visit only once. But in a world of long-term relationships there is a far greater incentive to be honest, as there is time for veracity or mendacity to be recognised and subsequently rewarded or punished accordingly.

But while the long-term relationship gives incentives for honesty, it won't succeed in generating that behaviour if people think little of the future and treat every relationship as more akin to a one-night stand. So let us examine the practicalities of lying in the short and long term in more detail.

The low road in practice

We observe lots of people lying or deceiving, or generally trying to get away with impressive-sounding nonsense, and many of those people have consciously or subconsciously opted for the low road, calculating that some gain can be derived from deception. In general, the biggest gains from this strategy are to be found where it is possible to cash in on a lie before any corroboration is possible, and where the vendor will never be asking for repeat business. The money is in the bank before the customer realises she didn't get what she had expected.

You can see the real-world validity of this proposition by examining the movie industry and the marketing of films. This is an industry that is innately short-termist because, like tourists visiting the Valley of the Butterflies, most movie-goers see a film just once, and have to make a decision as to what to see before knowing how satisfying the experience will be. If you manage to persuade people to buy a ticket to your film, your job is done, and it is then too late for the disgruntled film-goers to retract their custom if they find the film was not worth viewing. A film is a one-night stand, not a long-term relationship. When we look at what happens in practice we find that studios are not always completely frank in their public assessments of their films. (Have you ever seen a film advertised with the words 'it looked good on paper, but never quite delivered on screen'?) They are probably honest within their own private meetings, but somehow in public there is an irresistible urge to say what they would like to believe about the film, rather than what they do think about it. That is perhaps not surprising.

But there is a fundamental problem with a decision to follow the low road: the more incentive there is for you to take it, the more wary everyone will be of believing you at all. As no one is going to trust you anyway, when you sit down and do the cost–benefit appraisal of those short-term benefits of dishonesty you find they evaporate. We the public are not stupid; we know that studios want us to think their films are good, and we know that we have to commit to the purchase before we can be sure how good the film is. So we automatically discount what we hear from studios. They can say whatever they want about their product, but none of us will be listening, because unlike a car manufacturer, the film is in effect here today, gone tomorrow. In fact, this is a world of information anarchy, in which a lot of untruth is spoken and nothing is believed. It is close to the babbling equilibrium, which I mentioned in Chapter 4.

It is because that kind of world is so unattractive that humans will always strive to find other means of verifying truth and falsehood. The movie industry neatly demonstrates this point. Given that the movie-makers will generally review their own films positively, a whole slew of institutions have been invented to do the job instead: in particular, independent reviews, film prizes and word of mouth. And there is a form of long-term reputation and branding through big-name stars, directors and franchises like James Bond. The good news is that the market in film information works relatively efficiently, and somehow audiences do get to see the best films. Bad films do not seem to perform as well at the box office as good films.

A pretty good demonstration of this comes from the fact that mediocre movies, even those with the most brilliant marketing, don't achieve blockbuster success. Take the 2006 film *Snakes on a Plane* – it's hard to imagine a better-marketed product, and yet it didn't do particularly well. The film's premise (a crate full of venomous snakes are released on a plane) aroused a huge amount of internet and media interest before its release. Fans visiting the film website could arrange to send someone a call from the star, Samuel L. Jackson, urging them to see what he suggested could be the best film in history. There was so much buzz around it, the makers responded to bloggers' suggestions and did some extra filming to harden it up and give Jackson a catchline ('Enough is enough! I have had it with these moth-erf***ing snakes on this motherf***ing plane!). Given the hype, *Snakes on a Plane* was poised to be a huge hit. It opened to successful midnight viewings on Thursday 17 August, followed by reasonable audiences the next day, but it then slipped badly over the weekend. By Monday, it had already attracted the *New York Times* headline 'After Hype Online, "Snakes on a Plane" Is Letdown at Box Office'.[4] Audiences might have suspected that the film was going to be a let-down by the fact that the studio declined to allow critics to see it before it went on general release. The film just wasn't as good as its publicity, and the lesson is that in determining how many people go to see it, it is the quality of the film that matters, not the quality of the publicity.[5] Good marketing works in selling movies, but in this very best case imaginable it only gains you about twenty-four hours of success. And if that was true back in 2006, when social media was less developed, it is certainly true now.[6]

The basic rule is that you don't make a film successful by exag-gerating its merits, because you can't fool many people for very long. And that makes the more important general point that taking the short-termist low road offers only a limited upside. Consumers are well trained in seeking objective information about films from independent sources, or judging films on the basis of the long-term reputations of the stars or directors, and they are canny when it comes to knowing the difference between quality and hype. Overall, movies provide a great case study of an industry in which truthful information flows relatively freely and accurately.[7] And we shouldn't think of this success as being a matter of mere good luck; it is because reliable information is so important in the market (otherwise we'd simply have no idea which films to see) that in its absence, mechanisms for furnishing it have been nurtured. As a result, the truth prevails and there is little short-term benefit to be derived from exaggeration.

I don't want to pretend that opportunistic bullshit never works. We see people falling for scams all the time, handing money over to strangers before receiving a promised benefit in return; we see people hiring cowboy workmen to resurface their drives even though they have no comeback if the tarmac degrades before it should; we see people believing pre-election promises; and we see people responding to the marketing hype of film studios. But I do think that there is real-world evidence that most people have a natural immunity to opportunistic bullshit.

And the same point is made by my original example, the Valley of the Butterflies. Its ability, or that of any other tourist sight, to brand itself in a spuriously attractive way is far more constrained than you might think. Tourists everywhere know that they are vulnerable to exaggerations and lies, and they take requisite precautions as a result. They take care with taxis by reading up on how much it costs to get from the airport to the town; they check TripAdvisor – or, in the past, guidebooks – to see reviews of hotels before booking them; they are wary of those peddling souvenirs and turn their noses up at what they perceive to be touristy restaurants. And as they know the authorities have an incentive to over-sell their local attractions, they automatically discount what they are told by tourist officers and rely on independent sources for their information. This prevents those trying to sell a particular attraction from gaining customers by false representation. You can't successfully over-sell, even in the short term, as no one will believe you if you try.

That is undoubtedly the case with the Valley of the Butterflies. No one complains about the island of Rhodes's misdescription of moths only because it is so minor, and the tourist site so dramatic. Just imagine a case where the authorities decided to take a cynical turn and really overstate the excitement of an excursion to the Valley of the Butterflies by choosing to rename it the Valley of the Hippopotamuses. Assuming more of us want to see hippos than butterflies, you might argue this would be ingenious branding, because only after the coachloads of tourists had paid their entry fees would they discover there were in fact no hippos there. But this shows how limited the power of misdescription is, even in the short term. The sheer implausibility of the claim that there are hippos on Rhodes would induce tourists to check, and this would take no time at all as publicly available reviews abound. No one would go to the valley without advance knowledge of what to expect. I suspect that bus operators would advertise tours with phrases like 'There are no hippopotamuses in this strangely named valley, but it makes an exciting trip in the summer as it is populated by millions of moths.' The word hippopotamuses might catch the eye, but it would not hoodwink anyone.

These industries that live or die by their short-term encounters perfectly demonstrate the logic of an equilibrium: when it pays you to lie, it pays people not to believe you. There are two of us in a communication, the sender and the receiver, and the strategy of each has to be compatible with that of the other.

Where credibility is inevitably missing, it pays the two of us to invent ways for reliable assertions to be made and believed. There is still plenty of short-termist hype and exaggeration, but that is not because it achieves very much; more, it is because it costs so little to produce and does no harm. I would call it noise rather than deception, and those who are deceived by it are the exceptions rather than the rule. Short-term opportunism is limited in its power to influence.

The film and tourist industries are trapped in this world of brief encounters. However, that is not true of all businesses or all communicators, most of whom have a life that is longer than that of the average movie or holiday. They have a potential solution to the problem of lack of credibility, which is to establish it over time in the form of a reputation; they have the option of building a brand name that stands as a certificate of integrity, quality or honesty. And this, of course, takes us to the high road.

The long term: building a reputation

Baroness Philippine de Rothschild reportedly tells visitors to her château near Bordeaux, 'Wine-making is really quite a simple business – only the first two hundred years are difficult.'[8] You might view the creation of a reputation in the same way. It's a long slog, because to create one, you have to resist the temptations of short-term opportunism, not once but consistently, until everyone recognises that is what you are doing. But they may treat you as disreputable until the evidence that you are not becomes incontrovertible. Good companies understand that they have to invest in building their brands; they know it takes time and that you can't expect to make much profit during that investment phase. But they also know that once you have established a name for yourself, sales and profits follow.

It is the relationship between time and reputation that explains why many old businesses like to tell us when they were established: it is evidence that we can trust them. If they were ripping people off, the logic goes, they would probably not still be around; we can deduce that they are honest from their longevity.

The story of the way Japanese and Korean cars conquered the world exemplifies the way that reputation can be viewed as an investment. Think of them as the precise opposite of the makers of *Snakes on a Plane*. Instead of trying to hype a mediocre product in order to grab short-term sales, they strived to secure long-term sales by creating a product worthy of hype. It took time, of course; first they had to go through the pains of developing world-class cars, and secondly – thanks to the time it takes for the truth to come out – it took a while for car buyers to catch on to the fact that the cars were worth buying. It required patience to invest in that reputation, waiting for the reward to follow. But the business ethos of the high road was prevalent in Japan and Korea when they first became global car market players in the 1960s and the late 1980s respectively.

Because it takes time for quality to be recognised, their cars were initially priced well below the rest of the market. They had to be, given that they had no reputation. Faced with a choice of car, most consumers would opt for a familiar brand unless there was a good reason not to. Why believe in the cars of an upstart company only just coming into the market? In those early days, the marketing emphasised that you got more for your money. Honda advertised its coupé with the word 'Onedownsmanship'. Hyundai ads told you that you could 'Drive like the well-to-do and still be well off' or 'Show the world how much money you still have', and that 'For the average price of a new car, you can get a Hyundai Excel . . . and a spare.'[9] To build valuable companies,

Honda and Hyundai followed a successful strategy that was to be cheap in their early days, and then as the reputation of their products slowly came to reflect their quality, the margins and prices could converge on those of other manufacturers. At that stage, the marketing could reflect the upscale position, in a way that would come across as believable. And once the reputation had been sealed the products sold very well.[10]

You could think of the natural life cycle of high-quality products as a simple two-phase model: in Phase One, before they are known and recognised as quality products, they sell at the same price as low-quality products. As the truth comes out and people slowly learn that they are in fact high quality, they enter Phase Two, in which prices can be raised to reflect the true value. The brand then carries on profitably in perpetuity, as long as it sustains its reputation.

It is easy to see the benefit of having a reputation, but the obstacle to the creation or maintenance of one is the temptation to degrade it by engaging in short-term opportunism. At some point it is just too tempting to make a quick buck, or it is too difficult to live up to the standards you have set yourself, and so credibility is flushed away. At around the same time as the Japanese and Korean cars were starting to be recognised for their true quality, the British car industry went on a journey in the opposite direction. They entered the optional Phases Three and Four of the brand life cycle. These are the phases where you run your reputation down. In Phase Three, the dominant player, British Leyland, produced relatively low-quality cars but it took time for consumers to register just how bad they were, so they carried on selling better than any other manufacturer in Britain for some years longer than they deserved to. Phase Four was reached when consumers finally caught up with reality and stopped buying the cars, and their market share dwindled.

During that time, British Leyland found itself in an advertising war with new entrants to the market – a war that it lost because the product being advertised was simply not as good.[11]

The decision as to whether to create or maintain a reputation seems easy; everybody is in favour of long-termism, we are all against opportunism and everybody would rather have a Japanese car industry than a 1970s British one. But you have to remember that the immediate costs of an investment are often unbearably high. The British car industry in the 1970s was facing multiple problems and was way off the global pace, and it was not really in the gift of strategists to take a long-term view. They couldn't have guaranteed product reliability even if they had wanted to. All British Leyland could do was manage its decline by advertising its poor cars in as positive a way as it could, in the hope that they would carry on selling for as long as possible, and that something might come along to get them back in the game before it was too late.[12]

The dismal cycle

So, we've seen the difference between the high road and the low road. On the former, everybody behaves with integrity and is trusted accordingly. They know that their reputation matters and is rewarded, and so they have no incentive to undermine it. They know that for the sake of one small transgression they threaten their reputation for ever, and they know it's not worth it. On the low road, by contrast, nobody behaves with integrity and no one is expected to. The low road is easy at first, but becomes rather hard going later on. But let us examine in more detail the reason why anyone takes the low road, because it is this that explains why we encounter so much bullshit. What desperation is it that induces otherwise sensible people to suspend their normal good judgement and think, to hell with the consequences tomorrow, I'm going to talk bullshit today?

Well, the answer is clear. In many professions, in order for you to be there for the long term you have to survive the short term, which makes the short term the only period that matters. Let us return to the very real dilemma of an ordinary politician running for election. From a selfish point of view, should they be completely honest with people during the campaign, confronting the voters with the uncomfortable truth that they intend to put up taxes? The short-termist devil on one of the candidate's shoulders tells them they should lie or obfuscate (saying things like 'I have no plan to raise the rate of income tax', even though they plan to raise other taxes) because by the time their deception is exposed they will be in office. Even though the electorate may not find the claim persuasive, given the candidate's incentive to lie about it anyway, a few people may be fooled and it won't do any harm. And to say otherwise would be to scare the voters with a promise of something positively awful.

On the candidate's other shoulder stands a long-termist angel, urging them to be frank with the voters to avoid a backlash when they win and the public find out they have been deceived. 'Be honest and the voters will believe everything you say at the next election,' the angel says. 'Build a reputation for honesty as it will be useful once you are in office.' Now, much as it would be nice for the angel's plea to be listened to, you have to have some sympathy with the politician who listens to the devil instead. After all, if politics is your profession, the only election that matters is the one that you are facing now. The politician might want to be more frank and straightforward, but if the consequences of dishonesty will only come to bite them later, and if there is an election to be fought in the meantime, it takes a pretty exceptional person to resist. They feel trapped by their own circumstances. When I have spoken to politicians about how much better it would be from their own perspective if they sacrificed short-term point scoring to look more honest and statesmanlike, they explain that if you don't win the short-term points you don't last long enough ever to become a statesman.

It's not just politicians who can get stuck in a rut of short-termism in regard to their handling of communications. There is ample data to suggest that company executives are willing to make bad decisions simply because good long-term decisions would be hard to explain to their shareholders. In a revealing paper called 'The Economic Implications of Financial Reporting', academics John Graham, Campbell Harvey and Shiva Rajgopal published the results of a survey they carried out of 401 financial executives.[13] It makes painful reading: for example they find that 34 per cent of the executives they survey admit that they would probably turn down an opportunity that was good for shareholders in the long term, if it lowered their earnings in the short term to below the market expectation. The average probability of such a project being pursued was found to be 59 per cent. That has got to be mad – in principle, the figure should be 100 per cent. But the executives view the crucial earnings per share figure as more than just earnings; they see it as some kind of device to communicate with shareholders, and show how well they are doing. Massaging the earnings up is an executive way of spinning the news. And a large minority of executives do not want to communicate bad news, even if it is in the shareholders' long-term interest that they should. The authors report findings from an additional twenty detailed interviews:

One CFO [Chief Financial Officer] candidly admits that his/ her company would defer or eliminate maintenance spending to meet earnings targets, even if such deferment would accelerate the need to replace the asset in the future. The CFO went on to illustrate that retrenching trained personnel might be economically sub-optimal in the long run, but that his/her company has taken such actions to meet the earnings target. Similarly, another CFO mentioned that his/her firm would perform 'band aid' maintenance for several years to protect earnings, even if a decision to take a hit to earnings and refurbish the plant all at once would have been NPV [a measure of long-term financial value] positive.

The executives doing these things know it is silly, the shareholders do too, but still this kind of behaviour persists. Corporate executives fear that if they don't deliver good quarterly results they will be shown the door, notwithstanding the long-term value they have created. This inevitably drives the executives into the imperative of generating short-term returns, which is not to the long-term benefit of anyone. It is unfortunate that this particular form of incompetence is felt necessary for executives to communicate their competence and keep their jobs. One of the pithiest business quotes I have encountered came from the management guru Peter Drucker: 'The long term is not simply the adding up of short terms.'[14] In other words, maximising your annual returns for twenty years is not the same as maximising your twenty-year returns. The fact that so many executives feel they have to maximise the short-term returns rather than the long-term ones is pretty horrible for them and their shareholders.[15]

This phenomenon of looking after the short term, to the detriment of the long term, also occurs in politics, where it is particularly unfortunate. When it arises, it can be characterised as a dismal cycle in which politicians spend every election campaign treating it as though it is their last, desperately trying to raise expectations as to what can be achieved and then spending the subsequent period in office letting people down. That can create a circle of disappointment: one political leader does it and in response to the inevitable public disenchantment the next comes along doing the same, promising change but failing to deliver.

In the US, there is data that could be said to support this proposition, in the form of consistent Gallup polling on approval ratings. Since the end of the Second World War, the public have regularly been asked, 'Do you approve or disapprove of the way _____ is handling his job as president?' and we can look at the 'before' and 'after' ratings of the post-war office-holders. Harry S. Truman had come to the presidency on the death of Franklin D. Roosevelt, but he won the 1948 election with approval running at 67 per cent; he left office four years later at 32 per cent – a fall of thirty-five points from election to leaving office. Eisenhower came after Truman, with approval falling nine points across his term; Kennedy fell fourteen points before his assassination. Lyndon B. Johnson fell twenty-one points between his election victory in 1964 and leaving office. Jimmy Carter fell thirty-two points, George W. Bush fell twenty-three points, Barack Obama fell nine. Both Richard Nixon and Gerald Ford had big falls in approval too, but I'll exclude them from consideration as the former was driven by Watergate more than his disappointing performance generally, and the latter was never elected. Only three presidents ended their period in office with more public regard than when they started: Ronald Reagan (up twelve), the first George Bush (up five points, but strangely only in the weeks after he'd lost the 1992 election) and Bill Clinton (up eight). The average change in approval over the ten presidents is about –12 percentage points. The default form in democratic history appears to be one disappointment after another.[16]

We can see this phenomenon in Britain too. The adulation

that was given to Tony Blair on his arrival in office, followed by vilification after he left, is just the most extreme example. He was perceived as a new start and ended up being branded an old-style let-down. And everybody can remember the next new broom, which followed soon after in the form of Nick Clegg. The Liberal Democrats' 2010 election-campaign video showed him strolling through Westminster with bits of paper blowing around him, talking of broken promises. 'There have been too many in the last few years, too many in the last thirty years,' he said. 'In fact, our nation has been littered with them, a trail of broken promises.'[17] Mr Clegg then found himself in a coalition government; he took some tough decisions, and within months was accused of the biggest betrayal of election pledges that anyone could ever remember.

Over the decades, a sequence of political disappointments inevitably helps create a cynicism with politics, and endless public complaints that 'they are all the same' and 'they always break their promises'. What I'm describing here is not a system run by dishonest or particularly cynical people. It is a game with rules that dictate the way the players think they should behave. They may personally want to be more frank, but their careers are generally not long enough for them to take the risk that they think total honesty represents; they are driven to focus on relatively short time horizons by factors quite outside their control.

I don't want to overstate how broken the system is, and whether that explains the public disenchantment or anger that led to the rise of populist challenger parties in the 2010s, but it is quite possible for societies to become trapped on the low road, in a pattern of low trust and low integrity that fuels and is fuelled by short time horizons and then encourages voters to look for candidates of a different, and more decisive, character.

For an extreme and timely example of how this can persist,

it is worth looking at a book published in the 1950s about life in an Italian town. *The Moral Basis of a Backward Society* was written by Edward Banfield, an American political scientist who spent nine months with his family in Chiaromonte, 120 miles south-east of Naples.[18] (He tried to anonymise the town by calling it Montegrano.) He wanted to explain why the community remained so miserably poor and failed to implement basic and obvious measures to improve the welfare of its citizens. Why was there no hospital, when the nearest one was five hours away by car? Why was the schooling so bad, to the point that nearly 30 per cent of those aged between ten and forty were illiterate? Why, indeed, did no one try to change the bus schedule to make it possible to send local children to the superior school in another town near by? Banfield posits a problem stemming from the short-term and self-interested behaviour of those involved in public administration, which fuelled public cynicism and then fed back to the politicians, who found they could never benefit from taking a long-term public-spirited view.

> In Montegrano and nearby towns an official is hardly elected before the voters turn violently against him. As soon as he gets into office, his supporters say – often with much justice – he becomes arrogant, self-serving, and corrupt. At the next election, or sooner if possible, they will see that he gets what is coming to him.

If you are going to be treated as corrupt, you might as well cash in as best you can while you have the chance. The lack of trust feeds short-termism; the short-termism feeds the lack of trust. Banfield used the label *amoral familism* to describe the rule by which he believed everybody subconsciously operated:

'maximize the material, short-run advantage of the nuclear family; assume that all others will do likewise'.

> The amoral familist who is an office-holder will take bribes when he can get away with it. But whether he takes bribes or not, it will be assumed by the society of amoral familists that he does.

As one local man who was interviewed for the study put it:

> If I decided that I wanted to do something for Montegrano, I would enter my name on the list at election time, and everyone would ask, 'Why does he want to be mayor?' If ever anyone wants to do anything, the question always is: what is he after?

Banfield's study perfectly describes a society stuck on the low road, and he suggests that this long-standing ethos had made fascism more appealing to the poorer peasants than it would otherwise have been. He quotes from several interviews with locals condemning fascism but commending some of the attributes of the Mussolini administration: the enforcement of the law or the fact that employers couldn't cheat their employees. The fact that opportunistic dishonesty was outlawed by a strong external force was a clear component of several of the comments. One merchant, for example, said:

> Cloth was grade-labelled and marked with a fixed price along the selvedge. Everything was controlled. You knew what you were getting for your money. Now, unless you really understand cloth, a merchant can sell you inferior material at high prices. It was good for the customer and good for the

merchant too. The customer knew what he was getting and the merchant could count on his twenty or thirty percent.

Banfield argued that the economically disadvantaged would always see attractions in strong leadership to counter the selfish anarchy of amoral familism.

Most of us in the West would probably rather our societies do not emulate Montegrano, but to avoid that low road we need to find ways of rewarding those who take the high road and behave with long-term integrity. We don't want company executives to believe their contract will be terminated too quickly, because it induces them to milk the company for everything they can while they are there. And we don't want politicians to believe that honesty is the wrong tactic during an election campaign.

Later on we shall come to look at whether the political class can do better, and whether they are overstating the benefits of short-term dishonesty and underestimating the benefits of long-term credibility. I think they are, but I appreciate how difficult it is for them. And there is an additional problem that makes it much harder for them to break out of the dismal cycle by being more honest. Even if they as an individual want to do that, if their opponents stick to the practices of short-term opportunism they may find themselves punished rather than rewarded for their honesty. What one person does is influenced by what others choose to do, and it takes particular bravery to break out of the habits of an embedded short-term culture. It is this issue of the social norms of honesty and bullshit to which we now turn.

Culture and Norms

If everyone else bullshits, it's hard not to follow

The importance of culture

Even with the best intentions, it is sometimes difficult to be frank and honest. It all hinges on what policy everybody else follows. If all the builders in a town are in the habit of understating how long it will take for a job to be completed when competing for a contract ('It'll be done by Christmas') then the honest one ('It'll be done by next Easter') is at a huge competitive disadvantage. In fact, if customers understand the culture of understatement, it is positively misleading to tell the truth. If customers know that 'four months' means 'six months', they will assume that 'six months' means 'a long way into the future'. In fact, it's fair to say that if everybody lies consistently enough, words lose none of their meaning; they simply have different meanings. Just as the word 'literally' also means 'figuratively' (even the *Oxford English Dictionary* acknowledges that the 'incorrect' form is informally acceptable[1]), if everybody uses the word 'average' to mean 'below average' and 'good' to mean 'average', then why should anyone want to use the word 'average' to mean 'average'?

The implication of this argument is that, once embedded, a culture of mendacity is extremely hard to dislodge. It becomes a convention or standard of behaviour that is hard to break.

We all understand that there is a general culture of bullshit when we are looking for a job and come to construct our CV. Most people willingly conform to the conventions of CV-massaging, making the best of those awkward gaps or obvious weaknesses. We do it within limits – we try not to spin so hard that we would face serious censure on being exposed – but we do want to keep our CV up to standard. Fortunately, the people who read CVs know this.[2]

There is another context in which the same considerations apply, and it has been examined in some detail: online dating. One of the academic papers that has analysed this closely captured the honest person's dilemma perfectly in a quote from an interview with one male user of a dating site:

> I'm such an honest guy, why should I have to lie about my age? ... Everybody lies about their age or a lot of people do. So I have to cheat too in order to be on the same page as everybody else that cheats. If I don't cheat that makes me seem twice as old. So if I say that I am 44, people think that I am 48. It blows.
>
> —*RealSweetheart, Bay Area Male*[3]

Once the deception has taken root in online ads, it is hard to outlaw. It becomes self-sustaining, even in a situation where long-term honesty is recognised as a goal by each and every one of those joining the community of advertisers. They all have to fit in to the mendacious norm in order to compete on a level playing field.

As it happens, there is a casual perception that deception on these sites is rife, and this is reflected in the old gags about what people really mean when they use certain words online ('sociable' means 'drunk'; 'sensual' means 'pervert'; 'outdoor type' means 'doesn't wash'; and 'adventurous' means 'married'... you get the drift).[4] Clearly, on certain platforms, where role-playing is part of the game, deception is a requirement and it would spoil things to be honest. In these cases, there will rarely be an offline meeting to expose the reality and destroy the magic of the online encounter. In most cases, though, the goal of the dating site is to initiate a meeting in the flesh and so deception has its pluses and minuses: if you fail to exaggerate your positive features, you might expect to be overlooked, to the benefit of other people who are no better than you; if you exaggerate your positive features too much there is likely to be a quick reckoning once a face-to-face meeting occurs. In these forums, you simply have to behave in line with the norms followed by everybody else.

Analysis of online dating suggests that misrepresentation is widespread – in one study, about half of those interviewed admitted to it. But crucially that study suggests that most of the deception took the form of exaggeration, and in particular 'exaggerations that they thought others were probably also doing in their profiles', which adds weight to the argument that people simply respond to the culture in which they think they are communicating.[5] Here is an extract from an exchange between the interviewer (I) and a case study, Suszi (S):

S: Actually, it's quite funny that there is, you can pick, there is a thing for body type and you can pick 'slim, average, athletic, a bit overweight'. Do you know any chick that is going to tell you that they are a bit overweight?

I: I wouldn't know, I guess not?

S: That is right, so I just say average.

I: It's like the idea of perception of what is 'average', and average is, you know, probably a bit overweight anyway.[6]

The findings of this academic research make complete sense. The deception is usually limited to that which is thought to be socially acceptable, and which will not alienate or disappoint a partner on a date. Women are more likely than men to use older photos of themselves; men exaggerate how senior they are at work. On some occasions people blatantly lie; the lies are exposed and annoy their would-be partners. What also emerges from the research is that people use sophisticated techniques to establish credibility in this difficult arena: 'For example, one participant made sure that her profile photograph showed her standing up because she felt that sitting or leaning poses were a camouflage technique used by heavier people.'[7] The example demonstrates how subtle the communication strategies are, and how hard people will strive to find credibility.

But the overriding message is that bullshit is infectious; when one person does it, the next person quite rationally feels they have to do the same – or more – to keep up. This all derives from a need to position ourselves relative to everybody else; the more they up the ante, the more we need to. In this chapter we'll examine the relationship between the general culture of communication, and the behaviour of those within it.[8]

The Lombard effect

We have all had the experience of sitting in noisy restaurants, struggling to catch the words of the person across the table. We put up with the noise and perhaps even enjoy the atmosphere, but few of us devote much time to thinking about restaurant clatter. Fortunately, there is a group of people who can do that for us: acoustic engineers. And they've made a very simple observation about noisy restaurants – that as the noise level around us rises, we tend to speak more loudly.

Like all the most important observations, it sounds obvious once it is spelt out, but it carries the important lesson that other people's behaviour affects our own, and this creates a feedback effect. You shout, I shout, you have to shout a little more and so on. The phenomenon has a name – the Lombard effect – and a lot has been written about it. In fact, studies have shown the Lombard effect is present in cats, bats and whales, as well as in birds ranging from chickens to songbirds (but, strangely, not in frogs).[9]

It is named after Étienne Lombard, an otolaryngologist at the Hôpital Lariboisière in Paris. He was particularly interested in the internal ear, and it was while working in that field that he noticed the raised-voice phenomenon. He first discovered it in 1909, and published his findings two years later in a paper called '*Le signe de l'élévation de la voix*'.[10, 11] It turns out that we not only speak more loudly when there is background noise, we also subtly change aspects of our speech, and it appears to be an almost involuntary reflex. In fact, it takes training to stop doing it. The immediate application of Lombard's work was to produce a simple test to detect deafness, or those trying to fake it. Just put a noise in their ear and talk to them to see how their speech changes. (History doesn't record how many people have been caught out by this.)

Acoustic engineers have been dealing with the Lombard effect ever since their profession was invented. Andrew Parkin is one of Britain's senior practitioners in the field. He got into it almost by accident: 'I was going through the careers book and I didn't like accountancy, and acoustics was next,' he says. He knows nothing about the history of Étienne Lombard, but is aware that human behaviour is key in designing good building acoustics and the Lombard effect complicates things, particularly in a restaurant. 'You want it to be lively enough that you're aware that there are other people, there's a babble going on in the background, but not so lively that that babble starts to encroach on what you're trying to do, meaning that you've got to then speak over it.' Once that starts, it's hard to stop. 'It just escalates. It turns into a bit of a battle and ultimately it just ends in a racket. The other problem there is that as people start to raise their voices, they're not speaking with their clarity, their voices become more harsh and distorted and therefore it's more difficult to understand. So if you can make a space calm, then people won't be as inclined to start talking over each other. They'll talk more naturally quietly and then you don't run into all these problems.'[12]

If you read those sentences again, you might agree that the Lombard effect stands as a pretty good metaphor for angry public discourse, and the bullshit fed into it. In loud arguments we want our own point to be heard above the din. It becomes a kind of arms race: we all want to keep up with everybody else, and in the process we collectively act in a detrimental way. More noise, less information.

But the Lombard effect is not just a metaphor. It demonstrates that when it comes to human communication, we are pro-grammed to make ourselves heard. In whatever form we choose to communicate, through words, speech or action, the instinct to speak up kicks in and just as it can lead to a cacophony in a noisy bar, it can create a shouty argument on social media.

Before we delve deeper into that, it's worth taking note of the views of Mr Parkin, whose job is quite literally to calm everyone down. He thinks too many restaurants overlook acoustics in favour of aesthetics. 'Ceramic is noisy,' he says. 'It looks lovely.

It's very durable. It's very easy to clean, but it's noisy, and so for every bit of ceramic, you have to have something soft and squidgy to offset it, which is not always so easy, especially in a restaurant, where you want hygiene.' But restaurants are not his most important clients. Schools and hospitals increasingly recognise that by installing noise-reduction technology you get a double impact: the physical reverberation of the original noise reduces, which then induces a lowering of noise production, to the benefit of students and in particular hospital patients. 'If they're in a calm environment, then they will feel calmer, they will sleep better, they will recover more because they're not constantly stressed. Noise is a stressor, and if you can reduce stress then that has a direct impact.' Mr Parkin is not one to downplay the benefits: 'They'll require less medication and so the financial implications rattle right the way down the chain. You could even say that better acoustics equals less NHS waiting times.'

The dynamic of us each raising our voice above those of everybody else in the form observed by Lombard comes out of the workings of the inner ear and its instinctive response to noise. It leads to competitive shouting. And, funnily enough, that can be detected in some form in many different kinds of communication. The lights in Las Vegas, each trying to outshine the rest; competitive conspicuous consumption between people who have too much money and too little to do, and who feel compelled to show off their relative status; or cities trying to break records for the tallest building. These are areas where people are, in some metaphorical form, trying to yell above the crowd, and the presence of others doing the same raises the volume of all.

You might argue that the Lombard effect is what makes for the pleasing hubbub of human life and is to be celebrated. The lights of Las Vegas may not be to everybody's taste, but they certainly have their attractions. But the shouting usually has some negative effects. Let me focus briefly on three important areas, all highly relevant to current concerns about fake news and post-truth politics. In each there is a useful comparison to be made between shouting in a restaurant and the production of noise, and often nonsense.

Competitive shouting in journalism

All of us in the business of reporting news crave attention, and that shapes the way stories are told, creating incentives to exaggerate. The logic of how this comes about is impeccable. Just assume that these three plausible features of the media landscape hold:

- Journalists want their stories to be read.
- When it comes to serious news, readers tend to prefer important stories to unimportant ones.
- Journalists have to use some subjective professional judgement in determining how important to make a story sound when writing it up.

Those three factors taken together imply that journalists have an incentive to over-write stories in an attempt to grab attention. That would be true even if there were just one monopoly newspaper competing with other products for the public's time and money. But in a fiercely competitive media environment all journalistic instincts are naturally to 'big up' the news. 'First simplify, then exaggerate'[13] is the old adage, and it is born of a need to get attention in the same way that we speak up in a noisy restaurant. Look at the headlines on a slack August day when there is little news to report: from the tone and language of the headlines, you'd barely spot that there is nothing to see.

There is no area in which this kind of hype is more evident than in the reporting of clinical trials, or, more specifically, in breakthrough cures for cancer. It is difficult for journalists to keep a sense of proportion at the slow, steady progress being made in oncology, and it is tempting to lure readers with headlines that cut through the frustrations and constraints, like *Time* magazine's *HOW TO CURE CANCER* emblazoned on the cover, with an asterisk attached that took you to the sub-heading: *Yes, it's now possible – thanks to new cancer dream teams that are delivering better results faster.*[14] It's not untrue as such, but it is stripping out the nuance.

And don't just blame the journalists; look at the people who work in universities, and who want to get their science into the crowded news agenda. They too feel pressure to get their stories noticed. One study looked at 462 press releases on biomedical and health-related science, and concluded that 40 per cent of the press releases contained exaggerated advice, 33 per cent contained exaggerated causal claims, and 36 per cent contained exaggerated inference to humans from animal research.[15] Unsurprisingly, the majority of the news coverage of the stories written from those press releases reflected their exaggerations. The people who wrote the press releases probably worked in modestly sized communications departments at academic institutions and undoubtedly took pride in the fact that their work made news; their job was to get the team noticed, and they assumed that exaggeration is just part of the process.

It's not just science reporting that is subject to this phenomenon. Close to my own field is the excessive weight placed on certain pieces of economic news. Much bread-and-butter economic reporting is based on the release of a statistic of some kind: how the economy grew in the third quarter of the year, for example. Unfortunately, a lot of economic data turns out to be rather volatile; you can have an outlier in the series one month that will be cancelled out the next month by boring data fitting the regular pattern. To be frank, the only intelligent policy is to avoid getting too excited by any one economic statistic, and instead to keep a close eye on the overall pattern as it changes over time. However, if you are reporting the economic news and you want people to listen to what you are saying, there is always a journalistic impulse towards suggesting the news is significant. It's really not helpful to tell the audience that a particular statistic is less important than it looks, but the Lombard-type result – of talking up the news – generates a potential media bias towards over-reporting flaky statistics. The more interesting a figure looks, the more attention it gets, but the more likely it is to be an outlier and so less deserving of attention.*

I don't want to exaggerate the problem of this kind of media exaggeration. One press defender told me that 'the price of a free press is excess', and he is to some extent right. Just as noisy restaurants have their merits, a lively media can be to the social good, grabbing the attention of people who might otherwise have little interest in public affairs; anyway, most consumers are quite aware that the press has an incentive to hype. Screaming headlines are well understood and automatically discounted. And just as there are quiet restaurants to go to if you hate noise, there are plenty of calm media outlets that you can turn to if that is your taste. The growing audience of BBC Radio 4 and the enduring popularity of the less sensational newspapers are signs that people can find what they need if they are motivated to do so.[16]

---

* There is a similar effect in the reporting of house price rises in times of boom. Because there are many different measures of house-price inflation that are released regularly, you can find that the increase in prices in one month is excitedly reported five different times, as the press vie to show they are keeping up with the apparent speed at which prices are accelerating.

Competitive anger on social media

The discourse on platforms like Twitter is often sadly conducted at a high volume of low quality. This is more than just the normalisation of a shouty culture: like kids in rounds of competitive name-calling ('You're stupid' ... 'Well, you are more stupid' ... 'No, you're stupider'), there are ways in which the extremity of others induces more extremity in those with whom they converse. It is quite simply a natural emotional response to up the ante in arguments. Even among intelligent debaters who use Twitter without resorting to anonymity, restraint is sometimes abandoned and out-of-character behaviour results;* it is made to look positively reasonable compared with the hate and nastiness of those on the anonymous fringe.

Particularly interesting in this regard, though, is the idea that anger has a certain infectiousness. This has been observed on Sina Weibo, the Chinese social media platform. For six months during 2010, researchers collected seventy million posts from nearly three hundred thousand users and put them into four emotional categories: joy, sadness, anger and disgust. They then looked at how those posts spread across the network. For example, if I get a joyful post, how likely is it that I will send a joyful one myself? A paper called 'Anger is More Influential Than Joy: Sentiment Correlation in Weibo' empirically demonstrates the point made in its title.[17] As the authors say,

> Our results show that anger is more influential than other emotions like joy, which indicates that the angry tweets can spread quickly and broadly in the network ... We conjecture

---

* I could mention one or two names, but to do so would only provoke a silly argument.

that anger plays a non-ignorable role in massive propagations of the negative news about the society, which are always hot trends in today's internet of China.

It has also been observed that anger can be manipulated by those who simply want to attract attention. It is barely an exaggeration to say that there exists a professional class of controversialists who seek to be outrageous and to then watch their social media presence grow as people queue up to condemn them.[18]

Just as with journalism, I do not want to overstate the degree to which this is a problem. The Chinese have a lot to be angry about, and it is possible that allowing people to give vent to their discontent in electronic form prompts social change without people having to take up pitchforks and fight each other on the streets. And anyway, if anger isn't your thing, or you have better things to do than read other people's rants, it is not hard to avoid the conversations in which they occur, and to interact with those who prefer to do so more calmly. But there is no doubt that, thanks to the ways human emotions spread, the technology of social media is highly efficient at generating bullshit.

Competitive identity politics

There is a third area where Lombard-type feedback effects arguably play a role, and where, in the process, they can end up promoting myths and nonsense. This is in the area of group rivalry and identity politics. I have already suggested that there is a link between bullshit and tribalism. First, the question 'whose side are you on?' becomes more important than 'are you speaking truth or nonsense?' In a world where we are all acutely sensitive to social and political divisions, we look for subtle linguistic cues to ascertain other people's allegiances. For a politician, for example, adherence to the reassuring shared myths of a particular section of society can become a qualification for office. Secondly, there is the bandwagon effect, in which we take confidence in our own feelings by looking at the beliefs of others, and this can foster groupthink.

But there is a Lombard-type effect that fuels this process too. One group asserts its interests with a certain intensity, but in doing so provokes a reaction from another group, which defines its interests as somehow counter to those of the first. It could be Catholics and Protestants in Northern Ireland, or Sunni and Shia militias in Iraq; it could range from gangs of football supporters to nations setting out their interests without regard to those of other nations. In all these cases, highly varied as they are, there is a tendency for escalation; when one side makes an advance the other – with good reason or bad – feels a need to fight back out of a fear of being overlooked (even if the success of the first is simply symbolic rather than substantive). It is reminiscent of Jim Malone's line from the 1980s movie *The Untouchables*: 'You wanna get Capone? Here's how you get him. He pulls a knife, you pull a gun. He sends one of yours to the hospital, you send one of his to the morgue! *That's* the *Chicago* way, and *that's* how you get Capone!'[19]

In these situations of group rivalry – whether actual or perceived – it is the relative position of each side that matters, so an advance by one needs to be met by a similar or greater advance by the other.

There is another familiar word that captures the essence of identity competition: backlash. If one group shouts loudly, another may strike back. If the slogan Black Lives Matter is seen to be gaining traction, someone white will inevitably feel a need to pipe up 'White lives matter too'. They are like the attention-seeking child who, on seeing love being lavished upon a sick sibling, concocts a pain of their own. Justified or not, the backlash can be seen as a Lombard-style raising-of-voice in response to the raised voice of the other.

This kind of idea was the core of an important argument about the success of Donald Trump in 2016, that it was a white reaction to the attention bestowed upon excluded groups and minorities. One argument was put by Mark Lilla in the *New York Times* just after the presidential election, in an article called 'The End of Identity Liberalism'.[20] It was a criticism of the Hillary Clinton campaign, and of the direction of liberal politics:

> [Hillary Clinton tended to] slip into the rhetoric of diversity, calling out explicitly to African-American, Latino, LGBT and women voters at every stop. This was a strategic mistake. If you are going to mention groups in America, you had better mention all of them. If you don't, those left out will notice and feel excluded. Which, as the data show, was exactly what happened with the white working class and those with strong religious convictions.

In Lilla's account, liberal politics had an admirable preoccupation with righting the wrongs faced by certain disadvantaged groups, but that turned into a fixation that manifested itself in disproportionate attention being given to relatively specialist problems (like the use of transgender-sensitive pronouns). This had nothing to offer large numbers of people who felt that their own more pressing concerns needed to be addressed. Not surprisingly, those people voted for something different. I find the analogy of the Lombard effect a useful one in understanding the mindset that gets you there.

Incidentally, Lilla's account of voter behaviour is distinct from the argument that the Trump victory was a 'whitelash',[21] a protest fuelled by bigotry and anger; a reaction to the way the US had changed under eight years of a black president and the rising status of minority groups. But whether white voting behaviour was underpinned by old-fashioned racism or by a legitimate and explicable sense that liberalism had drifted off course, it is still possible to view the political struggles of 2016 as emanating from a form of competition for relative attention of certain groups.[22] And what is clear is that the result has been a politics more polarised than ever, and as bullshit-ridden too. As I have stressed elsewhere, that means attributes which might generally be regarded as important, like a grasp of the facts, no longer seem important to voters when their group's standing is at stake.

There is an important implication of this analysis. It suggests that if we want to reduce the volume of bullshit in politics, we have to de-escalate the sense of identity struggle and instead focus on things that matter to everybody. Society is not a zero-sum game, with the gains for women or people of colour or the LGBT population necessarily coming in the form of losses for white straight men. But by arguing in a zero-sum form, we give everyone the impression that you have to fight or be slain.

Acoustic engineers know how to handle this kind of problem: noise-dampening measures need to be taken to reduce the volume of myth-spreading tribal argument. In the words of Andrew Parkin, something 'soft and squidgy' needs to line the walls of the space in which political discourse occurs, to take the intensity out of the sense of rivalry. That sometimes means arguing more softly, not more loudly; showing more empathy with other points of view, not less.[23]

Unfortunately, this is opposite to the reaction of many protagonists, who enjoy nothing more than ramping up the volume, arguing their case ever more strongly and failing to appreciate that winning a point may not be contributing to their overall cause. Whether or not one supports Lilla's argument that liberal politics has been overly obsessed with identity, he makes an interesting tactical point for his liberal side of the debate: to avoid a backlash, you had better have something to say to the people who are not part of the groups you have identified as marginalised, and thus in need of special attention. You don't have to win them all over, and you will certainly never quieten the merchants of hate who try to stir up anger. But you need to win over some.

Other ways that culture prevails

The shouting struggle, whether it be in restaurants, journalism, social media, public discourse or any other form, describes one way that other people's tendency to bullshit affects our own. There is a vicious circle by which the conduct of one communicator inevitably induces a response from another, which feeds back into the behaviour of the first. But while this competitive effect is certainly the most powerful way in which culture influences behaviour, it is not the only one. You can find noisy habits unrelated to those Lombard-type dynamics. Social norms shape behaviour in non-competitive ways as well. We might, for example, just have a social norm of being loud, with no competitive element to it at all. In some countries and cities, car drivers have a habit of hooting literally every few seconds as they proceed along the roads.[24] Clearly, the fact that everyone else hoots all the time makes it more acceptable for me to do it; and if I've been brought up in such an environment I might simply assume that the right way to drive is to beep the horn every time I encounter another car. This can be a part of a driving culture and, like all cultures, once it is embedded for good or ill, it is hard to remove.

But this is not a competitive process: the fact that others hoot all the time does not force me to do it more. It just makes it easier. A social habit becomes entrenched.

Economists have written much about this kind of issue, taking the use of the traditional QWERTY keyboard for English typing as an example. It has been claimed that there are better keyboard designs out there, but they simply can't break into the market. Once the QWERTY model had settled in, it inevitably became the one we were all taught on and the one that was used in offices around the country; it thus became hard to buy anything else. Its widespread acceptance was self-reinforcing, in that it justified the decision of the shops to keep selling it. It has become locked in, and it would now require a gargantuan effort to shift us all to something else. Moreover, it would be relatively hard for any one individual to make that change unless other people were to do it at the same time, as only a mass movement could prompt a change in the installed base of keyboards.[25] Now it is true this account has been challenged by the suggestion that the QWERTY keyboard is hard to improve, but you can see the general point it makes.[26] Standards are hard to shift once imposed.*

If this point is true for physical products like keyboards, it is surely also true of social norms. We all have a strong tendency to conform to them, and if society has evolved to normalise nonsense, who are we to challenge that individually? If good manners or social ritual demand that we lie, most of us will lie. If everybody exaggerates stories to make them more entertaining, so will we. If defendants are generally expected to wear a suit in court, it takes a brave defendant to turn up in jeans. If flowery

---

* Obviously they are not impossible: we moved from the vinyl disc and cassettes to the CD, with a rapid change in the installed base of music players. But this did represent a huge jump in the prevalent standard.

rhetoric is expected in a big set-piece political speech, that's what ordinary politicians will feel they need to serve up in order to avoid disappointing party activists. These are not cases where we are *compelled* to follow everybody else for fear of otherwise being drowned out, but where we *choose* to follow everybody else because … well, because it's just what we do. And when it comes to honesty and bullshit, there are three particular reasons for us to behave this way.

First, if we are lazy, it gives us a default form of behaviour that requires little imagination or effort. You have to say something to the neighbour that you bump into occasionally; in the absence of anything better to comment on, the weather provides a harmless enough topic for a brief episode of small talk. It is not because the weather is very interesting; it is more because convention offers us an off-the-shelf solution to the problem of what to say.

Secondly, when it comes to lying or deceiving we tend to use the behaviour of others as a guide to our own ethical standards. If everyone at work fiddles their expense claims just a little bit, we will feel that it is acceptable to do the same. The psychologist and behavioural economist Dan Ariely has shown that cheating is contagious, and that while most of us act in dishonest ways from time to time, we do so in minor and conventional enough forms that we can still think of ourselves as basically honest.[27] At a college dorm, Ariely left cans of Coke and dollar bills in a fridge to see which were stolen first. It was, of course, the cans of Coke. He points out that most of us think it is better to steal a ten-cent pencil from a friend than to steal ten cents from their purse to buy a pencil. We have a preconceived view of what is acceptable and what is not, and that plays some part in our deliberations as to what we can get away with while keeping our self-image intact.

But the third and most important way that culture affects our behaviour is through other people's expectations of us, which are determined by the conventions within which we operate. To behave unconventionally is liable to be misinterpreted. To return to the horn-hooting example above, if other drivers learn to expect to hear a hoot when a car passes, they may be taken by surprise by a driver that fails to hoot. Not hooting can then be hazardous. Or, in the British system of adversarial politics, the party leader who turns up to Prime Minister's Questions (PMQs) each week and asks a constructive question in the expectation that there may be an answer to it will be seen not as clever but as weak. You are meant to be hostile and score a point, and your supporters will be frustrated if you fail to deliver. It doesn't have to be that way, but it has evolved in that direction and now it is hard for anyone to break out of the custom. Several have tried, most notably Jeremy Corbyn, the party outsider who became Labour leader, and who tried to do things differently.[28] But even he largely had to revert to the more traditional adversarial model. That is just the way things are. Again, all this indicates that a culture, once embedded, is very hard to dislodge.

The challenge of non-conformism

Is any of this of relevance to a politician choosing whether to over-promise in an election campaign? Are professional communicators who hype, lie, manipulate their words or talk nonsense simply conforming to the standards of behaviour expected of them? The answer to this question is a partial yes. And to make the point, I'll finish this chapter and this section of the book by taking a little time to relate the story of the late James Bond Stockdale, who will go down in history as one of the most straight-talking gentlemen the world has ever produced.

And who, partly as a result of that, will also be remembered as having made one of the least successful forays into politics that has ever been attempted.

Jim Stockdale was a vice-admiral and aviator in the US Navy who had the misfortune to be involved in the 1964 Gulf of Tonkin incident, which played a large part in driving the US into war with North Vietnam. The 'incident' refers to two episodes on 2 and 4 August, in which it was alleged that North Vietnamese torpedo vessels attacked US naval destroyers in international waters. It led to the Gulf of Tonkin Resolution, which gave President Johnson congressional cover for the deployment of troops in the defence of South Vietnam. Troops were of course then sent in their tens of thousands and the rest is history. The war didn't end well, but it didn't start well either, because there was always something fishy about the Gulf of Tonkin incident. Questions came to be asked as to whether it was all it seemed, or whether it had been concocted. Certainly a battle occurred in the northern arm of the South China Sea on 2 August, although it might have been the US that fired first, contrary to the impression given by initial reports. Stockdale was involved in that – and in a sense he was thus among those firing the first bullets of the Vietnam War. But the 4 August episode was most bizarre: the Americans engaged in battle for a second time, firing on the North Vietnamese torpedo boats. Yet there is scant evidence that the North Vietnamese were there to be fired upon. Stockdale was in the air above the theatre at the time, and later wrote that 'I had the best seat in the house to watch that event, and our destroyers were just shooting at phantom targets ... There was nothing there but black water and American firepower.'[29] He was a witness to and participant in one of the post-war period's most consequential abuses of the truth. And he was most uncomfortable with it.

I went through it with Stockdale's son Taylor: 'He was shocked when he woke up and Johnson had basically announced that they were going to start committing troops to Vietnam as a result of that.' The US was retaliating against North Vietnam, but for what? Stockdale of course could say nothing. 'It was tough, because it was classified information,' Taylor told me. 'So for many years after coming home from Vietnam he couldn't talk about it.'[30]

But before he got home, Stockdale endured the most horrific treatment at the hands of the Vietcong. Shot down in 1965, he was locked up for seven and a half years in the notorious Hanoi Hilton where he was tortured, held in solitary confinement for extremely long periods, and maltreated. The Vietnamese kept trying to connect him to the Gulf of Tonkin incident but he kept making up stories about being in the Indian Ocean at that time and managed to do a good job of evasion during his time in prison.

At one point, in order to stop himself being used in any propaganda, Stockdale bashed his face with a wooden stool and broke some glass with which to cut his wrists. It was a gesture that had a dramatic effect on his captors, who scaled down the cruelty they inflicted not just on Stockdale but on the other US prisoners too. He survived it because, as Taylor explains, the Vietnamese wanted him to. 'They didn't want him to die at that point because he was such a prominent figure in the prison. He woke up in a pool of blood and they were able to save his life. He had terrible scars on his wrist as a result but he just knew in his heart he had to do something to just stop everything.' His actions earned him a Congressional Medal of Honor.

While in prison, Stockdale made an interesting observation about the mindset that prepares you for survival when facing an ordeal of that kind, and it was later labelled the Stockdale

Paradox. It relates to optimism and honesty to oneself. Stockdale observed that the people who had the toughest time were those with the rosiest view; they were ground down by constantly finding their optimistic expectations dashed. The most resilient inmates turned out to be the ones who had enough optimism not to lose all hope that the ordeal would end, but who did not have so much that they built up unrealistic expectations. 'You must never confuse faith that you will prevail in the end – which you can never afford to lose – with the discipline to confront the most brutal facts of your current reality, whatever they might be' is the way he described it many years later, to the author of a book about leadership.[31]

Leadership was something that Stockdale had in spades. The highest-ranking American in the prison, he managed to institute an internal coding system based on tapping out letters, allowing the Americans to communicate with each other. And he was inspiring to his fellow inmates. As Taylor explained, 'They would get tortured and they would break down and they would give classified information after a while as anybody would. And my dad would say, "Hey listen, just do your best. If you do your best you're going to feel good about yourself. Don't beat yourself up," because he knew that the biggest enemy in those circumstances is people's own minds and their own sense of guilt.'

He got home in 1973. Taylor has a vivid memory of the occasion. 'I had always dreamed about hugging my father and thinking he was a big burly man, this military guy, and I remember when he got off the plane in San Diego and we came up to hug him, I remember hugging him around his waist and just nothing was there. It was like his uniform was on but he was so thin from being in the prison that I remember hugging him and it was like a ghost.' But he was in good mental shape. 'They were horrific conditions, worse than anybody even knows,' Taylor says. 'I read some of his personal diaries and it's just unbelievable. I always thought it was remarkable that a guy could come home like that and be loving and be caring and be warm and gracious after having had that set of circumstances to contend with.' And Taylor thinks his father's mental resilience was partly explained by his 'deep philosophical connection with the classics and with stoic philosophy. And most notably from there with Epictetus, a slave from roughly around the birth-of-Christ era, who developed a philosophy that you have more control than you think you do. You need to understand that once you become the victim then you're sunk. So you're not the victim of anything. You have control in your mind to decide how you're going to function during the most perilous times of your life.'

In 1985 Stockdale and his wife wrote a memoir, *In Love and War*, about his Vietnam experience. It included his account of the Gulf of Tonkin incident, which has long been seen as an important piece of honest testimony about the events of 4 August 1964. 'He was able to come out with the full truth to say there was nothing there and it was just a very confusing evening,' Taylor says.

Back in the US, Stockdale held a number of posts, including a short stint as President of the Citadel, the august military college in South Carolina. He was a controversial head of the institution, in particular attempting to reform the brutal student practice of hazing – putting freshmen students through dangerous bonding rituals.

I have given quite a bit of space here to an account of Admiral Stockdale's life, in order for you to see just what kind of man he was. I defy you not to be in awe of him to some degree, for his values, his honesty and his behaviour. It is surely hard to imagine anyone who could be regarded as better qualified to serve in a top job in politics, if he could ever be persuaded to take one. So one of the great ironies of his life is that when he was persuaded to put himself forward in 1992 it went so badly.

It was an era well before populism was a talked-about phenomenon, but the businessman Ross Perot decided to run for president as an independent candidate. He was a friend of the Stockdale family, having actively campaigned on behalf of American POWs in Vietnam, and he asked the admiral if he'd mind being named as a candidate for vice-president on his ticket. Initially it was envisaged that Stockdale would be something of a placeholder to allow Perot's name to be put on the ballot; it was never Stockdale's intention for it to go much further. He certainly didn't intend to wind up in a national televised debate with the two main candidates for vice-president, Dan Quayle and Al Gore. But one thing led to another and soon enough just such a debate was in prospect, and then it was too late for Stockdale to back out.

Unfortunately, Stockdale was not a conventional politician, armed with the standard tools for winning this kind of contest. Taylor remembers the debate well. 'I had my mom on my right and I had Mrs Quayle on my left, who was lovely. My brothers were on the other side of my mom and we're just all in shock. It was at Georgia Tech, down in the south. It was surreal. It was like, "This can't be happening. There's no way it can get this bizarre that we're here in this debate hall."' It didn't go well. Stockdale's gentle self-deprecation turned out to be a huge disadvantage when set against the slickness of the professional politicians. He gave a moving but stuttering performance in his two-minute opening address, starting with the words 'Who am I, why am I here?' It initially attracted a laugh, but as *Time* magazine said, his performance 'left viewers simply wondering whether he knew the answer to either question'.[32] It was all made far worse by his overly honest response to a question from Hal Bruno, the moderator of the debate: 'I didn't have my hearing aid turned on. Tell me again.'

Poor Taylor Stockdale watched in extreme discomfort from his front-row seat. 'The debate hall was big and it was loud and it was very hot, and I remember being in there and the debate didn't end. It was, like, a ninety-minute debate and it was, like, endless. In fact, I thought he did worse than he did. I mean, because at one point he was wandering ... Admirals like to walk the deck and he was kind of wandering, and I was like, "Get back to the podium".'

Stockdale's hapless performance has gone down as among the worst in the history of US televised debates. '"Who am I? Why am I here" got us off to a terrible start,' Taylor says. 'I think it was just his unease. Quayle and Gore would be just fighting like little kids and my dad wasn't little, and he didn't know what to say. "Is this an intellectual discussion or what is this?" So just watching his unease during that whole process was hard for me.'

After the debate, the family and the Stockdale team had to get to the spin room, as is the convention on these occasions. 'So they get me and my three brothers in this small room and this guy – I don't know where he was from – and he said, "Okay, here's what we're going to say. Your dad did great. He spoke well." And I remember my brother Sid finally just erupted and said, "What are you talking about? He was terrible. He was totally a fish out of water. We're not going to say that shit. Everyone knows. Everyone saw what they saw, okay, so let's be honest about it." It was so cathartic. We were all just like, "Yeah, we're going to say what we want to say. Get out of our way." And we went out there and it was good. I think we were able to say "Our dad's very smart and a hero, and it was totally not his element and clearly he's not a politician, but he speaks from the heart."'

With the night over, Taylor and the rest of the family retired to a hotel. 'I forget where we were staying, somewhere in Atlanta – and he went right over to the room service and he called up and he said, "I'd like to order a case of Jack Daniels, please, to room whatever ..." He was joking about it, but we stayed up all night and we just talked and we just came together as a family in a weird way. You looked out over these lights over Atlanta and just thought, What did everyone just see tonight? It was kind of a powerful night for the family, actually, and we did laugh, just sort of recalled all the craziness of the evening, et cetera, but beyond that it wasn't something you laughed about. It was never a laughing matter. It was a big deal for him and he knew how it went.'

You might put it down to his age – Stockdale was sixty-eight at the time of the debate. You might suggest he should have been better prepared on his key lines. But the truth is the skills that serve you in Vietnam are not the ones that prepare you for a televised political debate. Bear his story in mind when you berate politicians for being over-scripted and repeating their stock phrases. Here was a man who was a reluctant bullshitter. 'Yeah, he could do it, but it was not natural to him at all,' Taylor says. 'I mean, there was no guile in him, no guile.' As for Donald Trump, the outsider who *did* make a success of an election campaign, Taylor is pretty clear about what his late father would have thought of him. 'I don't think he'd be able to stand him. He wouldn't like Donald's bravado and brashness and his reckless behaviour, his reckless talk. It's just counter to everything my dad believed.'

Stockdale defied the political norms and went unarmed into battle with those who stuck to them. He was everything that we say we want in politicians, but he would have clearly been better off with the slick slipperiness we hate than uncalculated, unrehearsed straightforwardness. He is an object lesson in how hard it is to be a rule-breaker.

All this being said, we know that some people thrive on being unconventional. And when the rule-makers and rule-compliers become too stifling or dull, it is the outsiders who suddenly look most attractive. Being part of the prevailing culture becomes a disadvantage. It is fair to say that Western politics had not reached that point in 1992, but it had by 2016. The traditional politicians found themselves challenged by eccentric candidates who didn't speak in the dreary tones of the incumbents, but who spiced things up with simple ideas and direct language. But they did it with a new kind of bullshit of their own.

Which brings us to a set of new questions. Can we do better? In politics, business and life generally, is it possible to be more honest, more authentic and successful? And as consumers, is it possible to process the messages we are sent in a more intelligent way, to discourage the mendacious from even trying? How should we respond to the sense that we are in a post-truth era? It is these questions that I will try to answer as we move into the next three chapters.

SECTION THREE

HOW

A look at how we can improve our
relationship with bullshit, and navigate
our way through a post-truth era

9

Limits to the
Power of Persuasion

*Recognising what it is that clever
communication can and cannot achieve*

When good professions turn bad

What the last few chapters have shown is that bullshit is something of a social institution. It can sometimes be informative or persuasive, and it is often inevitable. But no one would say that it's all for the good, so in this section it's time to think about how we are using bullshit, and whether we could do so more effectively. Never has this issue been more important than now. This is not just because there is currently intense concern that truth is under attack from fake news and alternative facts, and that trust is low. It is that even before these post-truth anxieties, there was clearly a problem in the way policy-makers, politicians and businesses communicated with the public. Indeed, you might argue that the failure of the existing establishment to connect to the people helped trigger the challengers to that elite who emerged in 2016.

Chapter 11 focuses on the public. What responsibility do we each have – either as individuals or more collectively – for encouraging more honest public discourse? In Chapter 10, I'll mainly be concerned with those whose job is to persuade or sell a message, looking at the mistakes they should avoid and asking how they can do their job better.

This chapter also concerns the communicators, but it is a little more general. Having explained why bullshit makes sense, this chapter is all about its limitations. We know bullshit works, but how far can you push it? Can it really persuade anyone that black is white? Can a populist president convince people of something untrue merely by repeating it? Did the political spin that we became so accustomed to in recent decades really fool us? I confess to some scepticism that bullshit has such power. There is an old adage in banking that you should only give a loan to someone who has enough money not to need one. Maybe there is an equivalent proposition in communication and public relations that you only have the power to persuade people of things that they already believe, or at least are ready to believe or will soon believe anyway, when the truth emerges. Or is my scepticism unjustified? I suppose the basic issue here is whether good advertising really can sell a bad product. Or whether a lick of paint can transform a slum into a château.

The central message of the next few pages is that while it can, on occasion, pay to be less than straightforward, far too many professional persuaders have overestimated their ability to achieve a lasting change in our beliefs through their communication strategies. This is particularly true of professional spin doctors who all too often have been trying to sell a government policy they know is failing, and public affairs consultants who get paid for making a phoney case in defence of some company's interests. They should put PR back in its place and recognise that the most powerful weapons in the communication armoury are – in the long term – puny in comparison to the facts. They have put too much effort into the messaging, and not enough into the thing being messaged. In short, they've become enchanted by their own skill and deluded by their own science, and have thus taken bullshit way beyond the optimal level. They would be doing themselves a favour, as well as the rest of us, if they would scale it back.

If the communications profession has tangled itself up by deploying a sophistication that has become counter-productive, it is hardly alone; it is a well-established pattern in the modern human era. Our species has an instinct to strive for efficiency in everything it does. In any activity, we observe what works, and then develop systems that economise on effort and maximise impact. We take complex processes and hone them into a routine that is altogether simpler and streamlined. This impulse has served us well. It explains how we invented agriculture, how we managed to replace cottage industries with large factories, and how we gave the average Western citizen today a better living standard than that of a medieval king.

But sometimes, in trying to progress, industries can become too clever by half, refining their practices to such a degree that they end up losing sight of what it was they were trying to achieve in the first place. Dog breeders, for example, have taken their science to a level at which we now find them producing show animals that are physically unnatural and ill-adapted to basic functions like breathing.[1] Or look at mass-produced school dinners: until Jamie Oliver came along to point out what was happening, we had so perfected the industrial process of school-lunch manufacture that we had saved money on employing qualified chefs in school kitchens and squeezed the cost per meal down to barely imaginable levels; but in doing so, we had somehow overlooked the purpose of eating.[2] I could go on. From battery hens to formulaic reality shows, our ability to make a lean, mean industrial process out of a gentle craft can go too far.

Not all of the communications business has succumbed to this error, but parts of it have, explaining why there was a widespread sense that we had reached a point of peak bullshit before the word post-truth became popular. In making that point, let me start with a warning from elsewhere, because for me, there is a striking and useful similarity to be drawn to another modern industry, one that faced its own day of reckoning when its pursuit of sophistication eventually rebounded upon itself: finance.

Comparing PR to finance: striving to create value from nothing

It was the financiers who made mistakes in the sub-prime mortgage market who triggered the financial crisis that first erupted in 2007. The bankers, helped by their associates in the large ratings agencies, believed that with a bit of clever financial packaging they could turn sub-prime mortgages into prime assets with a safe AAA rating attached.[3]

This is hardly a place to go into the origins of the crash and the vanities of bankers, but it provides a useful cautionary tale, as the people involved were in every conventional sense very intelligent. No one could say their financial engineering was anything but extremely sophisticated. Taking a bunch of sub-prime mortgages, bundling them up into asset-backed securities such as collateralised debt obligations and applying techniques like 'tranching', they somehow produced a bundle of loans that appeared to have an average risk lower than the ones they'd started with. Safety had been conjured from thin air. Unsafe assets went into special-purpose vehicles; safer assets came out. At no point was this achieved by tighter credit standards or more careful handling of the sub-prime mortgage holders.

As it happens, financial engineering can on occasion produce miracles like this, but this was not one of those occasions. The loans made to sub-prime borrowers turned out to be riskier than anyone involved had imagined, and many of the apparently safe loans that had been created genuinely turned out to be indistinguishable from the sub-prime ones from which they had been fashioned.

At its narrowest, that sorry tale reiterates the message that you should start with the working assumption that the value of a bundle of sub-prime loans worth, say, a billion dollars, is still a billion dollars however much you dice it up, re-package or re-label it. You might sell it for more than a billion dollars to some misinformed buyer in the short term, but eventually the truth comes out and the underlying value reasserts itself. You can't transform a loan by very much simply by tinkering with it; to make it a better loan you need to change the behaviour of the borrower or lender in some fundamental way.

There is a second lesson too: that no matter how sophisticated, complicated and mathematical an activity it is, and no matter how smart the people pursuing it, if it is fundamentally misconceived it will achieve nothing.

The instruments at the heart of the sub-prime crisis were just an extreme example of financial sophistication going too far, but finance has a long and illustrious tradition of this kind of alchemy – trying to create value without the dull tedium of tilling soil or building factories. If juggling the financial structure could really make us all rich (as opposed to just those who work in it), financial engineering would be the best thing ever. But it can't and it isn't. Yes, finance has a place; but no, it can't replace substantive production when it comes to making a country prosperous.*

Fortunately, in finance, there is a history of academics examining exactly when and where its practitioners have the ability to genuinely create value, and sometimes the finance professors have been able to demolish the woolly thinking of the practitioners and expose the myths on which their trade is built. One of the most devastating findings in the academic study of finance emerged in the 1950s. It was so central to everything that had ever been understood about companies it later earned Nobel Prizes for the two professors who articulated it. They observed that a lot of work was done by corporate finance directors, whose job is to sweat over the financial structure of their company – things like how much debt to carry, what kind of debt and how many shares to issue. And they asked a very basic question: can you make a company more valuable by changing its financial structure? For example, if a company borrows money, can it become worth more to its shareholders? (If it borrows a million pounds, a company now has a million more pounds in the bank but it also has a million more pounds of debt, so it's interesting to ask if the overall value of the company stays the same or not.) It was a basic question, but for years the business of finance had gone on without anyone rigorously examining it. And then along came the professors with a theorem that said that under certain very simplifying assumptions, financial engineering can achieve nothing at all. In the simplest models, if you assume away all the everyday complexities of the real world like taxation, administration expenses, costly bankruptcies, messy business arrangements and so on, then finance is irrelevant

---

* Unless the country is selling financial services to foreigners who pay for them with valuable products.

and so are financial engineers. Those finance directors really need not worry too much about all those questions they struggle with – the amount of debt, the kind of debt, the number of shares – none of it makes any difference, because the value of the company is the value of the company, however you cut it up. In these terms, debt and equity are almost as irrelevant to the value of a company as whether you choose to express the share price in terms of dollars or cents. They are just different ways of getting to the same thing.

The implication was that finance guys should stop wasting their time on paperwork and be redeployed towards things that do affect the value of the company, like devising superior products and cheaper ways of making them.[4]

The two professors who developed this work were Merton Miller and Franco Modigliani of what was then the Carnegie Institute of Technology in Pittsburgh. Interviewed in 1999, a then rather elderly Modigliani said about it:

> The theorem, which by now is well known, was proven very laboriously in about thirty pages. The reason for the laboriousness was in part because the theorem was so much against the grain of the teachings of corporate finance – the art and science of designing the optimal capital structure. We were threatening to take the bread away, and so, we felt that we had to give a laborious proof to persuade them ... Nowadays, the theorem seems to me to be so obvious that I wonder whether it deserves two Nobel Prizes.[5]

In fairness, not all is lost for corporate finance directors: Miller and Modigliani also found that in the untidy real world where there are taxes, administrative costs and market irrationalities, there are plenty of occasions when financial engineering can create value. For example, increasing the amount of debt the company holds will possibly reduce its tax bill and make it more profitable. There are always wrinkles to be ironed out, quirks of everyday life that have non-negligible implications for our decisions, frictions that need to be factored in. So yes, down on Planet Earth, where taxes do exist and the assumptions of the simplest economic models don't hold, finance has a purpose, but it is still helpful to start with the default assumption that finance can achieve little and then think about the departures from that basic insight. That approach gives a role to finance, but a more limited one than its proponents have generally imagined.

So much for the work of finance professors. Is this of relevance to the professional communications business? Yes, I think it is. There are many similarities to be drawn between those in finance who hope that value can be conjured out of thin air, and those in PR who believe that reputations can be built on the back of great image-building. The sub-prime crisis was the financial equivalent of a government believing that it can use spin to take a sub-prime policy and turn it into a political triumph, or a business trying to sell a sub-prime car by spending more on advertising than its rivals. The idea that you can enhance reputations or win votes without doing the hard work of creating fundamental value has always been seductive, but is quite similar to the idea that you can create value and make money through financial engineering.

And if there is a similarity between finance and PR in that both strive for a magic that can take a rat and sell it as a squirrel,* is there an analogous proposition in the field of communications to that of Professors Miller and Modigliani in finance? Can we argue that it is only in a limited number of circumstances that

_____

* As the adage goes, a squirrel is just a just a rat with good PR.

clever PR can achieve much in pushing a message that deviates from the frankest, simplest presentation of the truth? This has to take us into a conversation about how far you can persuade someone of something untrue, or which they do not want to believe is true.

Can you hoodwink the public?

The last four chapters set out four basic reasons that bullshit may thrive and survive. In order, those chapters suggested:

- That the kind of bullshit and the tone it is delivered in can be genuinely informative, in particular signalling the allegiance of the communicator.
- That by exploiting our psychological foibles, clever communicators can frame messages in more believable and more powerful ways.
- That in the short term, in the absence of any attempt to build a reputation for honesty, bullshit may be able to achieve something before it is detected. (And anyway, it won't do any real harm.)
- That once a culture of bullshit is entrenched, it is hard for any individual to break out of it, particularly in an environment where communicators feel they are competing with each other for attention.

The first reason carries no implication of deception at all; the information buried in the bullshit is true, and that explains why it is accepted. The third only implies a temporary phase of deception, in the short period between a lie being told and its detection. There is no doubt that it is possible to deceive or confuse people for a while and that sometimes you can make a handsome profit before they realise they've been fooled. But that does not explain all the bullshit we see, by any means. The fourth explanation – based on social norms – is a more complex one, but is not underpinned by trying to fool people of anything. It is more about a competition to be heard.

It is really the second of those four explanations, the psychological one, that suggests a canny communicator can manipulate our feelings to make a message more believable than it would otherwise be. They can apply the techniques outlined in Chapter 6: using emotions to override our intellect; telling stories that provide an appealing narrative; whipping up a crowd to exploit the bandwagon effect; managing expectations to make small numbers seem big or big numbers seem small; and framing issues in a way that suits their argument. The pessimists who fear that a lot of us are born suckers might cite those devices as evidence in their favour. Are these – and other even more sinister methods – not the legendary PsyOps that can work subliminally on our feelings and sentiment?[6]

The answer to this question is, 'Up to a point.' The problem for those who want to manipulate our feelings and beliefs is that while we do have psychological vulnerabilities that can be exploited by those who are crafty with their words and actions, we also have psychological strengths that offer some protection against those who want to manipulate us. It's harder to break through our mental defences against bullshit than you might think. There are two key mechanisms here, habituation and recognition. *Habituation* describes how the more something is tried, the less effective it can become (the drugs no longer work). *Recognition* is how a technique can fail once the fact that it is a technique has been spotted (a trick is no longer magic once we see through it). Neither stops these psychological devices having an effect altogether – after all, shops have durably benefited from charging £9.99 for things even though we are habituated to it and recognise what is going on. But it is worth asking how far habituation and recognition provide immunity to the use of psychological techniques to manipulate our thoughts.

Self-protection through habituation

Habituation is not unique to human beings. I found an excellent account of it in a book on dogs:

> The simplest kind of learning is *habituation*, defined as the waning response to an event that turns out to have no consequences. Most animals have sense organs that pick up far more information about the world than they can possibly attend to, and dogs are no exception to this rule. To avoid wasting time, animals need a mechanism that allows them to avoid responding over and over again to something their senses are telling them they might want to attend to, but does not actually need to be bothered with. It is a very primitive and universal ability. Even animals without nervous systems can do this, or something like it.[7]

Just as dogs get bored of toys, humans tire of messages that have no connection to the observed world. The first time you ever heard a car alarm it screamed out that a crime was being committed. By the hundredth time, when not a single car alarm you had ever encountered pointed to a robbery, you ignored it. Well, that is really no different from the message that was propagated to the people of the former Soviet Union, that life there was wonderful. Once the public had the chance to see that the message deviated from the observed reality, it was the observed reality that won the day. Similarly, take those low-cost air fares advertised by Ryanair and other value airlines. These often have supplementary charges, which you don't discover until you are some way into the booking process. Most notorious was having to pay an additional fee for using a debit card to pay for a ticket. These extras mean the fares are not always as cheap as they first appear. But the point is that it doesn't take long for us to get wise to these devices and understand that the advertised price is not quite the same as the one you end up paying. The habituation neutralises any beneficial effect that Ryanair might derive from advertising low prices.[8]

The habituation effect is not just strong, it is irresistible. It means that messages that are potent in some contexts become normalised and then impotent in others – it all depends on whether they are externally validated. Newspapers whose stories don't quite justify their headlines will in the long term find that their headlines are taken with a pinch of salt. People know the difference between a sensationalist tabloid and an upmarket broadsheet. Or if you are a government spin doctor and pre-leak misinformation in order to flatter the real news when it is finally announced, you might succeed for a decade or so, but eventually we all stop taking leaked information at face value. We will assume that the message is being spun, and that the news will be better than the pre-release implies. There are so many examples of this. You can get attention at home or in the office by getting angry, but if you do so too often your anger will be cheapened, appearing synthetic or uncontrolled. It is then more likely to be ignored or despised. You can entice people to donate to good causes by showing them pictures of hungry children in far-off countries, but arguably, if you show too many, you risk making people feel anaesthetised to pictures of hungry children in far-off countries.[9] You can make yourself look 'down with the kids' by giving a speech against a multicultural backdrop of young people on stage behind you (as politicians are wont to do these days), but the five-hundredth speech presented in this contrived way will have less impact than the first. You can try to make an unpunctual person turn up for things on time by setting their watch so that it runs five minutes fast, but there's a danger that after a short period of time they'll adapt and roll up ten minutes later than the watch tells them to.[10] In all these cases, the contrived or false message has an effect, but it can wear thin.

Habituation doesn't wipe out the impact of an apparently effective communication altogether, but it does weaken it over time. All this is to say that we have an innate ability to observe correlations and patterns, and it is impossible for us not to make a connection between the words that are used and the reality they are attached to.

Self-protection through recognition

Recognition is a separate and altogether more conscious force to protect us from manipulation. If we recognise the techniques being used to persuade us of something, are we less likely to be seduced by them? When you realise that the charming Italian lover used the same pick-up lines on someone else, they have no effect at all. Or do they? We like to think we are clever beings and can use our intellect to see through the enchanting techniques deployed against us, but in practice how far does recognition help us?

In the modern era, in countries with a free press and social media, it has become hard to use any subtle technique of persuasion without it being exposed for what it is. But the general issue at stake here is how far mechanisms that work on our psychology are undermined by a conscious understanding that there are psychological mechanisms at play. Can the reasoning of our System Two thinking wipe out the subtle effects that work on our System One intuition? Does propaganda work even if we know it is propaganda? If you want to buy a house and visit a property with a coffee pot steaming away in the kitchen, pouring out a sensuous coffee aroma, does it entice you to buy, even if you know it is there to do just that? Who knows how deeply the psychological bias runs?

At a first glance, it is tempting to think we are unable to resist the appeal of a clever propagandist, even if we know that is exactly what they are. For years, door-to-door salesmen succeeded in charming home-dwellers with well-worn sales techniques, notwithstanding the fact that most people were aware of the legendary powers of door-to-door salesmen to secure a sale. Maybe understanding their tricks makes it easier to compensate for any effect they have on you, but it is hard to assess how much compensation that requires, and you may believe that in any particular case the product really *is* worth buying. You are never a neutral observer of these subliminal effects. Daniel Kahneman, the man who has done more to promote the understanding of System One and Two thinking than anyone, is deeply pessimistic that we can empower our rational System Two brain to overcome the impulses of our System One brain. 'I've been studying this stuff for about forty-five years and I really haven't improved one bit,' he has said.[11]

Kahneman has some evidence on his side. For example, we all know there is such a thing as a placebo effect, but does it still work if you tell someone they are taking a placebo? Answer: yes, there are indications it does; our conscious brain can't override the subconscious effect. Researchers at Harvard Medical School carried out a controlled study on eighty patients with irritable bowel syndrome and found the group who were administered a placebo – and who were told it could potentially work through the placebo effect – reported a greater easing of symptoms than those given nothing.[12] It is only a small indication, but it shows that recognition of a psychological technique does not give you immunity to its effects. And if placebos can work their magic on us when we know they are placebos, propaganda can work too, even if we know it is propaganda.

Another piece of evidence that conscious recognition bestows no protection against unconscious appeal comes from our responses to communication that is not trying to persuade or sell. Consider film or television entertainment; ask yourself how far recognition of the method deployed backstage changes your appreciation of the product. To me, a joke is funny even when you know it's a joke, just as a James Bond film is entertaining, even though you know the plot formula to which it is adhering. My enjoyment of comedy quiz shows is not reduced at all by my belief that the contestants get told the questions in advance.[13] Who cares? Recognition of the production techniques used to make the programme is irrelevant to whether I find a joke amusing or not.

All of these points suggest that our ability to recognise a psychological trick is unable to override its subconscious effect on us. But wait; think about it more carefully. The examples of placebos and James Bond movies just cited are ones where we are willing participants in the process. It is quite different if we actively try to resist the sales pitch tugging at our subconscious. Try this thought experiment. Think of a political movement or party that you hate. Now imagine that it produces a cute ad along the same lines as those of a company you like – perhaps something rather like a John Lewis Christmas commercial. Nice music, a good story, a little boy perhaps waiting to make a gift to his parents, who in this case are keen supporters of the party you hate. Now do you think you would weep at the sweet child's desire to please his parents? Or would you now feel new disdain at the cynicism involved? Irritation at the attempted manipulation? My guess is that you would not sob at the ad if you hated the cause it was supporting. Instead, your System Two thinking kicks in to alert you to the danger of manipulation, and all the ad can thus do is entrench your pre-existing view. Incidentally, for supporters of the party it would cement their view too, making them feel a little more passionate about their cause. But that is because they already believe and want to believe, not because they have been freshly persuaded of something that isn't true.

This implies that recognition does offer some protection. An audience that is aware of what is being done to it can at least partially stand up for itself – *if it wants to*. I concede that much of the time we are rushed, unsure or easily led, and recognition that we are being manipulated offers little protection. But when it comes to issues that really matter to us? Surely we are better-informed, self-aware and appropriately sceptical, and no attempts at brainwashing (short of administering mind-changing drugs) will alter our thinking. The propagandist is, in short, having to work with the grain of the target audience's predisposition.

Hoodwinking the public: the ambiguous evidence

If the existence of habituation and recognition suggest that we are partially protected against lies, what evidence is there that we are gullible? It's easy to find evidence that you can fool some of the people some of the time; it's easy to find evidence that you can fool the bulk of the people for a short time, or the bulk of people for a long time, about something inconsequential; but it's harder to get evidence that you can fool the bulk of people about anything significant once reality has time to impose itself. Chapter 6 showed that a well crafted message can change our behaviour; the nine-ending pricing succeeded in lifting sales by 8 per cent relative to the round number ending. But is 8 per cent a lot or a little? And would you get an 8 per cent uplift if the items being purchased were important? I doubt the effect of psychological pricing would be that great if it was applied to a car or a house.

The truth is those asserting that the public are hoodwinked often clutch at anecdotal evidence, which proves very little. It's always possible to point to some powerful piece of propaganda and show how effective it has been at tricking a hapless population into buying the wrong product or voting the wrong way. But that is to look at the most observable phenomenon – an advertising or political campaign – and to connect it via causation to an outcome. Unfortunately, it is always possible that there are other unobservable things going on that explain the outcome, or connect the campaign to the outcome in a non-causal way.

For example, we know that advertising works, but we are not careful about linking that evidence to the appeal of the product being advertised. When we see Nescafé is advertised more and sells more than other brands of instant coffee, it is all too human to assume that the advertising sold the product. But who's to say Nescafé isn't better than its rivals? Maybe it is advertised more heavily because the company sells more and can afford more ads. Remember, for bullshit to be a powerful persuader, the real question is whether it works regardless of the rubbish being advertised. The Institute of Practitioners in Advertising's famous and widely respected IPA Effectiveness Awards look at all sorts of metrics in measuring the impact of advertising campaigns, but the actual quality or attributes of the item being advertised are not explicitly among them.[14] So yes, the methodology used in the awards shows that advertising is effective, but not that it can work regardless of the product being advertised.

I was struck by a headline in *Forbes* magazine: 'How Come Bad Ads Sell Good Products, But Good Ads Can't Sell Bad Ones?'[15] I generally stick to the view that the producers of reasonably good products have more incentive to advertise than other producers, and that makes it hard to know whether it is the advertising or the product or the interaction between the two that is driving the sales.

At this point, some will cite Silvio Berlusconi, Vladimir Putin or Donald Trump as evidence that public opinion can be manipulated. They would say each could only ever have been elected on the back of lies. Again, I am happy to concede that people can be fooled in the short term, and that the short term can be very important if it means winning an election or referendum campaign, so it is quite possible that their voters were gullible. But on the basis of what evidence? Who knows to what extent Italian, Russian or American voters were manipulated in these cases, or to what extent they had prejudices, hopes or fears that pre-dated the election campaign? Maybe the campaigns were a canny response to the existence of those sentiments rather than leading them. The economist and *New York Times* columnist Paul Krugman wrote a piece called 'The Populism Perplex', in which he pondered why Donald Trump got so many white working-class votes in the 2016 election, when for him it seemed obvious that people were voting against their own interests.[16] Krugman speculates that it may have been that Trump's lies paid off; he suggests that it can't have been Mrs Clinton's policies that lost her the election, as media gave little attention to policy during the campaign; and he concludes that Trump managed to stir up resentment of the attention liberals devote to non-white and other excluded voters. But is it possible that voters use a different definition of their own interests from that of Paul Krugman? Perhaps they wanted a big change, disliked the existing way things were done and were being smart in voting for a proper shock to the system in the way they did. Perhaps they weighed up whether Donald Trump would be a disaster or an effective antidote to a system that was annoying them. Who is to say? The truth is, it is hard to be sure and there is a raging debate about why Trump won, and whether his voters will be any more disenchanted with him than they are with other presidents. But, logically, you cannot infer the public have been hoodwinked simply because your candidate didn't win.[17] Instead of asserting that a candidate won by lying, you sometimes have to ask, why did that candidate's lies appear more persuasive than my candidate's ones?

Needless to say, this discussion does not do justice to the huge literature on propaganda or other forms of persuasion and their effectiveness. And I don't want to deny that there is such a thing as group hysteria, and that it can be incited by clever propagandists. Hitler did come to power, after all. But personally, my default assumption would be that a good propagandist can only work with our pre-existing values and beliefs, which are in part moulded by the evidence that we have encountered. Reality imposes itself, disposing us to accept some messages more readily than others, and it constrains the ability of propagandists to shape our views.

This is supported by some of the academic work on persuasion. One mainstream academic model posits that you can move opinion, but not a million miles from where opinion already lies. The literature says that when people are engaged with an issue and hold a specific position on it, they usually regard a range of views near to theirs as reasonable. Anything within this tolerance range is labelled the *latitude of acceptance* (with some people having broader latitudes than others).[18] When we are confronted with a proposition we first ascertain whether or not it is within our latitude of acceptance. If it is, we are inclined to accept it; if it is not, we tend to reject it. According to this theory, changing people's minds is a rather special skill, akin to a parachutist landing in a specific field. You have to land your desired message on exactly the right spot within the target audience's latitude of acceptance. If you miss the space altogether (hitting the *latitude of rejection*), you present your audience with a message wholly unacceptable to them and just alienate them. But equally, if you want to shift their attitudes you don't want your message to be bang in the middle of their latitude of acceptance; that would just confirm their present view. The goal is to frame a message that deviates from their pre-existing view, but which is nevertheless acceptable. This way you can gently move or widen the latitude of acceptance in your favour. That's the theory anyway, and it is one which has achieved a very prominent place in training courses devoted to communication and persuasion.

But it's important to remember that something determines the range of acceptable beliefs in the first place, and that is to some extent dictated by people's observations of real life – in other words, the truth or the merits of an argument. Do these not have a place in determining where the latitude of acceptance lies? Slowly shifting opinion on issues as varied as same-sex marriage or whether to build a high-speed train line takes not just patient, gentle campaigning (though that helps) but the substance of the case to shine through. If there is no case, you are unlikely to persuade a majority of the population there is one.

The latitude of acceptance is not dissimilar to another concept talked about in political science, the *Overton window*.[19] This represents the range of socially or politically acceptable views on any issue. Again, if you want to shift debate radically you somehow have to move that range. It isn't easy – but it can be done. But contrary to the argument usually proffered in talk of the latitude of acceptance (that you can only influence people if you are inside the boundaries of acceptability), it is often suggested that to move the Overton window, you have to stand outside it shouting loudly. Eventually more extreme opinions are normalised and the range of socially acceptable views moves. Donald Trump, it is suggested, managed to shift this range markedly in 2015/16; by being so extreme in his talk about Hispanics and Muslims he caused previously unacceptable views about foreigners to become publicly expressible.

Even here there are questions as to how far Mr Trump did genuinely and sustainably shift public opinion. Did he move it, or simply make more vocal the opinions that were already there? Was it his campaigning that achieved a shift in opinion or was a shift occurring anyway, given the frustrations felt by Trump supporters? And has he achieved a *sustainable* change, or will the public let events dictate their views of foreigners once they see how things pan out?

Where does all this leave us? For me, the burden of proof is on those who want to argue that the voters or the consumers are stupid. I'm sure they can be, and I'm sure they make mistakes, as we all do. But you can't assume they are in any given situation or over any lengthy time period. And overall, what we know is that there is a complex interconnection between truth and belief. Faced with any case of persuasion, there are five distinct propositions: what you say ('our policy is working'); what the truth is (the policy is failing); what people are disposed to believe ('the government is on our side so we'll give them the benefit of the doubt'); what they actually believe now ('the policy is working'); and what they eventually believe, when the evidence becomes clearer ('the policy failed'). What you cannot expect to do is plug any kind of message in at the beginning of this chain, however well crafted, and get the particular belief you want out the other end. The intermediate steps matter and they are not all in your control.

Comparing PR to finance: the Warren Buffett approach

I started this chapter by comparing the professional communications business to that of finance, arguing that in both there are some who have a desire to turn base metal into gold. If that attributes more power to PR than it truly has, how should the practitioners of PR view their trade?

To demonstrate a perfectly practical alternative, let's return to the world of finance and a more favourable analogy than that of sub-prime manipulators. Warren Buffett is generally regarded as the world's most successful investor and has a rather different view of investment from many others in the business.

He is famous for amassing a fortune of tens of billions of dollars for himself and his shareholders simply by buying stock in the right companies. For many years, it was possible to look at his success and argue that he was simply lucky – perhaps he had simply benefited from the fact that repeated throws of the investment dice happened to fall his way. But as his career continued successfully decade after decade it became less and less likely that he was the beneficiary of some kind of long-running sequence of coincidences. After all, he always has a clear rationale for his decisions, he has adopted a particular approach to investment which stands in marked contrast to most other professional investors, he is happy to tell you what it is and which book to read to learn it yourself (*The Intelligent Investor* by Benjamin Graham), and his approach sounds sensible to most people, focusing as it does on the fundamental value of companies rather than the latest quarterly earnings. Buffett and his partner Charlie Munger generally buy and hold shares in companies for long periods rather than trading them all the time. In short, Mr Buffett has been a success by eschewing the spuriously sophisticated analysis and short-termism of others in his industry.

Warren Buffett is not just the world's most successful investor ever, he also happens to be one of the nicest. He has never let success go to his head and is remarkably unflashy for one as successful as he. Unlike the bankers and oligarchs with whom we have become familiar in recent years, he sustains a relatively modest lifestyle and avoids ostentatious consumption. He pays himself a salary of $100,000 a year[20] (his wealth comes from his investments); he lives in an unremarkable family house ('I'd move if I thought I'd be happier someplace else,' he says, 'but I'm five minutes from where I work, I've got great memories associated with it, the kids grew up there, the neighbours are fine. I don't know why the hell I'd be happier if I flitted around and had a place in London and Los Angeles and so on. If I'd wanted to become a superintendent of housing or something of the sort, I could have gone into that as a profession.') He drives to work in an ordinary car and his favourite restaurant is Gorat's Steak House in Omaha, Nebraska. When asked about his success, he is ever modest: 'When I was born I was wired in a certain way,' he says. 'It works wonderfully in a capitalist society but it wouldn't have worked so well if I'd been some place where they'd have valued physical ability or whatever it may be. But I get paid enormously at no great credit to me. I just was lucky at birth. I shouldn't delude myself into thinking I'm some superior individual because of that. In the end, a market system allows me to get this enormous disproportionate amount of the country's resources into my hands. One way or another, a fair amount should get back to society.' He is true to his word, committing billions of dollars to philanthropy and not even asking for his name to be attached in bold letters to prestige projects. ('Charities can get money by naming things for people, so why waste a building on me? They're going to get my money anyway.') He talks of how, in an earlier era of human history, he would not have flourished if, for example, the most valuable skill was that of running away from lions. Being good at investing would have counted for little. ('I'd say I allocate capital and the animal would say, well those are the kind that taste the best.')[21]

Of course, Mr Buffett is a human being. He has made mistakes; there are those that have found reason to criticise him; some say he is less folksy and down-to-earth than he likes to pretend. But for all this, no other investor has ever come close to matching him in terms of the wealth, the respect and the trust he has accumulated.

My purpose in describing Warren Buffett here is not just to highlight his success as a financier, but to discuss his brilliance as a communicator. Certainly, no other investor is quoted as often as he.[22] But interestingly, his approach to communication matches his approach to finance: he has made a success of himself by doing what others don't do. He is more straightforwardly honest than most, speaks more casually and manages the process with far less ceremony. Crucially, because he is not trying to manage a message, he does not have to think about what he says: he just has to say what he thinks. I can testify to his idiosyncratic style, having had the opportunity to interview him for a BBC documentary in 2009.[23]

If he were an ordinary senior manager in a large company, I would have expected to be given a time and duration for the interview, to be asked for question topics to be sent over in advance, and to show up to find one or possibly two public relations advisors present. But multi-billionaire Warren Buffett is not as self-important as the average senior manager in a large company. When we sat down together there were no PRs in tow, no limits to the question areas, and at no point was he looking at his watch to indicate the interview was going on too long. As for the quality of his responses, we covered far more ground than I expected because he didn't waste time obfuscating and trying to avoid answering questions. He just made his points and made them well. I'm not pretending it was easy to get an interview with him in the first place. The programme's producer, Charles Miller, had to work hard to persuade him to give us the time. Having done so, Mr Buffett explained in an email that he wouldn't be able to give us very long because, 'from an actuarial standpoint, I only have about four thousand days left on this earth, and I'm trying to keep various activities in proper proportion'. When it came to the day, though, he gave us more than two hours and let us wander freely around his offices unaccompanied in order to pick up television shots.

For a taste of the contrast between communication Buffett-style and business-as-usual, you can look at the website of Berkshire Hathaway, the company that holds all his investments. It is comically austere – specially designed to be positively anti-design – which makes the point that the company's emphasis is on the content contained therein rather than the look. The documents sitting there are disarmingly honest, in marked contrast to the usual annual report. Buffett's yearly letter to shareholders, which is by now something of an institution, uses lines like 'I've run out of good news. Here are some developments that hurt us during 2011 . . . ' or 'Last year, I told you that "a housing recovery will probably begin within a year or so". I was dead wrong.'[24] An ordinary chairman's letter to shareholders would probably phrase the same thought along the lines of 'Developments in the housing market have not proceeded as we had forecast ...' Buffett's 'Owner's Manual', a guide to shareholders of what to expect from Berkshire Hathaway, explains how Buffett himself has 98 per cent of his personal wealth tied up in the company. '[When] I do something dumb, I want you to be able to derive some solace from the fact that my financial suffering is proportional to yours,' he writes.[25]

This informal and reassuringly honest prose must come, in part, as a direct result of Buffett not trying to manage his message. Of course, he is lucky in having plenty to say (which puts him at a huge advantage over most people, who do not) and he has little to hide, but because he generally allows himself to say what he thinks he makes his life – and his text – far more straightforward than would be possible using more sophisticated approaches to communication.

Which brings me to what might be termed the Warren Buffett Rule. He formulated a version of it in a single sentence, delivered without much forethought, in response to a question from me as to why he didn't employ a professional PR team as most other people in his position would. His answer was: 'When you get to be old, you have the reputation you deserve.' In other words, in the long run, however you try to manage the message the truth will out, so there is no need to think too hard about presentation. People will like you if you deserve to be liked and they'll hate you if you deserve to be hated. No amount of PR effort in the meantime will make any difference. Buffett followed this up by adding, 'That's true with businesses too: you get the reputation you deserve.' More generally, one might extend this rule beyond reputations to say that truth will ultimately prevail.

This is the exact PR equivalent of the assumption underlying his investment policy, that in the long term underlying value will be recognised. Whether it is the financial value of a company, or its reputation, ultimately the truth will emerge. You may make things look good by dressing them up in the short term, but as the truth always comes out eventually, you are just putting lipstick on a pig, to use that colourful phrase. The message for companies – and for us all – is, first be good; then carry on being good; and then, finally, a good reputation and corresponding rewards will follow. And if this rule holds, it means that where a reputation is bad, the long-term problem is likely not to be the reputation but the underlying behaviour. The problem of the pig is that it's a pig, not that the public misunderstand it.

To me it is very striking that the man who I would suggest is the best interviewee I have encountered in my broadcasting career adopts an approach to communication that is the exact opposite of that of almost everyone else, in that he avoids trying too hard. He obviously knows that in the short term, reputations can deviate from reality, just as share prices may for some period fail to reflect the true strengths of companies. But just as the key question for an investor is whether the fundamental value of a company is currently reflected in the share price, the key question for a public relations advisor is whether the real behaviour of a person is currently reflected in their reputation. If Chile's late President Pinochet is thought of as evil, is that because his behaviour and reputation were misaligned or is it because he was evil?[26]

This is tantamount to asking whether it is really communication at issue, or whether it is the underlying situation. If, in a particular case, the Warren Buffett Rule is breached and a bad reputation is undeserved you should bring in the image-makers to sort out what genuinely is a presentation problem. But if the rule holds and you have a bad reputation that *is* deserved, don't waste money on image-makers trying to persuade everybody to

think more highly of you, as communication doesn't have the
power to make people believe things that are not true.

Not everybody in finance appreciates this as clearly as Warren
Buffett. This has been brought home to me by several lunches
and dinners with senior figures in the City of London, at which
the conversation is inevitably steered to the poor public perception of the financial sector. The hosts invariably invite me – a
figure from the media – to speak to them about what can be
done to improve the image of the City. My problem is that I
genuinely have nothing useful to say about the image of the City,
believing as I do that there is nothing wrong with the City's PR.
The low esteem in which it has been held by the public has been
quite understandable. After all, the banks have played a big part
in causing a prolonged depression in the West; they paid many
of their staff millions of pounds while robbing shareholders of
value and driving their institutions to insolvency; they mis-
sold products worth billions of pounds to consumers; and they
invented complicated charging structures for their services in
order to obscure the real price being paid for them. One doesn't
need to think very hard to fathom why nobody likes them. The
City's problem has not been that it was given a grade D by the
public while deserving an A. It had been awarded a D for a D-
grade performance. No amount of re-marking would be likely
to change that grade. What can I say, other than to explain as
politely as possible that there is no problem in the communication department? It is not a good media strategy they need, but
a complete change of personality, culture and behaviour. My
advice has always been that if the behaviour changes, the public
image will also change, although probably with a five-year lag.

At the risk of labouring the point, if you are regarded as bad
and you *are* bad, you don't have an image problem, you have a
badness problem. The communications challenge in the City is

not to change the public's mind about the banks, but to change the banks' minds about what they do.

My City hosts were focusing on the symptom rather than the cause. They overestimated the power of communication to solve an underlying problem, which it could never do. Armed with this kind of faulty analysis, the temptation for anyone is to hire consultants to refine their message, but without any change in the underlying behaviour that tactic will lead nowhere. In no time you would be writing the kind of stuff that we saw in the Barclays annual report back in Chapter 2, boasting of great customer service with no regard to what the customer service is actually like. After drafting a few meaningless claims that impress no one, you'll drop the consultants and blame the media for your poor image.

In contrast, what is interesting about the Warren Buffett approach is that it in effect conforms to the rational model of economic theorists who assume that bullshit can't get you far. For them, only substance matters. Personally, I'd rather put my money on those following the Warren Buffett approach. It's not that his proposition that you have the reputation you deserve is always true (and indeed I doubt he meant it to be taken too literally); it's simply that it is true enough to make it the best working assumption.

A struggling company that sells bad products should not put its effort into finessing its advertising, but into improving its products. A government confronted with difficult questions on a policy that is failing should have a frank reassessment of the policy rather than spend its time spewing out selective statistics in an attempt to show that the policy is working after all. Even the best communicators can't make bad products good or failing policies succeed, and yet the sad fact is that too many people in business and politics appear to have fooled themselves into thinking otherwise. They have locked themselves into the habit of devoting too much effort to the art of communication rather than to product design or policy formulation. Rather than keeping things simple by saying what they really think, admitting their weaknesses and discussing their vulnerabilities, they contort their words into lies, half-lies or obfuscating nonsense. Yet it is to no useful effect at all, because instead of persuading us that things are as they would like us to believe, they simply persuade us they are not to be trusted.

That is not to say that communication does nothing. You can obviously buy time by affecting people's short-term beliefs if they are disposed to trust you; and above all you can communicate the truth in more or less effective ways. That will sometimes involve a bit of bullshit. But the four previous chapters, which set out explanations of why bullshit exists or persists, have not offered a magical, sustainable way of persuading the bulk of people to believe things when the evidence says they are not true. They may provide good reasons for deploying bullshit, but only in the same subtle way that the existence of taxation justifies thinking about debt levels. They do not justify talking nonsense in the hope of dressing up dross. However good you are at communicating, you surely do not have the power to persuade people of anything you want. You can only successfully communicate those things that people are capable of believing; and as mentally stable people are mostly only disposed to believe things that are either true, plausibly true or that they want to be true, your powers are at best modest.

If you are interested in long-term reputation and performance, start with the assumption that manipulative communication can achieve very little in persuasion, and then you are more likely to devote your attention to the things that matter. To return to an analogy I offered earlier: if you are the coach of an Olympic swimming relay team, the real task is to make the team members swim fast. Communication is equivalent to the bit where you think about the order in which the team members swim. It's not nothing, but it can't work miracles either.

10

Better Bullshit

How communicators can raise their game

Lesson One: Donald Trump

The message of the last chapter was that while bullshit might work up to a point, it has its limits. That has always been true. So it's time to get more practical and to look at how the communicator class can do better. How can people in politics or public relations, whose profession involves selling a message, do so more effectively? How can they be more authentic or more like Warren Buffett? And how can they avoid coming across like victims of excessive media training?

These questions seem particularly important for the old Western political establishment. In 2016, their world changed. In Britain, most political leaders tried and failed to persuade the public to vote for membership of the European Union. They found that there was widespread scepticism of the arguments they offered, and they had insufficient credibility stored in the bank to draw on. In the US, Donald Trump came along and smashed the prevailing rules of political communication, and in so doing dragged the mainstream media and social media into a new phase of scrutiny and self-examination. While he has been criticised for being a bullshitter of the highest order,[1] he will probably be judged in the long term on his performance in office rather than on his rhetoric, extraordinary as it is. But in some ways the most important thing that Trump did was to expose a problem in the system that preceded him. The year 2016 could perhaps be seen as a contest between two kinds of bullshit – the old and the new – and in that contest Donald Trump's fresher form of it won. So the issue now is what communicators can learn from 2016 and the stagnation that had gone before. Without imitating Donald Trump directly, how can they raise their game?

The theme that runs through this chapter is that while we are all in the business of selling (whether we are selling a company, its products, a programme of government or ourselves), there has been a tendency to try too hard in doing so, and this is counterproductive. We are all aware that if you are looking for love, it pays not to come across as desperate; and it is similar for those in the business of communication. The best advice is to relax, not to over-think, and to avoid coming across as too studied. In fairness, this is easy advice to give, but difficult to put into practice. Just as anyone who's been desperate for love knows, it's hard to hide that fact from prospective partners. And anyway, if you want to come across as sincere, what are you meant to do if you are sincerely desperate? However, there are no absolute rules in communication – there are often trade-offs or dilemmas. This chapter is simply a nudge in the direction of softer selling and more authentic presentation.

The first lesson, though, is the negative one: that phoney message-management of the kind that has dominated public discourse should be put back into the box from which it came.

Having a good story to tell is important, and presenting it
consistently, clearly and without clutter is also helpful. But that
is not the same as devising a slogan and endlessly repeating it
without any regard to context.

Let me take one example of that way of communicating, as it
illustrates how far it has drifted away from naturally engaging
language. In 2013/14, the Labour Party wanted to make the
argument that Britain was experiencing an unpleasant squeeze
on living standards, which was largely the responsibility of the
coalition government's misguided austerity. It was an intellectually plausible line and an obvious one for an opposition to
take, pinning the blame for any hardship on the incumbent
government. But Labour adopted the modern habit of encapsu-
lating the core message in a key phrase and then trying to ram
it home as hard as possible.[2] The goal is to ensure that even the
disengaged public pick up the message and so the key phrase
has to be used without deviation or hesitation, but with plenty
of repetition. A leading party member is shunted in front of
the cameras and feels compelled to repeat this key phrase even
when it is not really truly relevant. The practice is even more
evident in the quotes that are inserted into press releases. In
the case of Labour in 2013, it was 'cost-of-living crisis' that
was shoe-horned into as many soundbites and quotations as
possible.

On the privatisation of the Royal Mail, for example:

Taxpayers have been left hugely short changed at a time when
families are being hit by a cost-of-living crisis.
                    —Chuka Umunna, Shadow Business Secretary[3]

On the government's Help-to-Buy scheme, designed to give
support to home-buyers struggling to raise a deposit:

You can't deal with the cost-of-living crisis without building more homes. We need a Help-to-Build policy to boost housing supply and tackle the cost-of-living crisis, alongside a reformed Help-to-Buy scheme. That's why Labour has committed to getting at least 200,000 homes built a year by 2020.

—Emma Reynolds, Shadow Housing Minister,
who gets double points for using the phrase twice[4]

On measures to curb payday lenders:

At a time when families are being hit by a cost-of-living crisis, if Ministers were serious about action they would back Labour's plans to give Britons the protection they deserve from these legal loan sharks.

—Stella Creasy, Shadow Minister
for Competition and Consumer Affairs[5]

There may be nothing wrong with the phrase in those three examples, but the same words were stretched when used in a reaction to the Financial Conduct Authority's report on the annuities market:

David Cameron's government have ignored this problem for far too long, refusing to fix the broken annuities market and rejecting Labour's changes to the Pension Bill which would have helped hard-pressed savers facing a cost-of-living crisis get a better deal.

—Gregg McClymont, Shadow Pensions Minister[6]

What about on the National Audit Office's Progress Report on the Regional Growth Fund?

To grow our way out of the cost-of-living crisis we desperately need to see better-balanced and sustainable growth across the UK's regions, but the Tory-led government's flagship Regional Growth Fund has been plagued by chaos and delay.

—Toby Perkins, Shadow Minister for Small Business[7]

To the party, this looks like delivering a consistent message. It's considered a sign of discipline that everybody is singing from the same hymn sheet. But it stops the party's protagonists speaking in natural English. No single instance taken on its own is too egregious, but when taken together they exhibit a pattern that debases the term 'cost-of-living crisis' altogether. It ends up with this instance, on the cost to government of the student loan scheme caused by low graduate repayments:

As a result of the cost-of-living crisis, earnings have been far below the government's expectations and many graduates have been left unable to find a job at a time when more than 900,000 young people are out of work.

—Chuka Umunna again[8]

The words have become so devoid of meaning that here it is asserted that earnings are low *because* of the cost-of-living crisis. Surely low earnings are the same thing as a cost-of-living crisis? And then, did the Shadow Health Secretary Andy Burnham really mean to explain pressure on NHS Accident and Emergency services by reference to the same phenomenon?

And this brings me to the third reason for the pressure on A&E – the cost-of-living crisis.[9]

Or did he just need to slot the phrase in somewhere? An even starker example is from Jon Cruddas, who managed to spoil an otherwise thoughtful speech:

> Many people worry that the country is in decline; some don't think politicians can sort out its problems. They feel powerless to make their voices heard. They are right, we have locked too many of the British people out. People have lost trust in the political establishment of all parties. At the heart of our cost-of-living crisis is the question of how the country is run and who it is run for.[10]

If we are asking questions about how the country is run and who it is run for, framing it in terms of a cost-of-living crisis can detract from a far bigger message.

Finally, how about this example, in which the Labour leader Ed Miliband wedged the phrase into a cumbersome quote about his plans to revamp competition policy:

> I am determined to lead Labour into the next election as a One Nation party of the consumer, small businesses, working and middle-class families who never thought they would be struggling with this cost-of-living crisis.[11]

Here, he has inserted a second significant phrase into his sentence. Although the use of the words 'One Nation' represented astute political positioning (as they had mostly been associated with a moderate wing of the Conservative Party), they made his sentence almost completely unintelligible to a normal human being. He outlined the groups whom he saw Labour as supporting – which turned out to be almost everyone.

Among professionals, far from being seen as contrived, this

kind of messaging is considered best practice; the way that proper professional politicians work. I could easily have taken the Conservative Party's use of the words 'long-term economic plan' at about the same time as an alternative example of the same conduct.

The defence of this kind of approach is that message discipline is important, because without it no one knows what you stand for; and that repetition is vital because most people are not following the minutiae of everyday politics and so will miss the point unless it is made many times over. That is all true, but no one should think that just because you have a phrase, you have a credible message. If a message is not particularly convincing, reducing it to a slogan and awkwardly repeating it on every occasion is not going to make it so. And the danger of this approach is that the effort may go into enforcing the use of the slogan, rather than into producing a compelling story that can be told in a powerful and authentic way.*

Donald Trump provides an interesting contrast. Compare the way the cost-of-living crisis phrase was deployed with the way he infused his campaign with the slogan 'Drain the Swamp' in 2016. Of course, his politics was more unruly and his signature phrase was coarser than anything the Labour Party wanted to say. But Trump ingeniously managed to sound sincere in his use of the phrase, by deconstructing his own attitude to it:

> You know when I first heard that term, I hated it. I said, oh, that is so hokey. That is so hokey. But I said, look, let's give it a shot. The place went crazy. I said, maybe we'll try it again. The place went craaaaazy. And now I like it.[12]

---

* A second, more convincing, defence of this kind of approach is that if you don't have a compelling story to tell, this kind of messaging is probably the best you can do.

The crowd, of course, were cheering before and after those words. Somehow, the fact that Trump had constructed a little story around the phrase gave it a significance and memorability that the average overused slogan lacks. His willingness to talk about his own use of the phrase – a kind of superficial deconstruction of his own rhetoric – also imbued it with a meaning it would otherwise have lacked. And acknowledging the role of his audiences in persuading him that the phrase was useful was also a clever touch.

Trump's effectiveness in the campaign also derived from a willingness to speak more directly than ordinary politicians. He was prepared to ask basic questions that sounded to ordinary people very reasonable: why should the US be obliged to stand as a defender for many different countries if NATO allies don't pay their fair share of the defence burden?[13] He didn't just ask questions like this, but he expressed himself in very vivid ways that were in stark contrast to the self-taming of most politicians; he never tried to downplay his points to make them sound less offensive and more reasonable, but quite the reverse: he ramped up the rhetoric. So, for example, talking about the USA obligation to defend Japan, he put it like this:

> You know we have a treaty with Japan where if Japan is attacked, we have to use the full force and might of the United States. If we're attacked, Japan doesn't have to do anything. They can sit home and watch Sony television, OK?[14]

The 'Sony television' is the touch that says he is not trying to run away from controversy; he really wants you to get it. Again, there was plenty of nonsense in his campaign, but to many ordinary people the directness exemplified in this paragraph has an honesty that contrasts with familiar political discourse;

that is why it should be of no surprise to anyone who listened to him that, despite all the accusations that he was lying, Donald Trump's trustworthiness ratings were not dissimilar to those of Hillary Clinton.[15]

More generally, outsider political forces have managed to make great strides by smashing the old conventions of restraint, and being willing to call a spade a spade. You don't have to like their politics to recognise that they are, in part, a force that has emerged out of a failing of traditional politicians to speak a language that engages the wider public. At its best, the idiom of traditional politicians across the West is designed to reflect a certain maturity and cognisance of the world's complexity; at its worst, it has become rehearsed, often defensive, obfuscatory and unwilling to entertain radical ideas. And in the process, the professionally crafted messages of expert political advisors, which are designed to hammer home a consistent, clear and simple message, have come to sound unnatural.[16]

To me, the message of Trump's success in 2016 is that the tired old language which had come to dominate political discourse had become worn out. Much of the expensive work by professional communications teams was easily exposed as empty by more natural communicators. It may have carried the day once, but it could now be ditched in favour of something fresher. If that is true in politics, it is true in other areas of life as well. And this is the first practical lesson for those that have been peddling the old bullshit for so long: you can move on. This is a chance to say that we've reached a peak of that kind of thing and can explore fresher, more direct, honest and natural ways of communicating. That's not to say that everybody has to become unprofessional and shambolic in the pursuit of authenticity; it is just that if you are stuck in old-phoneyism, you need to do something different.

The case for honesty

The next point follows quite logically: communicators should, *as a default*, say what they really believe in as straightforward a way as possible. I'm not a believer in simply exhorting people to do that if they have an incentive to behave differently. If there is a compelling logic to lying – i.e., if the benefit of doing so exceeds the cost (measured by the severity of the punishment for lying weighted by the probability of detection), then you would expect people to lie, or at least to be less than frank.

But there are plenty of cases in the public and private sectors where there is no real logic to bullshit at all, and it is not even in the bullshitter's own interests to peddle it. Why did Transport for London feel a need to hide the reduction in Circle line services when they publicised the increase in services to Hammersmith? Why do so many annual reports not give a sensible and honest assessment of the strategic challenges facing the company? Why do governments pass legislation enshrining their own targets, knowing that they can de-legislate later if they miss them? Why are chief executives who come on to the radio so often incapable of admitting to weaknesses in their company's performance? Why do politicians persist in arguing that their private polls show the results are going to be much better than the published polls suggest? Why is there so much knee-jerk defensiveness in corporate and government responses to criticism? These are all examples of the routine verbiage that litters the airwaves; it's the communications equivalent of filler in packaging – a small amount of content lies therein, but you have to get through a lot of Styrofoam to find it.

There are plenty of good reasons to exaggerate, embellish or decorate your beliefs, or to be economical with the truth, or to spin: that is what Section Two of the book was about. You may do these things to emphasise a point, to make it colourful, or to be theatrical and grab attention; or to keep up with the prevailing standards of bullshit elsewhere in a competitive situation; or because your life, or that of your company, is in mortal danger and you need to get out of a hole right now and worry about the future later on. Or maybe there is some other reason, such as to spare someone's feelings. But in so many of the cases we observe, I'm unable to think of any good reason, from this list or any other, for being less than straightforward. In so many cases, I honestly think that the bullshit is at best useless and at worst damaging, and it is thus odd that it is so pervasive.

I suspect this banal verbiage stems from two main cognitive problems, each of which needs resisting. The first is habit – that once we have an established course of behaviour, it is much easier to follow it than to think afresh about what to do each time. Habits are one of our mental short cuts and are fabulously useful. Recycling is a real nuisance the first few times you have to sort through the different plastics for the different bins; once it is a habit, it is easy. In fact, once it is a habit, it is positively hard to break it. Habits allow System One intuition to govern our behaviour, without having to muster the tiresome effort involved in System Two reflection. And when it comes to many routine examples of bullshit, habit is the key. No one has really thought through any good strategic or tactical reason to be fatuous; they haven't asked themselves why they need to depart from complete honesty; they haven't gone through a checklist of the kinds of reasons outlined in Chapters 5 to 8. No, it's basically just the way things are.[17]

This is important, because if communicators did think it through they'd realise it wasn't achieving anything, mainly on account of the fact that few people are going to believe them anyway (and if anyone does, they'll soon discover they were wrong to do so). They would also realise that, despite achieving almost nothing by being insincere, there is a cost in forgoing the benefits of establishing credibility, which comes as a reward only to those who are honest over the long term.

But there is a second cause of routine bullshit, which is self-delusion. The messengers come to believe the message they are paid to propagate. Almost all the press officers, PR officers and spokespeople that I've talked to over the years have given the impression of being sincere in what they say. On occasion, they'll give a wink or have a lilt in their voice that suggests they are just reading a script that they know is rubbish. But more often, when they say things that are silly it simply seems as though they have lost the ability to distinguish between what they think is true, what they want to be true and what they want me to believe is true. These all fuse into one and the same.

It is tempting to think they come to believe in their own spurious lines because of a cognitive dissonance: that there is a pain in their brain caused by the gap between the nonsense they say and their perception of reality, and the gap resolves itself by a change in their perception of reality. If you say something enough, you'll come to believe it. But it seems that good communicators have a more basic instinct to self-delude. They start believing their message before they've even started repeating the lines that they are saying. Ian Leslie's book *Born Liars* offers the best summary of this topic: the most effective people, he suggests, are blessed with malleable beliefs because that allows them to make sense of the world; it motivates them to get things done and it allows them to lie without looking insincere. Leslie reports one academic as pointing out that what some psychologists call self-deception is what sports coaches call championship thinking. Leslie also quotes Benjamin Franklin: 'So convenient a thing it is to be a reasonable creature, since it enables one to find or make a reason for everything one has a mind to do.'[18] This captures it perfectly. A good PR knows they are a member of a team, they want to do their best for the team, and if it is useful for the team that something be true, then for all intents and purposes they'll do their best to make sure it is true. And thanks to confirmation bias – that we tend to only register the evidence that supports our pre-existing view – once the line is in their brain it will take a lot to dislodge it.

Although I see the advantages of self-delusion, I confess to not being a fan of it. I accept that for an individual it can be psychologically useful to operate under various illusions. But for governments, big companies and society at large there are risks from people making decisions on the basis of what they want to be true, rather than on what is actually the case. And the worst of it is that you can end up in the ghastly position where the only people persuaded by nonsense are those who are spinning it. The former head of the Financial Reporting Council, Paul Boyle, put it rather well when talking of creative accountancy back in 2008:

> The real problem with creative accounting is not so much that it misleads the market – there are many examples of companies which used creative accounting where the market was able to 'look through' the published numbers and reflect that in the share price before the creative accounting was formally exposed – the real problem is that it misleads management. It allows management to persuade themselves of the brilliance of their business strategy when in reality it is not successful and it delays the day when the strategic problems which the company faces have to be addressed.[19]

In other words, the analysts whose job it is to study the company's performance are not fooled, but the propagators of the nonsense – and who actually run the company – are.

It is quite unrealistic to think that we can exhort people to avoid self-deluding, any more than we can expect good public relations staff not to act as team players, promoting the best case they can for their organisation. But if we can persuade professional communicators to start out with a mindset that aims to be straightforward and honest with other people, they will probably become more honest with themselves as well.

The underlying point here – and it will come up in the next chapter too – is that honesty is often just a form of open-mindedness. It is a rejection of reflex defensiveness and a willingness to embrace the complexities of argument rather than to see things as black and white. It's as good for you to be honest as it is for those to whom you speak. There is no need to be absolutist about this – it is simply a matter for those working in communications to start from the view that straightforward honesty should be the approach to adopt on any particular occasion, unless there is a clear reason why it should not be.

This is no different from simply urging them to think long-term. Or, to be like Warren Buffett and to realise that, unless your life depends on it, simply getting through the next couple of days is not really that helpful. Although this may appear naive to many in the communications business, it is important to keep reiterating that it actually involves giving up quite little, because in a world where trust is low and bullshit is prevalent you are not going to be believed if you're peddling a line that suits your self-interest anyway. It's a risk worth taking.

Sell yourself, not your argument

The next practical implication of 2016 and the stale culture of phoneyism that preceded it is that those involved in communication should put less emphasis on a specific message and far more on coming across as a person or organisation worth listening to. Successful communication is less about winning a point than winning respect as someone who can be trusted to make the right call on that point. It is *who you are* that matters, more than *what you say.* If you are the right person, what you say will be accepted; if you are the wrong person, nothing you say will be accepted. This, incidentally, is why Donald Trump's novel approach to the 2016 election campaign did him so little harm. For many, it was all a sign that he was on their side, and so it strengthened his appeal rather than diminished it.

Sometimes you'll see politicians behaving like politicians do – jabbing their finger in a televised debate, speaking over their rival, desperately trying to prevail on some issue that matters little to the average voter, or speaking in a weirdly contorted and defensive way – and you can gaze upon their performance and ask, do they really think this is attractive? That it makes them look like the sort of person voters want to have around for the next five years? Their language and behaviour stems from a desire to get their key lines across, to push their point. But it fails to recognise that there is always an indirect message carried by their words and tone, which can come across as negative. Rather than making their point well, they are in fact sending an unattractive signal about the kind of person they are.

This argument that who you are matters more than the substantive point you are making is especially true of politicians. Voters focus on character rather than policy partly because they are better able to judge character and are relatively uninformed about policy, but also because they quite rationally understand that most of what their elected representatives have to do in office is react to things that haven't yet come up. Having the right person there is more important than having one with an impressive manifesto. So, for a politician, having a good reputation is worth a hundred quick victories in specific arguments.

This is not an original point. There is an old adage, often attributed to Theodore Roosevelt (probably incorrectly), that 'No one cares how much you know, until they know that you care'.[20] There is a variant, which belongs to the American political scientist Mark Schmitt: 'It's not what you say about the issues, it's what the issues say about you.' In both cases, the claim is essentially that what matters most is what you are demonstrating about yourself, your values and your selection of friends rather than the actual point at hand. Mark Schmitt explains it thus:

> ... as a candidate, you must choose to emphasize issues not because they poll well or are objectively our biggest problems, but because they best show the kind of person you are, and not just how you would deal with that particular issue, but others yet to rear their heads.[21]

Ezra Klein has picked up Schmitt's point on using issues to say things about character to suggest this is what Donald Trump did in 2016. He did not offer very well-developed policy plans, and they morphed from one thing to another during the campaign. But what they did do was consistently signal which battles Trump was interested in fighting, and whose side he was on.[22] This was particularly important given that Western society was in one of its occasional convulsions, with voters having the worst possible combination of fear (that their interests would be overlooked), anger (that other people were ahead of them in the queue) and uncertainty (as to who stood for what). At those junctures, being the right kind of person is everything. Winning a policy debate is not.

If this is all true in politics, it is also true of brands and businesses. For better or worse, corporations can have character; the tone and content of their PR can contribute to the perception of that. There are no absolutes here, but if the PR comes across as self-interested or selfish, it can be to the detriment of the corporation's overall image. Trust in the name is worth more than a single point well argued. This point has been firmly made by Robert Phillips, who was chief executive for Europe, the Middle East and Africa at Edelman, one of the world's great PR agencies. He quit and wrote a book whose name says it all: *Trust Me, PR is Dead.*[23] In it he said:

> There are no silver bullets. PR is not prepared, or even fit for purpose, in this age of activism, nor does it properly understand the restoration of trust ... PR is still too busy talking, not doing, and frequently advising its clients to do likewise. Talk is cheap and control is over. Message massaging and media management, once the mainstay of corporate PR folk, are no longer possible; reputation and issues management are easily broken open.

A good example was raised in a review of the book by the *Financial Times* writer Henry Mance.[24] He cited the case of the travel company Thomas Cook, and its handling of a tragic case in which two small children died of carbon monoxide poisoning on one of its holidays.[25] The company took the view that the deaths were not its responsibility, but that of the owner of the hotel where the children were staying. Thomas Cook refrained from apologising, lest it should be seen as an admission of guilt. One can see what the company was thinking – after all, it cannot check every boiler in every property in every country it sells holidays in – but it rather missed the point. By acting defensively, the company looked as if it was trying to wash its hands of the tragedy. To make matters worse, it received more compensation from the hotel owner for the costs that had been incurred as a result of the disaster than was given to the parents of the deceased children. The episode cost Thomas Cook dear. It should have taken the view that its overall reputation mattered far more than scoring a particular point, and it would have behaved very differently. Knowing when to let others win the point is an important social skill.

A similar argument, that it is people's perception of overall character that matters, applies to consumer-facing brands. Customers develop an allegiance to a particular brand not only because it is functionally competent and its values align with their own, but also because it appears to be aimed at people like them. The brand becomes more important to the buyer than any individual product within it. Sixty-somethings know not to buy their clothes at Topshop because they can tell that it is designed for teens and twenty-somethings; but they may well choose to shop at Marks & Spencer. Once customers have an attachment to a brand, its label serves as a short cut to decision-making: they can select from its offering rather than having to shop around. They know the brand works for them. Thus, for a company interested in long-term value, preserving the integrity of the brand is more important than making a fast buck. (That, incidentally, explains the point I've already made as to why the communication in advertising is often about sending subtle signals as to who the brand is for rather than the quality of the product.)

It goes without saying that whether it is a politician, a company or a brand, there are lots of aspects to having the right character, but whichever attribute is important, authenticity is a prerequisite for anything that's put on show. Most of us have a built-in phoneyism detector and we tend not to believe the things that insincere people say. We can distinguish words, brands, products that are authentic from those that are not. We inevitably come to a view as to who is sincere and who is artificial, and we usually get it right. So when it comes to putting on a best face, that face has to come across as genuine. And in most cases, the easiest way to come across as genuine is to be genuine.[26]

The weakness of the hard sell

Following on from the idea that character is as important as any specific message is the lesson that the people who come across well are usually the ones that don't try too hard to sell their message. As someone who talks to politicians and business-people off air as well as on, I'm often struck by how much more impressive they are when thinking aloud in private than when they assert their certainties in public. That is a truly remarkable state of affairs: people trying their very hardest to come over well somehow manage to come across badly when it actually matters. Then, as soon as they drop the 'must sell now' mentality and talk to fellow human beings with all the vulnerability and uncertainty that most of us have, they begin to sound convincing and trustworthy.[27]

It is a paradox of persuasion that the harder you sell, the less convincing you can end up being, but we are all familiar with it. Think of retired politicians, who no longer have their youthful desperation to win you over and who instead can afford to sound statesmanlike and objective. They are often more impressive than they ever were in office.

Why is the hard sell counterproductive? It's back to the point that when you communicate a message you are delivering information directly, in the content of what you say, and also indirectly, through your tone and choice of words. The hard sell may offer a strong direct message, but it does so while also indirectly alerting listeners to the fact that a hard sell is under way. The audience can tell that you are actively selling them something, and that you are not a friendly advisor. That immediately weakens the imperative to listen to what you are saying.

Imagine listening to a debate on the radio about the building of a new generation of nuclear power stations. What would be the most persuasive way of making the case for nuclear? The typical proponent would set out their arguments as forcefully as possible and dismiss with exaggerated certainty any counter-arguments. This means that you, as a neutral listener, will be in no doubt of the arguments in favour of nuclear power and will be clear as to the strength of belief of the proponent. But you will probably register the proponent as a keen advocate on that side of the argument, and that may cause you to discount what they are saying: after all, if they are a strong advocate, then they would say all the pro-nuclear stuff anyway. The unstated message they are sending by arguing too strongly is 'Do not trust me to come to an open-minded view on this complicated topic.'

So now imagine listening to someone adopting the softer sell. In this case, they conduct themselves more as an interpreter of the evidence on your behalf. It takes a completely different mindset, because they have to set out the arguments *against* new nuclear as clearly as any of their opponents might. They talk about the expense and the unresolved issues around decommissioning and nuclear waste; they may express these arguments perhaps even better than the opponent, but then they put their view that, on balance, other factors militate in favour of going ahead. They explain why. Now, they have shown that they understand the concerns of opponents; they have demonstrated genuine expertise and come out of the session as a trusted advisor. My suspicion is that, seven times out of ten, this is a more persuasive tactic.

The point is that the radio debate on nuclear power is not just won or lost on the basis of competing points along the lines of 'it's safe' – 'no it isn't'; 'it's expensive' – 'no it isn't'; and so on. It is also an audition in which listeners come to a judgement about the people on either side of the argument. Often, the protagonist making the case more softly will be the winner of that audition by virtue of coming across as less sure, but more trustworthy.

It is possible to go further and adopt the tactic of being publicly and surprisingly open-minded. It is remarkable how few politicians do, and how elevating it is when they try. Imagine that a disappointing economic statistic is released and the finance minister has to give a reaction. Which would you respect more, the one that defensively downplays the news and offers excuses as to why it means nothing and why the economy is really doing well? Or a reaction that acknowledges the disappointment and gives an honest account of what it means? Or think about the converse – a cheery economic statistic comes out. A finance minister who downplays it and who argues that it doesn't tell you much will earn credit in the bank when bad news emerges (as it eventually will). If you can bear to be so reasonable that you are willing to talk against your own self-interest, you gain credibility when you have to defend your own side in an argument.

You might argue that it is phoney for those who are fixed and passionate in their opinions to tone them down and pretend they are somehow objective. And I'd be the last to argue that faking open-mindedness will work. If you pretend to be open-minded when you are not, you are likely to be detected. But much of the time, the certainty is itself fake; it is often an acquired adherence to a point of view. Most people in public life are capable of realism, self-deprecation and respect for opponents, and those that are not would benefit from being so.

The challenge for politicians

Of all the people who have to sell a message, it is politicians who have the most challenging job. I have no illusions about the frustration that they might feel when outsiders suggest that they try to be more natural, eschew some of the overly sophisticated communications techniques taught to them by professional advisors, and connect in a more directly human way with their potential voters. Not only do they face all the problems outlined in the earlier chapters, but they already know that sincerity is desirable; their problem is that they have to impress lots of voters of many different kinds and their particular brand of sincerity may not be popular enough to do that. It's not surprising that they then have to try hard to appeal to those beyond their home crowd. What do you do if your personality or politics is not to the taste of enough voters to win? What if you like opera, and the voters prefer football? Don't you have to pretend that you are one of them? Politics, after all, is a profession of compromise, and those who fail to build a coalition with other near-minded folks will get nowhere. And building a coalition involves settling on a stance that may deviate from the one that each agreeing party would opt for individually. Insincerity is inevitable.

I can see the dilemma. On the one hand, you have the option of being a so-called professional politician, perhaps like Hillary Clinton. You might back a set of policies that you think are effective and which roughly conform to your values, and to fit in with the public mood you say a number of things that wouldn't come naturally to you. But as you are capable of self-persuasion you quickly tell yourself that those things are right, and you are soon arguing them with a reasonable degree of sincerity. And what do you get for that competence? You are told you come across as boring, a bit stilted, and possibly disconnected from real people. You are said to be a slave to opinion polls and focus groups, and have no conviction.

Then you have the other option, of bowing to no one and sticking rigidly to your personal views, but you might find yourself accused of failing to listen to the people or being uninterested in winning votes. In his career as leader of the Labour Party and as a backbench MP, Jeremy Corbyn has been criticised for many things, but insincerity has not usually been among them. Indeed, he has been so faithful to his personal views that on one occasion he ended up speaking in parliament against the policy on nuclear weapons of the party of which he was leader.[28] He's always had to resist pressure from colleagues who hold him to be unelectable and unprofessional, and who want him to yield to mainstream media and public taste.

Politicians must think they are damned if they are sincere, and damned if they are phoney. But there are two things to say about this dilemma. First, politics is a business in which sincerity is increasingly a *necessary* condition for success, but it is not a *sufficient* one. If your sincerely expressed views and personality are not what the people want, you can't expect to do very well. You are what you are, and if you are not popular I fear neither sincerity nor insincerity is likely to be a route to success. Take Mr Corbyn; there could be many reasons that he and his party were performing badly after his selection as leader. He is an untypical politician and his party was disunited. It's not clear that if he had spent his career paying lip service to views he disagrees with, he would have been more successful. As for Hillary Clinton, she would perhaps have performed better if she had allowed herself to come across as more human. Her professionalism counted against her. Jon Stewart, the former host of the *Daily Show*, said of her during the 2016 campaign, 'What I think about Hillary Clinton is, I imagine her to be a very bright woman without the courage of her convictions, because I'm not even sure what they are.' He suggested she would be in trouble if she didn't find her real self, but admitted, 'maybe a real person doesn't exist underneath there, I don't know'.[29]

The second point about the politicians' dilemma is that when you face it the correct – and sincere – thing to do is to articulate it. If you have to make a compromise, is it really that hard to say that's what you are doing? We all understand the need for tact, diplomacy, give and take, so where you have to be careful with your words or have to sign up to things that are not quite what you would yourself choose, just say that and explain why you think the compromise you are making is the right one.

It's perfectly possible to do this without creating a scene: take this comment by John Kerry, who in early 2017 was about to finish his term as US Secretary of State. He was asked by the BBC's Katty Kay for his reaction to some apparent criticism of him by Theresa May. It's one of those classic cases where you might have expected diplomatic obfuscation and denial, but Mr Kerry was obviously keen neither to bullshit nor to agitate an awkward situation, so he just said exactly the right thing:

Katty Kay: Were you surprised by Prime Minister May's reaction?
John Kerry: Well again, you know, an honest answer is yes, but I'm not going to get into going back and forth about it, we move on.[30]

In a one-sentence answer, he said both that he felt surprised and that he didn't want to make a meal of it. It was a perfectly straightforward, direct and sensible way of answering a question, and quite comprehensible to anyone that heard it. He spoke straight, and no damage was done. The overall message of this chapter to those in politics and public relations is to emulate that style more often.

Pushing rather than pulling

There are many areas of life where it is easy to get things wrong. Not just a bit wrong, but the complete opposite of right. If you have a flawed model of how things work, you push when you should pull, tighten when you should loosen. It's all too easy to think that you can discipline a dog by hitting it; whereas the evidence is that this can provoke an aggressive response, and you are better off using rewards to encourage good behaviour. It's all too easy to think happiness is about enriching oneself; but the evidence is that happiness is more likely to come from enriching someone else.[31] It's all too easy to think you steer a motorbike to the right by pushing on the left handlebar as you would on a pushbike; whereas in fact you push on the *right* handlebar to lean the bike into the direction you want to go. It's all too easy to think that governments should save money in a recession to balance the budget, even though, as John Maynard Keynes pointed out, at times the government will help itself and everyone else by spending more and stimulating the economy. It's all too easy to think that if you open a fridge door the room will become colder; whereas in fact the fridge will heat the room more than it cools it.[32] In all these cases, the mistake comes from a lack of understanding of the basic mechanism at play, and the resulting error points you 180 degrees away from the direction you should take.

It seems that professional persuaders have perhaps got the wrong model themselves. They push their point harder when it would be more persuasive if it was put more gently. They think that the way to gain authority is to make opponents look small, whereas they'd look more commanding if they acknowledged their rivals' strengths. They try to look certain when open-mindedness would be more impressive. They disguise their feelings when the public crave honesty and authenticity. They try to look confident by sticking firmly and defensively to their line, whereas genuinely confident people tend to be more open to criticism. These are points that, in hindsight, might have been useful for the Remain side in the UK's EU referendum. The public were craving honest guidance as to the issues at stake, but felt that they got it from none of the protagonists. It is just possible that if the leaders of the Remain side had conducted the campaign by making the case *less* forcefully rather than more, they would have been more convincing to undecided voters.

I again concede there are no absolutes here: it's not my intention to propose a new set of decrees, to replace the old set by which communication was conducted. Communication is a complex business and as soon as a rule is made its meaning begins to evolve and its purpose changes. But if 2016 proved anything, it was that rewards go to those who have a fresh way of thinking and communicating; not just a little different, but very different from what has gone before. For me it's obvious that there are ways to improve on the old bullshit; it'll be interesting to see how significant the disruption to it is. We've already seen some change: in her first year, Theresa May demonstrated a marked contrast in communications terms to her recent predecessors as UK prime minister. She appeared keen to keep the government out of the limelight with fewer public pronouncements than we have been used to and she presented herself as a politician who is straightforward and reluctant to play political games. While she has been criticised for failing to live up to that ideal, she has enjoyed good poll ratings. But who knows if her approach will be robust in the face of more severe stresses.

So much for the politicians. If they, or any other category of communicator, want to raise their game and present themselves in a more natural way, the rest of us can make it easy or difficult for them to do so. Communication is a two-way business, after all. We have a part to play in this, so as we turn to the final chapter we must examine ourselves.

The Discerning Listener

The clinician

Rob George has thought far more about honesty than most of us. As a Consultant Physician in Palliative Care at St Christopher's Hospice and Guy's and St Thomas' Foundation Trust, he has one of the hardest jobs in the communication business: confronting patients with bad news. Rob is also a Professor of Palliative Care at King's College London and a one-time senior lecturer in Ethics at UCL, and he writes about the dilemmas that arise in his field and about how honest to be. Rob is not a bullshitter by character, nor by profession. His line is that 'when we're dealing with hard facts like cancer or heart disease or something like that, when there's something that's verifiable and objectively true, then we have to tell the truth when asked'.

But his work is far more complicated than that because often it is not hard facts that patients are seeking; it's a medical assessment as to how much longer they have to live. Here, Rob has to use his judgement in deciding how frank to be. Some years ago I had the chance to interview him as part of a series for Radio 4.[1] I asked him if he sometimes felt he had

to obfuscate. 'Yes, we have to,' he told me. 'We have to maintain a relationship in order to take somebody down a road of
discovery, which may be the discovery of an unpleasant truth.
My duty of care is to act in your best interests ... That doesn't
mean that I'm going to tell you an out-and-out lie. But maybe
if somebody says, "Oh, my God, I've got cancer. Am I going to
die from this?" then the answer is "I don't know." Now, actually
in the back of my mind, I might think, 99.9 per cent certain,
but now is not the time to go there. So in this situation, I am
likely to say, "That's not the conversation we need to have right
now. The conversation we need to have right now is what are
we going to do to manage this?"'

So on what basis does Rob decide how blunt to be with a
particular patient? His answer is that it all comes back to the
patients themselves: 'I'm going to respond to you in the way
that you place a question to me. Now, that sounds like I might
be planning to deceive you or something, but it means that I'm
matching how I respond to you according to what you're signalling to me as to how much of the truth you want now, how you
might want it delivered and how you're going to respond to that
when I give it to you.'

What Rob is doing is reading the patient and formulating
a communications strategy accordingly. He will tell them the
unvarnished truth if they clearly want it ('If somebody does
want disclosure and they demand disclosure then I think you
have to give it, even if you think it's against their best interest');
he will tell them nothing if they insist on that ('Autonomy means
you're free to say no to the truth as much as you're free to say "I
want the truth".') Very occasionally, he will actually tell people
the bad news even if they don't want it, if he thinks, for example, that they need to get their affairs in order. ('If somebody is
busy denying away and saying "This is not happening. I'm going

to beat this," then there may come a time where you say, "Do you know what? I think we really do need to sit down and talk about this." That's the difficult conversation.') Rob has a range of options and tailors them to patients based on the responses and needs he observes.

I don't envy Rob his job or the decisions he has to take about how – or how fast – to break bad news. It's a serious business, and I deliberately refrain from using the word bullshit in relation to the delicate choices of words Rob has to make. But I mention that interview because it alerted me to two very important truths about the bullshit we are all fed in other areas of our lives. First, that we the recipients have some part in shaping what is directed our way. The more we lap it up, the more it flows; the less attention we pay to facts, the more non-facts will be deployed. Even Donald Trump – the man with little self-doubt, who carved out his own, unique kind of election campaign and who specialised in eschewing expert advice – gave the crowds what he thought they wanted as he looked at the enthusiastic expressions on the faces gazing up at him. The second observation is that our hopes and desires play a big part in shaping our beliefs. Some of Rob's patients don't want to hear what he has to say because they want to hang on to their hope that things will turn out all right.

I hesitate to say we get the bullshit we deserve, but there is a little truth in that, so in this last chapter I'll focus on us, the listeners. What can we do to deserve better, and how should we protect ourselves against the worst mendacity and nonsense?

There are two kinds of answers to these questions. There are the ones that apply to us individually in the form of measures we can each take not to be fooled or manipulated – the equivalent of putting an alarm on our house to prevent a burglary. The second kind relates to our collective response, the measures that society or its institutions can take to improve public discourse. This is the equivalent of a country finding ways to reduce crime. We'll take a look at both, starting with the individual.

Hope and open-mindedness

When Rob George has to break bad news, his challenge is to handle the hopes of his patients that things will turn out well. Our desires play a big part in shaping our response to news, so just as cancer patients have to handle their hopes and fears in order to come to a realistic view of their prognosis, we all have to manage our own as a way of protecting ourselves against nonsense and mendacity. The simple advice is: where you have a craving for something to be true, apply a double dose of scepticism to anybody telling you that it is. In many ways, hope-mongers are more likely to manipulate opinions and beliefs than fear-mongers.

Let's take a case in point: the market for male baldness cures. A lot of men are desperate to thwart their loss of hair. It is an area where self-consciousness can override rationality. You can look on web forums and find men who really believe their life is ruined by hair loss. As one man put it in a post entitled 'Want to shoot myself in the head':

> I just feel helpless against this thing we all fight. To any other male who says 'oh, it's no big deal' I say how about we cut off your testicles and see if you feel the same way. To any woman who says, 'it's no big deal', why don't we cut off a breast and see if you feel the same way … I'm feeling in the dumps. I'll get over it (that's what we do), but man … right now I'm really hating life.[2]

As it happens, I am one of those other males who would say to him, 'It's no big deal,' and would add that comparing baldness to castration shows an unreasonable loss of perspective. But I'm also genuinely sympathetic because he can't help his feelings, however irrational they may seem to me or other happy bald men. This is not the place to talk about why we can have such an extreme sense of insecurity based on our looks, but we know that people do, and that with that desperation comes a yearning for something that might make a difference. It is that which leaves them vulnerable to exploitation.

Now let's be clear: hair loss can be reversed. There are two main approaches, the surgical and the pharmaceutical. Surgery relies on taking follicles from a hairy part of the head, and transplanting them (either in a strip or individually). It can carry some risk of scarring. Not all the transplanted follicles will necessarily work as desired. An acceptable success rate is said to be 85 to 95 per cent. The balding man quoted above explains in the discussion forum that he has been through surgery; he spent fifteen thousand dollars on 1800 individual grafts, which probably works out as about $3.75 per hair (as there is more than one hair per graft).[3] He was depressed because he thought that fewer than half the hairs had taken. That can be a problem with surgery, but another is that even if it works, it won't stop your other hairs falling out if that's what they are disposed to do.

There is also evidence that drugs to counter hair loss do work, but again not for all patients. And these tend to work only for as long as you take them. Minoxidil has been found to be 'very effective' or 'effective' in 64 per cent of patients after taking it for a year.[4] Of patients taking Finasteride for five years, one trial found almost two-thirds saw a maintained or improved hair-count; that was true of none of the men on a placebo.[5]

Personally, I would never go on permanent medication to counter hair loss, nor take the expensive risk that surgery may not work; I'd rather have therapy to deal with my self-consciousness issues as I'm sure it would be more likely to offer a lasting solution to any embarrassment I feel. But more desperate people may well choose treatment; the problem is that, being desperate, it's hard for them to make sensible treatment choices. The sheer strength of the desire for there to be a cure makes them seek out marketing material that fosters an optimistic view of the outcomes. The Belgravia Centre, a big treatment centre in London for those with hair loss, is upfront about the possibility that treatment may not work.[6] But its marketing uses myriad pictures of success stories. There is honest disclosure in that they are presented as 'Success Stories'; no one can be in any doubt as to what they show. But it takes a calm head to focus on the fact there is no equivalent page of failure pictures. A reflective buyer might also want to see evidence of long-term outcomes. Few of the success stories posted on the Belgravia website go beyond twelve months from initial consultation. The clinic told me it has many long-term clients but said it had not got round to posting long-term success stories.[7]

In addition to the recognised pharmaceutical or surgical treatments for hair loss at places like the Belgravia Centre, there are plenty of other therapies available, such as caffeine-infused shampoo or laser combs. In each case, it is possible to find research that purports to demonstrate the efficacy of the treatment, but it is hard for ordinary customers to appraise the quality of any clinical trial or scientific-sounding claim, such as this randomly selected statement:

Adenosine triphosphate is a molecule that carries energy from one cell to another. One typical example of its function can be found in photosynthesis of plants. The laser comb has a similar function to the cells found in your scalp. It carries energy to these cells that thickens existing hair and promotes hair growth.[8]

Some hair-loss therapists and many users of the laser comb say it has no effect at all, but to anyone wanting to believe in it, the science in the marketing offers a mental straw that can be clutched.

Treatment for baldness is just one case of a market in which people may find themselves giving credence to assertions that they would normally appraise more critically. The man desperate to counter the thinning of his hair might laugh at someone silly enough to buy a penis-enlargement kit over the internet, but his desire to believe that he can sustainably reverse his hair loss, allied with tantalising evidence offered in support of a particular therapy, makes him too credulous.

And that generalises to us all. We are subject to wishful thinking and confirmation bias. We are far more likely to give a favourable hearing to a slanderous assertion about a politician we hate than one we love. And we can be madly unrealistic about the fresh-faced politician who comes along promising to clean things up and change things. That's just our reflex. It takes awareness, and a full-on conscious System Two effort, to counter our instinct to believe. When someone offers an unverified proposition that is wonderfully self-gratifying, in business or in politics or at work, we just have to remember the example of desperate balding men overriding their normal good sense to grasp at an unrealistic hope. We need to tell ourselves not to let optimism turn into gullibility.

But our desire to believe things does not usually come from anxiety and self-consciousness. To a large extent, we subscribe to beliefs that fit our outlook on the world and our place in it.

I've already said that, in social media, our disposition to believe things is sometimes a form of bonding. Not only do we tend to reside in echo chambers online,[9] but we actively enjoy becoming closer to our friends by sharing views and agreeing with them. The act of consenting to someone else's beliefs, and have them consent to ours, is satisfying; and because it is so, it stops us questioning the nonsense that others post. It is fair to say that much of the bullshit fired our way comes from friendly sources; that is precisely what makes it so seductive.

There is also the problem of the *narrative*: a prevailing interpretation of a pattern of events. We all have these lurking around in the back – and sometimes the front – of our heads. They allow us to make sense of the world by imposing a structure on disparate events. Like-minded groups of individuals share a narrative about many things, as indeed does much of the media: that the French economy is sclerotic, that America's lack of gun control is mad, that a prime minister is inept, that Russia is evil, and so on. These narratives are sometimes true, sometimes not, but they are often like stereotypes: they have a germ of insight in them, yet are too simplistic. Once embedded in our minds, though, they can easily gain excessive traction and trample over truth as willing believers put too much weight on propositions that conform to their narrative without looking for evidence in support of them.[10]

To defend ourselves against this impulse, we need to be particularly sceptical of claims that make us feel good or satisfy our pre-existing beliefs. There is an inverse requirement too: we need to be willing to believe things that don't conform to our worldview. In the last chapter I made the claim that honesty is linked to open-mindedness, suggesting that the latter is a protection against self-delusion. But it also gives us some immunity to excessive credulity. Embrace the fact that most arguments have two sides, and that your outraged or joyful reaction to some piece of news may simply be predicated on your unwillingness to get the full picture.

It really is incredibly easy to fall for a story that fits your pre-existing prejudice; you want it to be true because it reassures you that your worldview is sound, and because your worldview is sound you don't question the story that conforms to it. I remember succumbing to a one-sided presentation of a story, the notorious case of Stella Liebeck, the woman who sued McDonald's for burning herself with hot coffee. Her burns were caused by a cup of coffee she had been holding between her legs in a car, and she reportedly won $2.9 million. The story ran round the world, as it appeared to confirm a widespread narrative that American courts were awarding absurdly high damages.[11] I swallowed it whole and can remember quoting it in disbelief (I'm not sure why we use that phrase, as I was in fact quoting it in credulous belief). It looked, at a glance, simply ridiculous: the spillage was surely her fault; she must have been cashing in; and didn't it prove that greedy lawyers have far too much power? But the case, of course, turns out to be far more complicated than I or most other casual onlookers appreciated from the second-hand coverage that was howling around the press. It was only recently that someone alerted me to the full story. Ms Liebeck – a non-litigious seventy-nine-year-old retired department store clerk – had very serious injuries when she spilt the coffee onto her lap by simply removing the lid from the cup. She was burned over 16 per cent of her body; some of that was third-degree burns, and she was in hospital for over a week. Contrary to much of the coverage, she had not been driving; she was a passenger in a parked car at the time of the spill. She had initially tried to settle the case out of court and asked McDonald's to cover her medical bills and her family's out-of-pocket expenses (reportedly between ten and twenty thousand dollars), but was only offered eight hundred dollars. The coffee had been served at over 80 degrees Celsius, far hotter than that which comes from home coffee machines. It turned out that hundreds of people had reported burns from spilt McDonald's coffee. Members of the jury – who heard seven days of testimony and were unanimous in their decision – had not taken leave of their senses at all; they made an award of two hundred thousand dollars for damages, but this was reduced to $160,000 because Ms Liebeck had spilt the coffee herself. In addition, the jury decided to set punitive damages against McDonald's of two days' coffee revenue, believing the company was wrong to serve coffee at a scalding temperature. That took the total to $2.9 million, but it was just a recommendation. The punitive award was subsequently scaled back and in the end McDonald's paid out something closer to six hundred and fifty thousand dollars.[12]

Before pontificating about the case at dinner parties, I would have done well to have acquainted myself with the details. Had I even thought about it at all, I would have asked very basic questions. What was going on to induce a jury of twelve people to make what I thought was such a stupid award? Didn't they know more about the case than I did? Why had I not bothered to find out what the opposite view to mine was before making a judgement? Too often we'll lap these things up, taking them on trust from a distant second-hand source.

This accords with the view of Stephen Greenspan, whose 2008 book, *Annals of Gullibility: Why We Get Duped and How to Avoid It*, offers some tips. One of his sections is entitled 'Cultivate skepticism but not cynicism'. It is a difficult balance to strike, but he is right to point out the twin dangers: if you are insuffi-ciently sceptical you are open to false belief, but if you are overly cynical you can end up believing the claims of charlatans rather than reliable sources. Greenspan talks about a character called Harold, who is so disbelieving of those in authority he sees conspiracies everywhere and is inclined to believe those instead. Harold's cynicism, Greenspan says, contributes to his gullibility, for example in that he champions alternative medicine as a way of saying 'screw you' to the medical establishment.[13]

Of course, we don't want to be open-minded to con artists; all we can do is look for reliable and unprejudiced sources of information, apply high standards of evidence to the claims that we hear, lean against our desires and hopes when it comes to assessing that evidence, and not attach too much weight to assertions that don't pass these tests.

Tough on the causes of credulity

It's pretty clear that hard-headed individuals can protect themselves from the stupidest fake nonsense if they want to, but what happens when they don't want to? What can a society at large do to create herd immunity to bullshit, and to nudge citizens in favour of processing the claims thrown their way intelligently? If people choose to accept fake news, believe outlandish claims and fall for swindlers, what can be done?

Obviously, societies can go some way to protecting people from lies. We try to outlaw scams and we have bodies like the Advertising Standards Authority to respond to complaints about inaccuracies in adverts. But there are always limits to how quickly any information regulator can keep up with falsehoods, and most of us don't want agents of the state to have too much power to proscribe free speech.

So if your goal is to prevent public misapprehension, rather than just hoping to regulate away any lies, you have to encourage personal responsibility in fending them off. In other words, you need to be as tough on the causes of credulity as you are on the spreaders of falsehoods. We know why people try to get away with lying; the question to ask is why people are disposed to believe the nonsense.

The issue came to the fore in 2016, when it was observed that what was unusual was not that more lies were told (on the basis that lies have always been told), it was that some voters demonstrated an inclination to accept them.[14] That was partly why 'post-truth' was declared word of the year by the Oxford Dictionaries.[15] As the announcement said:

> Rather than simply referring to the time after a specified situation or event – as in *post-war* or *post-match* – the prefix in *post-truth* has a meaning more like 'belonging to a time in which the specified concept has become unimportant or irrelevant'. This nuance seems to have originated in the mid-20th century, in formations such as *post-national* (1945) and *post-racial* (1971).

In the UK, the worry that truth had become 'unimportant or irrelevant' emerged during the EU referendum campaign, and in relation to the most notorious claim that was made during it, that Britain sent £350 million a week in membership fees to the EU. As I said in Chapter 1, this was a misleading claim because it represented a calculation of the country's notional contribution to the EU, but not the amount Britain ever actually had to pay. Britain had negotiated a discount, and the true figure paid was in fact £285 million a week.[16] (Even this could be said to be an exaggeration, because the EU also sends a lot of money back to the UK for agricultural and regional support, and so the net figure was £190 million a week.) The head of the

Leave campaign, Dominic Cummings, subsequently said the phrase 'we send the EU £350m' was used 'to provoke people into argument', which it certainly did.[17] And it is fair to say that its prominence in the campaign was noticed. A week before the vote an Ipsos MORI poll found that more than three-quarters of the public had heard the claim.[18] Almost half – 47 per cent of the respondents – thought it was true; and only 39 per cent thought it was false. Surprisingly, even a third of those intending to vote Remain thought the figure was correct. This was despite the fact that the Chair of the UK Statistics Authority, Sir Andrew Dilnot, had called it 'potentially misleading', and the media had challenged the claim on numerous occasions.[19] Somehow, a large proportion of the public accepted a falsehood, despite being offered ample authoritative evidence that it was not true. For many critics, this brazen £350 million claim was at the heart of the charge that something had changed in public discourse: a willingness on the part of politicians to stretch the truth on a basic point of fact, *and* the predisposition of so many people to believe it despite the prevalence of reliable advice to the contrary.

Now, we should not exaggerate the role of that claim in the history of the campaign. The same poll found that only 3 per cent of voters thought the issue of EU membership fees was 'very important' in determining their vote; the issues that actually mattered were the economy and immigration. And it is also not clear that if the Leave campaign had used the legitimate £285 million figure it would have made a material difference to the argument, because I think that, to most people, it would still sound like an incomprehensibly large number. But the central point remains, that it will always be hard to fight those who peddle untruths if the public has a predisposition to believe them and makes no effort at all to verify the reliability of information fed to them. It's a long way from the rational model of the economists who assume that we would never believe any cheap talk coming our way if it derived from a source that had reason to mislead. In practice, we evidently are quite happy to believe untruths.

In the US, the same arguments arose over the many implausible claims made by Donald Trump during the 2016 presidential election campaign. For some reason, the public seemed happy to ignore the fact he was weak on policy detail and in conflict with expert opinion, inconsistently veered from one position to another, and on some issues was accused of blatantly lying.[20]

So is there an explanation for the approach that some voters, in both the UK and the US, seemed happy to adopt in 2016? The answer is that people will go some way to accepting false-hoods if they seem to conform to known facts about how the world works. So in the British referendum, Leave voters were not duped by the campaign, they were predisposed to believe bad things about the EU; that could be said to have been the EU's fundamental problem in Britain. A lot had gone wrong in the EU in previous years, so it seemed quite natural to believe the negative stories. If things had been going well for the EU, then maybe there would have been a willingness to accept more positive claims.

But it is also interesting to ask whether there are some periods in which bullshit is more likely to be accepted than others. To me, the answer to this question is 'yes', there are times when truth becomes less important to voters and citizens, and other things seem to matter more. At the most extreme end, one might cite Nazi Germany: Hitler manipulated public opinion, but it was already a hideous time for the country and the pre-vailing conditions had given some citizens a predisposition to seek solace in myths and hate. You might call Hitler the cause of the evil that followed, but equally you might blame the pre-existing tensions that made conditions so ripe for a Hitler to come along.[21]

More generally, at fraught times in countries that are sharply divided and where people have a strong sense of loyalty to one side of an argument or another, there is perhaps an increased tendency for people to swallow a group line without questioning it. 2016 was just one of those troubled periods. There had been a long spell of stagnant living standards,[22] there was an unusual amount of public anger, there were major arguments about how to change things, and there was an exceptionally intense political sensitivity to issues of identity and nationhood. In the UK, there were well publicised arguments around the respect accorded to traditionally excluded minorities. There was a long-running row over the place of a statue of Cecil Rhodes at Oriel College, Oxford, and a controversy over comments by Germaine Greer about trans women.[23] In the US, the Black Lives Matter campaign emerged, and there were arguments about which bathroom trans people were allowed to use.[24] As we saw in Chapter 8, whatever the merits of the arguments on either side, those rows ignited a certain sense of a culture war. That undoubtedly contributed to voter behaviour. For those feeling intense and emotional about the issues at stake, the arguments can get rough, gangs form, and truth is dispensed with. If open-mindedness is a protection against misbelief, then periods in which people's minds are closed are more likely to be ones where lies can be more successful.

For example, when it came to the vote for Donald Trump, certain American voters obviously decided that the attributes that the political establishment traditionally considered desirable in a president didn't rate as important when compared to his stance in the great schism between cosmopolitan liberals and the rest of the country. Trump seemed to be on their side, and for many that was the priority in selecting who to vote for.

For what one might call the worried class – the liberals who are anxious that public opinion is peculiarly malleable and that people are dangerously vulnerable to manipulation – it might be that the most constructive effort should be directed at reducing the social and economic tensions underpinning people's willingness to believe untrue things. It's all too easy to say that the people were fooled by charlatans and thus voted the wrong way; that will always be true of some voters on all sides, but not all of them, and the outsider or populist forces are to a large extent *reflecting* public anger as much as stirring it up. Instead, their liberal opponents need to ask why people were so fed up in the first place.

In any event, we shouldn't exaggerate the degree to which the public are open to believing untruths. There is a lot of evidence that people are broadly untrusting of those trying to sell things to them. The Ipsos MORI polling on the EU referendum found that 46 per cent of voters considered the two campaigns to be 'mostly telling lies'; only 19 per cent thought that the campaigns were mostly telling the truth. The respondents were obviously far more likely to believe the claims of the campaign they supported, but still only about half of Leave voters thought the Leave campaign was mostly telling the truth. (Remain voters, by and large, were slightly more trusting than Leave ones.) This, to me, suggests not that the untruths persuaded people, but that the persuaded people were willing to go along with the untruths. I tend to agree with Dominic Cummings, who primarily put the Leave victory down to three big global events – the rise in immigration and concern over it, the financial crash and the euro crisis:

These three big forces had global impact and had much more effect on people who pay a normal amount of attention to politics than every speech, article, pamphlet and 'campaign' about the EU over 15 years, the sum total of which had almost no discernible effect.[25]

He was not denying that his referendum campaign had a big effect, but without the stark EU reality that lots of things had gone wrong, the campaign would not have got anywhere. The public did not, when they came to vote, simply take their instructions from mendacious politicians.

The media

Meanwhile, there has been some media angst at the rise of populist parties and associated talk of fake news and post-truth politics. The media in all its multifarious forms is an intermediary between those who create the bullshit and those who consume it. How should it react to recent developments, such as the controversial and sometimes unsupported assertions of the Trumps and their associates? How should it react when it is accused of spreading fake news by politicians, who may themselves have a tendency to spout nonsense?

These accusations have been all too common in 2017. It sometimes seems they are thrown around not to change minds about the truth or falsehood of any particular proposition, but more to deflect attention from counter-charges or simply to sow confusion and raise scepticism.[26]

Personally, I don't find it that difficult to see how the much-maligned mainstream media should react. It should simply do its job with the usual rigour and set out the facts as it always would; it should not allow itself to be intimidated and nor should it pick fights for the sake of it. Above all, it should distinguish itself from its critics by freely admitting when it gets things wrong, as it inevitably will from time to time. In other words, the media should stand firm – no more, no less. It should never fail to point out inaccuracies, or fall for the phoney impartiality that leads to reporting of the 'some people say the earth is flat, others say it is round' variety, because that is a disservice to the public.

But equally, if the media goes down the path of believing that it must lead some special crusade in defence of truth, setting out each morning to take on the liars in positions of authority, it is likely to accentuate the sense of tribal rivalry and, if anything, exacerbate the tendency for opposing forces to spread falsehood. The mainstream outlets have to remain fair to their accusers, even when the accusers are not fair to them. Anyway, if a newspaper or broadcaster that positions itself as impartial finds itself leading some giant campaign against a particular elected official, it is likely soon to succumb to its own groupthink about what is true and what is not. I veer towards the view of Ross Douthat, expressed in a *New York Times* comment piece about Donald Trump, called 'The Tempting of the Media':

> ... the press may be tempted toward – and richly rewarded for – a kind of hysterical oppositionalism, a mirroring of Trump's own tabloid style and disregard for truth.[27]

For Douthat, this would be gratifying in the short term, but disastrous in the long term.

> The danger for the established press, then, is the same danger facing other institutions in our republic: that while believing themselves to be nobly resisting Trump, they end up imitating him.

Such imitation will inspire reader loyalty and passion – up to a point. But beyond that point it's more likely to polarize than to persuade, which means it often does a demagogue's work for him.

Douthat's colleague on the *New York Times* Thomas Friedman puts it rather differently, saying of Trump that 'if you engage with him too much, too often and too closely, he will actually suck your brains out'.[28]

In addition, it's worth saying that when it comes to accusations of fake news, there is a tendency to think the responsible media has to be the guardian of the facts. This is true up to a point, but often the facts themselves are less at the heart of an argument than their selection, interpretation and use. Obviously, where facts *are* centre stage, sensible media outlets can't fall for the relativism of any political or corporate interest that tries to suggest 'alternative facts' are equally valid. Lots of media organisations have quite rightly taken it upon themselves to check facts and set the record straight when potentially misleading claims are made.[29] But while this is a worthwhile exercise (even if most people are not interested in it), it will never be as much a guardian of truth as a cool-headed, honest-hearted media making a decent effort to anchor public discourse in sense and truth.

So our final task is to ask what it takes to make a cool-headed, honest-hearted media in an age when so many people are challenging orthodox or expert views.

First, there are a number of tactical issues to be resolved when politicians are keen to suppress negative stories and propagate favourable ones. Should newspapers that purport to be objective use the world 'lie' in relation to what appear to be intentional mis-statements? The *New York Times* has taken the view that it sometimes should, and has done so in relation to Donald

Trump in its news as well as in its comment pieces.[30] The *Wall Street Journal* editor, Gerard Baker, has been more cautious, arguing that you have to set out the claim and the facts, and where they disagree let the readers decide whether the claim is an intentional lie or not.[31] This is not a very important issue, as the word is only ever likely to be used in news coverage with caution and restraint.

I think there is a more significant question around the role of the media in giving airtime to nonsense, even if only to debunk it. This was a problem with some of the coverage of the £350 million per week claim; it was much talked about, and through the reiteration effect the repetition probably added to the numbers of casual observers who ended up believing it. How much attention should we give to bullshit that is merely designed to attract attention or provoke an argument? How much repetition of a lie should we broadcast if we know that some passers-by will hear the lie and not the truth? There is no obvious answer, other than to say that if the purveyor of a lie is important or newsworthy it seems impossible to ignore what they say, as this at least helps engaged citizens tell who is truthful and who is not. At the same time, there are plenty of controversialists who provoke, exaggerate and embellish in order to get attention or to fill their newspaper columns. It is important that credible news outlets do not bestow the badge of seriousness upon them, even if they make good box office.

Many have worried that if respectable news organisations take President Trump or his ilk seriously, it is tantamount to normalising racism. For them, this is the path to perdition. But crucially, while the mainstream 'impartial' media outlets owe no respect to any particular politician, they do owe respect to the voters, not least because they ultimately pay the journalists' salaries. Any media organisation purporting to be impartial simply cannot be anything other than normally polite to a candidate; but at the same time, it can never be indulgent of lies or exaggerations. It just has to stand its ground with resilience and grace. Of course, a healthy media industry will have partial as well as impartial outlets, and they may choose to treat any politician however they want. They might even stamp the word 'fascist' over the photograph of a president or prime minister if they feel so inclined, but they will be judged on different terms if they do.

Otherwise, notwithstanding the challenges, I don't have much doubt that the media's job is just to get on with its job. However, for that to be done well there are three important features that characterise a flourishing media landscape, and each helps serve as a control against the worst excesses of the forces of untruth.

The first is that there are several competing, reliable sources of impartial news, with each seeing it as their goal to be fair to the facts and fair to all sides in an argument. There is a huge difference between those who try to be impartial and those who don't; it is the difference between the news pages of the *Guardian* or *Telegraph* and the comment pages, and it would be tragic if the news pages were crowded out by comment. But equally, no single impartial provider will ever be perfect, and each will potentially suffer from its own unconscious biases. The only thing that can stop self-appointed guardians of truth falling for falsehoods is competition between several of them. It keeps them all on their toes and it is also a protection against the critics, who in my experience rail against what they see as false impartiality in the mainstream media, but who sometimes then take refuge in the most nakedly biased publications available on the web. I know there are the critics who say mainstream media outlets are full of fake news, but the fact they all get things badly wrong from time to time does not invalidate their role at all, as long as there are several of them.

A second desirable feature of a media landscape is diversity in viewpoint and values, and in journalistic style. We don't want all media outlets to be striving to be objective – we want some that are adversarial, some that are sensationalist, some that take a risk with the facts while others that are sticklers for accuracy; some that are funny and some that are serious, and maybe one or two that are offensive. The key thing is that there is a diverse ecosystem, and that the public understand what they are getting, whatever they consume. As it happens, I think people are quite capable of telling the difference between, say, the *New York Times* and the *National Enquirer*, or the BBC and a random unsourced news story on the internet. If they can't tell the difference, it is usually because they don't want to, and in that situation we need to go back to the topic of the last section and ask why they make no effort to maintain good information hygiene.

The third point, without wishing to appear self-serving, is that it is desirable that there should be some media platforms that are shared by everybody. In the UK, the BBC is in this category, and although it might be criticised from any side and on any occasion for holding its own view on things, a country needs some shared space that stops factions retreating into their rabbit holes and losing all connection to the rest of the populace. Given the difficulty for a BBC or similar to serve the whole country when the people are divided in their views, it goes without saying that there should be competition in the role of serving as a mainstream and popular news provider, in order to ensure the job is done competently and fairly.

But overall, I can only reiterate the point that we don't need to agonise too much over the particular challenges to the media in the so-called post-truth era. The best it can do is get on with its job as honestly and effectively as possible.

One final challenge

All that being said, there is one last general point to be made about the media, and indeed the rest of us. It is not about how we all deal with lies, but how we handle honesty. Are we up to the job?

To understand the question, just imagine a well-intentioned public figure, with integrity, having to cope with a problem that is not of their making. Let's assume they do the best they can, but inevitably in a way that fails to satisfy large numbers of people. Would that public figure get a fair hearing in the media, and would they be rewarded by the public for being honest about the downsides of their actions? I suspect the answer is 'not always'. And as long as people in authority feel that they are not going to get a fair hearing, they will have an incentive to disguise their mistakes, and cover up the consequences of their actions.

This is a dilemma for the press, which rightly sees one of its main tasks as holding the powerful to account. This means challenging those in authority on the decisions they take and the damage they do to people; after all, we don't want to forgive incompetence or cruelty. But we can easily stray into making an error the other way by falsely convicting people of malfeasance, when really they are just doing their best in a set of trying circumstances. It's the 'we've had an earthquake, let's blame the government' phenomenon.

In broad terms, if a government knows that it will get the blame for everything, it will at least focus on doing its job well; it will have an incentive to prepare for the next earthquake in the sure knowledge that, when it comes, it'll be held responsible. But there is a problem if we end up with unfairly harsh treatment of those in office: it is that in order to escape punishment, perfectly decent people will try to hide their behaviour. In the end, we can drive policy-makers into a defensiveness that is conducive to bullshit.

Personally, I'm an admirer of the culture of the airline industry, which always regards identifying a problem as more important than identifying the culprit.[32] The industry recognises that to learn lessons from things that go wrong, you need people to feel comfortable opening up about their errors – which they won't if to do so means they'll be severely punished. Satisfying as it is to lock someone up when disaster strikes, it's often the wrong way to solve a problem. That suggests we should strive to have a culture that punishes cover-ups more heavily, but in return is more forgiving of mistakes.

It's a difficult balance. Too little accountability and we never get the best out of people, be they social workers, politicians, chief executives, campaigners or journalists. Yet too much accountability and we inevitably end up paralysing those people rather than challenging them. A vibrant media culture, populated with sceptics fired up with the self-proclaimed duty to 'speak truth to power', can ironically end up creating a hopelessly secretive culture of administration. The paradox is that journalists need to overcome bullshit to hold people to account, but in the process of holding them to account they can induce people to produce bullshit. There is no better example of this than the readiness to use the word 'gaffe' for a public statement that is too honest or straightforward.[33] The need to avoid a hysterical reaction to some careless mis-statement accounts for the overly cautious media practices of public figures.

This is not an easy problem to solve, partly because it's hard to draw a line between too much scrutiny and too little. But also there is no such thing as *the* media; no one controls it, or coordinates it, it is just an industry of disparate players, each doing their own thing, often in competition or outright conflict with each other. I'm reminded of Homer Simpson's famous characterisation of alcohol: it is, he said, 'the cause of, and solution to, all of life's problems'. When bullshit is the problem, the media is like a strong gin and tonic. It makes it more likely, but also makes it more bearable.

Final Words

When it comes to communication, things never change and yet things are always changing.

As a final reflection, let's ponder both halves of that proposition, starting with the claim that things never change. When it comes to bullshit, that principle surely holds. Mendacity and nonsense are not new and are not going away. The rational model of the economists, which struggles to find a justification for bullshit (because we are all too sensible to trust anyone who has a reason to deceive us), simply describes a world which doesn't exist. The most straightforward, honest communication will always be the exception not the rule. Myths, embellishment and exaggeration will always be used as a means of sending subtle signals, and why shouldn't they be? In addition, for as long as we are human beings with instincts and emotions they will be used to teach, influence or manipulate us. Plus, there will always be chancers who think they can lie and get ahead in the short term, before the long term catches up with them. And anyway, a culture that tolerates mendacity and nonsense, as ours does, will be self-reinforcing.

But there is something else that won't change: for all the rubbish we speak, ultimately the fate of human beings is driven by reality not words. The central guiding principle has to be that, in the long term, the truth will out. The geniuses who think that great advertising can sell any kind of junk will be proved wrong. In market economies, good products will tend to flourish and displace bad ones; in democracies, politicians who reflect the public's views will tend to prevail over the ones who don't. (And incidentally, the public's own views will tend to gravitate towards support for things that solve problems rather than create them.) Life is messy and crude; it might take a while for the truth to emerge, and irrevocable damage may be done before it does; there will be plenty of exceptions where people get away with lies. But in general, communication ends up being subservient to substance. In practice, it's probably best to make the assumption that the truth will come out before you die. While the rational model of the economists is not an accurate description of our world, it is a useful approximation of the long-term position.

Those are the basic principles underlying the nonsense to which we are exposed. But let's now focus on the opposite claim: that when it comes to communication, things are always changing. How so? The answer is that freshness and vitality are appealing features of all communication, and as a result the kind of language that works one day can fail the next. A style that sounds inventive at first can quickly be overused and come across as hackneyed. Something that sounds cool on Monday can be cringe-worthy by Friday.* Something that comes across as slick in one election can seem inauthentic in the next. Prose styles come and go like fashions in jeans.

Recently, we've been witnessing a particularly interesting

---

* I was impressed by a refreshingly amusing notice on Virgin trains, which said 'Please don't flush nappies, sanitary towels, paper towels, gum, old phones, unpaid bills, junk mail, your ex's sweater, hopes, dreams or goldfish down this toilet.' It broke the conventions we associate with such signs. But after you've seen it twenty-five times it is no longer funny, and you yearn for something more straightforward.

challenge to a prevailing political and business ethos, and to its stale approach to public discourse. It has at times felt like the collapse of an *ancien régime*, a farewell to the controlled, managerial style of communicating. It was effective once, but it has squeezed too much public communication into passionless, obfuscating messaging with an insufficient connection to reality. In the UK, it reached its height with New Labour, which used it as a successful response to the ragged and messy spontaneity of the party's wilderness years of the early 1980s. But it wore out in the 2000s, and then obstructed the party in connecting with its natural supporters.

It's not clear what will take its place. The rhetoric of Donald Trump is not to everyone's liking, but even for those for whom it has been a refreshing change it will probably wear out eventually. Indeed, it might expire quite quickly, depending on the success or failure of the substantive results with which it becomes associated. Whatever its failings, it will have taught old-style communicators a thing or two about how to break out of their rigid, self-imposed rules.

All that I would say about the talk of us being in a post-truth era, or one in which we have reached peak bullshit, is that yes, we are in a pretty strange period, but every cycle has its end. Bullshit ebbs and flows, returning in different forms for different occasions.

The downfall of Senator Joseph McCarthy back in the 1950s provides a useful tale for those who make the mistake of assuming that, once it embeds itself, bullshit is invulnerable and can never be toppled. McCarthy made his name by warning of communist infiltrators who were, in those paranoid times, supposedly subverting great American institutions from the State Department to Hollywood. For a while his stridently delivered message – supported from the wings by his young chief counsel,

Roy Cohn – resonated with a certain section of the public, insecure at the start of the Cold War and unsure as to how the world would develop. McCarthy's message was also a politically convenient one for Republicans, as it undermined the administration of the Democratic President, Harry S. Truman. But 1954 was the year in which it all went wrong for McCarthy. As chairman of the Senate's Permanent Subcommittee on Investigations, he took on the US Army, launching a probe into supposed infiltration of the Signals Corps. But during the proceedings he faced a counter-accusation that Roy Cohn had sought special treatment for a friend who had recently been drafted into the army. That prompted a new investigation, which then became a nationally televised showdown between McCarthy and the military.[1]

The inquiry exonerated Senator McCarthy (although it found that Cohn had engaged in 'unduly persistent or aggressive efforts' on behalf of his friend), and yet he was still destroyed by it. The hearings gripped the nation and were seen by tens of millions of Americans who were then able to judge his behaviour for themselves. What finished McCarthy off was the realisation by a fair-minded public that he was on the wrong side of civility and honesty. In a famous moment, which came to be seen as defining the end of McCarthy's influence, the Army counsel, Joseph Welch, turned to him and said, 'You've done enough. Have you no sense of decency sir, at long last? Have you left no sense of decency?'[2]

McCarthy's approval ratings plummeted; he was condemned in a Senate vote at the end of 1954 and three years later died of acute hepatitis generally ascribed to alcoholism.[3] Roy Cohn went on to have a successful legal career. He, incidentally, became something of a mentor to the young Donald Trump in the 1970s, before dying of an AIDS-related condition in 1986.[4]

The McCarthy story perhaps illustrates Winston Churchill's observation that you can always count on Americans to do the right thing after they've tried everything else. But it really makes the point that yes, bullshit can captivate and entrance us for a time, but good sense normally prevails in the end.

NOTES

INTRODUCTION

1 Jon Lovett, Keynote Address at Pitzer College, 18 May 2013. See 'Keynote Address by Jon Lovett', 18 May 2013, <http://pitweb.pitzer.edu/commencement/tag/transcript/>.

2 Laura Penny, *Your Call Is Important to Us: The Truth About Bullshit* (New York: Crown Archetype, 2005).

3 See Alan Rappeport, 'Donald Trump Laments Loss of Aerosol Sprays to Frame His Hair', *New York Times*, 30 December 2015, <https://www.nytimes.com/politics/first-draft/2015/12/30/donald-trump-laments-loss-of-aerosol-sprays-to-frame-his-hair/?_r=0>.

4 Sarah Cattle, 'Czech president says smoking is fine after 27 years old', *Daily Telegraph*, 17 October 2013, <http://www.telegraph.co.uk/news/worldnews/europe/czechrepublic/10386228/Czech-president-says-smoking-is-fine-after-27-years-old.html>.

5 Further reading: Craig Oliver, *Unleashing Demons: The Inside Story of Brexit* (London: Hodder and Stoughton, 2016); Tim Shipman, *All Out War: Brexit and the Sinking of Britain's Political Class* (London: HarperCollins, 2016).

6 Marc Fisher, John Woodrow Cox and Peter Hermann, 'Pizzagate: From rumor, to hashtag, to gunfire in D.C.', *Washington Post*, 16 December 2016, <https://www.washingtonpost.com/local/pizzagate-from-rumor-to-hashtag-to-gunfire-in-dc/2016/12/06/4c7def50-bbd4-11e6-94ac-3d324840106c_story.html?utm_term=.555ec7ffc6c2>; Henry Mance, 'Britain has had enough of experts, says Gove', *Financial Times*, 3 June 2016, <https://www.ft.com/content/3be49734-29cb-11e6-83e4-abc22d5d108c>.

7 Anthony Trollope, *The Way We Live Now* (1875; Portland: The Floating Press, 2009), p. 22.

8 Further reading: Peter Kenez, *The Birth of the Propaganda State: Soviet Methods of Mass Mobilization, 1917–1929* (Cambridge: Cambridge University Press, 1985); Maria Lafont and Sergo Grigorian, *Soviet Posters* (London: Prestel, 2015).

9 Harry G. Frankfurt, *On Bullshit* (Princeton: Princeton University Press, 2005). Originally published as an essay in *Raritan Quarterly Review*, 6:2 (fall 1986).

10 Robert Service, *A History of Modern Russia: From Tsarism to the Twenty-First Century* (Cambridge, MA: Harvard University Press, 2013, third edn).

11 Ibid., loc. 799.

12 Ibid., loc. 7136.

13 Ibid., loc. 7071.

14 Ibid., loc. 7139.

15 Salena Zito, 'Taking Trump seriously, not literally', *The Atlantic*, 23 September 2016, <http://www.theatlantic.com/politics/archive/2016/09/trump-makes-his-case-in-pittsburgh/501335/>.

CHAPTER 1

1 BBC News reports, including: 'Timeline of events', 18 August 2002, <http://news.bbc.co.uk/1/hi/england/2180946.stm>; 'Huntley guilty of Soham murders', 17 December 2003, <http://news.bbc.co.uk/1/hi/uk/3312551.stm>.

2 Steven Morris, 'Huntley – girls died in freak accidents', *Guardian*, 26 November 2003, <https://www.theguardian.com/uk/2003/nov/26/soham.ukcrime>.

3 Further reading: Nicci Gerrard, *Soham: A Story of Our Times* (London: Short Books, 2004).

4 Craig Silverman, 'Here Are 50 of The Biggest Fake News Hits On Facebook From 2016', BuzzFeed News, 30 December 2016, <https://www.buzzfeed.com/craigsilverman/top-fake-news-of-2016?utm_term=.noY667yKBB#.xvNnnQ30GG>.

5 For example, see the Advertising Standards Authority UK Advertising Codes, which 'lay down rules for advertisers, agencies and media owners to follow', drawn up by the Committee on Advertising Practice. On misleading advertising, the codes state 'Obvious exaggerations ("puffery") and claims that the average consumer who sees the marketing communication is unlikely to take literally are allowed provided they do not materially mislead', <https://www.asa.org.uk/codes-and-rulings/advertising-codes.html>.

6 Features in Phil Kuntz (ed.), *The Starr Report: The Evidence* (New York: Pocket Books, 1999), p. 359.

7 Further reading: Ken Gormley, *The Death of American Virtue: Clinton vs Starr* (New York: Crown Publishers, 2010); Peter Tiersma, 'Did Clinton Lie?: Defining Sexual Relations', *Chicago-Kent Law Review*, 79:3 (2004), 927.

8 Max Black. *The Prevalence of Humbug and Other Essays* (Ithaca: Cornell University Press, 1985).

9 Russell Hotten, 'Volkswagen: the scandal explained', BBC News, 10 December 2015, <http://www.bbc.co.uk/news/business-34324772>.

10 Jorn Madslien, '"Carmakers manipulate emissions tests"', BBC News, 14 March 2013, <http://www.bbc.co.uk/news/business-21759258>.

11 Jack Ewing, 'Diesel Scandal at VW Spreads to Core Market', *New York Times*, 23 September 2015.

12 The fact that a sin is not defined in absolute terms, but instead sits on a spectrum, always allows a degree of self-justification, best exemplified by an exchange in the *Simpsons* episode 'Bart the Murderer' (1991), in which the character Bart finds himself working for mafia boss Fat Tony. Bart is suspicious that he is involved in some kind of criminal tobacco smuggling operation and confronts Fat Tony:

>   Bart: Uh, say, are you guys crooks?
>   Fat Tony: Bart, is it wrong to steal a loaf of bread to feed your starving family?
>   Bart: No.
>   Fat Tony: Well, suppose you got a large starving family. Is it wrong to steal a truckload of bread to feed them?
>   Bart: Uh uh.
>   Fat Tony: And what if your family don't like bread? They like ... cigarettes?
>   Bart: I guess that's okay.
>   Fat Tony: Now, what if instead of giving them away, you sold them at a price that was practically giving them away. Would that be a crime, Bart?
>   Bart: Hell, no.
>   See <http://www.imdb.com/title/tt0701060/trivia?tab=qt&ref_=tt_trv_qu>.

13 Those involved in the Vote Leave campaign persist in 'vigorously disputing' any suggestion that the £350 million claim was misleading.

14 Edmund Burke, 'Letter I: On the Overtures of Peace', from Three Letters Addressed to a Member of the Present Parliament on Proposals for Peace with the Regicide Directory of France, in *The Works of the Rt Hon Edmund Burke*, vol. II (1841), p. 305.

15 Mark Twain, *Following the Equator: A Journey around the World* (Hartford: American Publishing Company, 1897).

16 Malcolm Turnbull, *The Spycatcher Trial* (London: Heinemann, 1988), p. 104. Lord Armstrong told me that there were broad grins on both sides at this exchange.

17 Christopher Hutton, *Language, Meaning and the Law* (Edinburgh: Edinburgh University Press, 2009), p. 172. See also Chapman Pincher, *The Spycatcher Affair: A Revealing Account of the Trial That Tried to Suppress a Book but Made It a Bestseller* (New York: St Martin's Press, 1987).

18 Alan Durant, 'On the interpretation of allusions and other innuendo meanings in libel actions: the value of semantic and pragmatic evidence', *Forensic Linguistics*, 3:2 (2016), 195–210.

19 Ross Lydall and Miranda Bryant, 'Longer waits and fewer trains after Circle line extension', *Evening Standard*, 16 March 2010, <http://www.standard.co.uk/news/longer-waits-and-fewer-trains-after-circle-line-extension-6746111.html>.

20 TfL have responded to my criticism with the following comments: 'The

changes implemented on the Circle line and those it shares track with have enabled us to provide a more robust service, so between 2009/10 and 2012/13 average customer delays on the Circle line have been reduced by around 48 per cent. Most importantly of all, the number of Circle line trains per hour that customers *actually* see is often no fewer than before, the overall number of services on all lines is much greater and reliability is much improved, as it is across the Tube network as a whole.

'This customer information was also just one part of a fully integrated package of communications, alongside engagement with media and stakeholders, and we were always frank about the reduction in scheduled trains on the Circle line from seven to six required to deliver the overall improvements to service.'

21 This figure has since been revised to +0.1 per cent. See Office of National Statistics, Gross Domestic Product: Quarter on Quarter growth: CVM SA %, 23 December 2016, <https://www.ons.gov.uk/economy/grossdomesticproductgdp/timeseries/ihyq>.

22 Andrew Porter, 'George Osborne blames snow for double-dip threat', *Daily Telegraph*, 25 January 2011, <http://www.telegraph.co.uk/finance/economics/8280664/George-Osborne-blames-snow-for-double-dip-threat.html>.

23 Office of National Statistics, Gross domestic product preliminary estimate, 25 January 2011, <http://webarchive.nationalarchives.gov.uk/20160105160709/http://ons.gov.uk/ons/rel/gva/gross-domestic-product--preliminary-estimate/q4-2010/gross-domestic-product-preliminary-estimate-4th-quarter-2010.pdf>.

24 Timeline of events: Mark Mardell, 'Tory leadership: Behind the scenes of Gove–Johnson drama', BBC News, 3 July 2016, <http://www.bbc.co.uk/news/uk-36693200>.

25 See, for example, Gordon Rayner, 'How Boris Johnson was brought to his knees by the "cuckoo nest plot"', *Daily Telegraph*, 1 July 2016, <http://www.telegraph.co.uk/news/2016/06/30/how-boris-johnson-was-brought-to-his-knees-by-the-cuckoo-nest-pl/>.

26 For example, on BBC *Newsnight* (30 June 2016), the Conservative MP Jacob Rees-Mogg said: 'I think Michael Gove has changed his mind and I think politicians ought to change their minds and announce it to the public, so I think what he has done is extremely brave; it came late in the day; nobody in their right mind would have plotted it this way. So I am convinced that it is genuine. He came to a conclusion, he told everybody and I think he would be an excellent prime minister.'

27 See also Tim Shipman, *All Out War: The Full Story of How Brexit Sank Britain's Political Class* (London: William Collins, 2016).

28 For a longer version of this argument, you will find a 2005 blog post of mine here: <http://news.bbc.co.uk/newswatch/ifs/low/newsid_4330000/newsid_4331800/4331893.stm>.

29 'Business: The Economy. Governor tries to douse north's fire', BBC News, 22 October 1998, <http://news.bbc.co.uk/1/hi/business/197995.stm>.

30 CIA, Iraq's Weapons of Mass Destruction Programs, October 2002, <https://

web.archive.org/web/20060426071800/http://www.cia.gov/cia/reports/iraq_wmd/Iraq_Oct_2002.htm>.

31 A useful pre-Chilcot summary of Tony Blair's claims comes from Mehdi Hasan, who does describe them as lies: 'Blair: truth and lies', *Guardian,* 29 January 2010, <https://www.theguardian.com/commentisfree/2010/jan/29/tony-blair-chilcot-iraq-inquiry>.

32 *The Report of the Iraq Inquiry: Executive Summary* (London: HMSO, 2016), p. 73, para. 536.

33 'Sir John Chilcot's public statement. 6 July 2016', The Iraq Inquiry, 6 July 2016, <http://www.iraqinquiry.org.uk/the-inquiry/sir-john-chilcots-public-statement/>. See also *The Report of the Iraq Inquiry: Executive Summary,* p. 46, para. 330.

34 Tony Blair, Statement to the House of Commons following publication of Hutton report, 28 January 2004. Quoted in 'Timeline: Tony Blair's statements on weapons in Iraq', BBC News, 12 December 2009, <http://news.bbc.co.uk/1/hi/uk_politics/8409526.stm>.

35 *The Report of the Iraq Inquiry: Executive Summary,* p. 73, para. 537.

36 'Sir John Chilcot's public statement, 6 July 2016'.

37 On the Iraq War: Thomas E. Ricks, *Fiasco: The American Military Adventure in Iraq* (London: Allen Lane, 2006).

38 Ian Leslie, *Born Liars: Why We Can't Live Without Deceit* (London: Quercus, 2011).

39 Nassim Nicholas Taleb, *The Bed of Procrustes: Philosophical and Practical Aphorisms* (London: Penguin, 2010), p. 66.

CHAPTER 2

1 Quoted in Neil Irwin, 'The real jobless rate is 42 percent? Donald Trump has a point, sort of', *New York Times*, 10 February 2016, <http://www.nytimes.com/2016/02/11/upshot/the-real-jobless-rate-is-42-percent-donald-trump-has-a-point-sort-of.html?_r=0>.

2 Based on data from the OECD statistical database.

3 The CNN poll can be found at <http://edition.cnn.com/election/results/exit-polls>. The question *Is Hillary Clinton honest and trustworthy?* saw responses of 36 per cent yes, 61 per cent no. The question *Is Donald Trump honest and trustworthy?* yielded 33 per cent yes and 64 per cent no.

4 Salena Zito, 'Taking Trump seriously, not literally', *The Atlantic,* 23 September 2016, <http://www.theatlantic.com/politics/archive/2016/09/trump-makes-his-case-in-pittsburgh/501335/>.

5 Harry G. Frankfurt, 'On Bullshit', <https://www.stoa.org.uk/topics/bullshit/pdf/on-bullshit.pdf>; *On Bullshit* (Princeton: Princeton University Press, 2005).

6 Ibid., p. 56.

7 For a recent application of his framework to Donald Trump, see Harry G. Frankfurt, 'Donald Trump is BS, says expert in BS', *Time,* 12 May 2016, <http://time.com/4321036/donald-trump-bs/>.

8   US Bureau of Labor Statistics, <http://www.bls.gov/>.

9   Reported in: Shaun Walker, 'Ukrainian president: Russian troops have crossed border', *Guardian*, 28 August 2014, <https://www.theguardian.com/world/2014/aug/28/ukraine-accuses-russia-invading-south-east-help-rebels>.

10 Examples from David Cameron's era as Prime Minister were helpfully collated by BuzzFeed and include Andy Coulson, Chris Huhne, Liam Fox, Maria Miller and Grant Shapps. See Alan White, '6 People In Whom David Cameron Had "Full Confidence"', BuzzFeed News, 21 March 2016, <https://www.buzzfeed.com/alanwhite/i-see-a-bad-moon-rising?utm_term=.rjRB9GjAD#.to0vgQDaB>.

11 Barclays was contacted in relation to this section but declined to comment.

12 Barclays Bank, *Barclays PLC Annual Report 07* (2008), p. 72, <https://www.home.barclays/content/dam/barclayspublic/docs/InvestorRelations/AnnualReports/AR2007/2007-barclays-plc-annual-report.pdf>.

13 Graeme Wearden, 'How the PPI scandal unfolded', *Guardian*, 5 May 2011, <https://www.theguardian.com/business/2011/may/05/how-ppi-scandal-unfolded>.

14 Jill Treanor, 'Barclays missold financial products to small businesses', *Guardian*, 29 June 2012, <https://www.theguardian.com/business/2012/jun/29/barclays-missold-products-small-businesses>.

15 James McBride, 'Understanding the Libor Scandal', Council on Foreign Relations Backgrounders, 12 October 2016, <http://www.cfr.org/united-kingdom/understanding-libor-scandal/p28729>.

16 The 2007 Barclays annual report was prepared by Pauffley Creative, a corporate communications consultancy specialising in corporate reporting. It was purchased by larger PR agency Fishburn Hedges in June 2009, which in turn combined with Fleishman Hillard in November 2015.

17 Lloyds Bank, *Annual Report and Accounts 2007: Building Long-term Relationships* (2008), <http://www.lloydsbankinggroup.com/globalassets/documents/investors/2007/2007_ltsb_group_ra.pdf>.

18 Further reading: Sonia Piotti, *Exploring Corporate Rhetoric in English: Hedging in Company Annual Reports – A Corpus-assisted Analysis* (Milan: EDUCatt, 2009).

19 See the poll conducted on the public's perception of the existence of WMD categorised by respondents' main source of news. Viewers whose main source was Fox were most likely to believe in the existence of WMD (33 per cent), those whose main source was NPR were least likely (11 per cent). See Steve Kull, 'Misperceptions, the Media and the Iraq War', Program on International Policy Attitudes/Knowledge Networks Poll, 2 October 2003, <https://web.archive.org/web/20060210232719/www.pipa.org/OnlineReports/Iraq/IraqMedia_Oct03/IraqMedia_Oct03_rpt.pdf>.

20 See Ronald F. Inglehart and Pippa Norris, 'Trump, Brexit, and the Rise of Populism: Economic Have-Nots and Cultural Backlash', Harvard Kennedy School of Government Faculty Research Working Paper (August 2016), <https://research.hks.harvard.edu/publications/getFile.aspx?Id=1401>; Jon Swaine, 'White, working-class and angry: Ohio's left-behind help Trump to

stunning win', *Guardian*, 9 November 2016, <https://www.theguardian.com/us-news/2016/nov/09/donald-trump-ohio-youngstown-voters>.

21 See 'Nixon's China Visit and "Sino–US Joint Communiqué"', Ministry of Foreign Affairs of the People's Republic of China, <http://www.fmprc.gov.cn/mfa_eng/ziliao_665539/3602_665543/3604_665547/t18006.shtml>.

22 Richard C. Bush, *At Cross Purposes: US–Taiwan Relations Since 1942* (Abingdon and New York: Routledge, 2015).

23 Bill Keller, 'Mitt and Bibi: Diplomacy as Demolition Derby', *New York Times*, 12 September 2012, <https://keller.blogs.nytimes.com/2012/09/12/mitt-and-bibi-diplomacy-as-demolition-derby/?_r=0>.

24 See Joseph I. Lieberman, 'Hillary Clinton – a strong leader for America and the world', *Jerusalem Post*, 3 November 2016, <http://www.jpost.com/Opinion/Hillary-Clinton-a-strong-leader-for-America-and-the-world-471652>.

25 'Renewing America's Promise', 2008 Democratic Party Platform, 25 August 2008. Transcript at the American Presidency Project: <http://www.presidency.ucsb.edu/ws/?pid=78283>.

26 *Newsnight*, BBC2, 13 May 1997, 22:30.

27 *Today* Programme, BBC Radio 4, 10 January 2017, 08:17.

28 Kate Proctor, 'Jeremy Corbyn calls for salary cap in attack on "grotesque difference" in pay', *Evening Standard*, 10 January 2017, <http://www.standard.co.uk/news/politics/jeremy-corbyn-calls-for-salary-cap-in-attack-on-grotesque-difference-in-pay-a3437001.html>.

29 Michael Wilkinson, 'Jeremy Corbyn suffers car crash "reboot" as he backtracks on pledges to introduce wage cap and curb freedom of movement', *Daily Telegraph*, 10 January 2017, <http://www.telegraph.co.uk/news/2017/01/10/jeremy-corbyn-brexit-labour-reboot-live/>: 'Jeremy Corbyn suffered a car crash relaunch of his leadership today when he appeared to backtrack on two key *pledges* within hours of *announcing* them' (my emphasis); Jim Pickard, 'Jeremy Corbyn rows back on proposed cap on wages', *Financial Times*, 10 January 2017, <https://www.ft.com/content/48f6bc34-d74c-11e6-944b-e7eb37a6aa8e>: 'Jeremy Corbyn has stepped back from a *proposal* for a cap on wages only seven hours after *announcing* it' (my emphasis).

30 Virginie Boone, 'Wayfarer 2014 The Traveler Pinot Noir (Fort Ross-Seaview)', *Wine Enthusiast*, 1 September 2016, <http://www.winemag.com/buying-guide/shelf-talkers/square/wayfarer-2014-the-traveler-pinot-noir-fort-ross-seaview>.

31 Traditionally it was thought that the tongue can taste four flavours – sweet, salty, bitter and sour. Then umami was added to make five, and now it is thought there are many more receptors in the tongue than had previously been assumed. So in fairness to the writer of the review, seven flavours is quite possible. But whether seven can be distinguished from each other simultaneously is a different point. Further reading: Adam Hadhazy, 'Tip of the tongue: humans may taste at least 6 flavors', Live Science, 30 December 2011, <http://www.livescience.com/17684-sixth-basic-taste.html>.

32 Quoted in Paul Levy, 'Pamela Vandyke Price: Wine expert whose acerbic writing scorned supermarket brands in favour of independent and

traditional makers' (obituary), *Independent*, 18 February 2013, <http://www.
independent.co.uk/news/obituaries/pamela-vandyke-price-wine-expert-
whose-acerbic-writing-scorned-supermarket-brands-in-favour-of-9134576.
html>.

33 See 'Matteo Renzi: 11 quotes on the future of Italy', World Economic
Forum, 21 January 2015, <https://www.weforum.org/agenda/2015/01/
matteo-renzi-11-quotes-on-the-future-of-italy/>.

34 'Donald Trump's Mexico wall: Who is going to pay for it?', BBC News, 6
February 2017, <http://www.bbc.co.uk/news/world-us-canada-37243269>.

CHAPTER 3

1 'The Legend of Dame Carcas', Tourism Carcassonne, undated, <http://
www.tourism-carcassonne.co.uk/discover/history-carcassonne/
legend-dame-carcas>.

2 Calvin Killman, *The Esoteric Codex: Cathar Heresy* (Raleigh: Lulu, 2016),
p. 38.

3 Pépin le Bref, or Pepin (or Pippin) the Short, was waging a campaign
in the Septimania region in the 750s. He laid siege to nearby Narbonne
from 752, capturing it in 759 (Archibald R. Lewis, *The Development of
Southern French and Catalan Society, 718–1050* (Austin: University of
Texas Press, 1965), p. 16). Sources are less clear in relation to Carcassonne.
Charlemagne may have been born in 742, but some say it was 747 or 748
(Rosamond McKitterick, *Charlemagne: The Formation of a European Identity*
(Cambridge: Cambridge University Press, 2008)).

4 For more, see Jeff Guo, 'Why people used to look so serious in
photos but now have big smiles', *Washington Post*, 1 December 2015,
<https://www.washingtonpost.com/news/wonk/wp/2015/12/01/
researchers-have-discovered-a-surprising-reason-we-smile-in-photos/>.

5 See, for example, Steve McKenzie, 'Archive body starts debate on smiling for
photographs', BBC News, 17 December 2011, <http://www.bbc.com/news/
uk-scotland-highlands-islands-16219211>.

6 This book is an exception.

7 See, for example, Will Smale, 'Do firms really need a social policy?', BBC
News, 1 December 2006, <http://news.bbc.co.uk/1/hi/business/6102108.
stm>; Matthew Lynn, 'Corporate Social Responsibility has become a racket –
and a dangerous one', *Daily Telegraph*, 28 September 2015, <http://www.
telegraph.co.uk/finance/newsbysector/industry/11896546/Corporate-Social-
Responsibility-has-become-a-racket-and-a-dangerous-one.html>; S. B.
Banerjee, 'Corporate Social Responsibility: The Good, the Bad and the Ugly',
Critical Sociology, 34:1 (2008), 51–79.

8 For example, David Cameron speaking about his party's proposal for a
married couple's tax allowance said, 'We are confident that it is the right
policy. We think it is a good strong announcement that reinforces our
message that society matters to the Conservatives.' (Quoted in Andrew Porter

and Robert Winnett, 'General Election 2010: Conservatives to give four million married couples a tax break', *Daily Telegraph*, 9 April 2010, <http://www.telegraph.co.uk/news/election-2010/7573263/General-Election-2010-Conservatives-to-give-four-million-married-couples-a-tax-break.html>); or Sussex Assistant Chief Constable Geoff Williams on the decision to put armed police on railway stations: 'We do not want to alarm people – it is purely a precautionary measure to reassure the public that we are here.' ('Armed police on patrol at station', BBC News, 8 July 2005, <http://news.bbc.co.uk/1/hi/england/southern_counties/4665909.stm>).

9 See generally Philip Cowley and Robert Ford (eds), *Sex, Lies & the Ballot Box: 50 Things You Need to Know about British Elections* (London: Biteback Publishing, 2014).

10 See James Bartholomew, 'The awful rise of "virtue signalling"', *Spectator*, 18 April 2015, <http://www.spectator.co.uk/2015/04/hating-the-daily-mail-is-a-substitute-for-doing-good/>.

11 See 'The Climate Change Act and UK regulations', Committee on Climate Change, undated, <https://www.theccc.org.uk/tackling-climate-change/the-legal-landscape/global-action-on-climate-change/>.

12 See 'Child poverty promise and Child Poverty Act', Child Poverty Action Group, undated, <http://www.cpag.org.uk/content/child-poverty-promise-and-child-poverty-act>.

13 'FS11: UK Fuel Poverty Strategy and the Warm Homes and Energy Conservation Act 2000', UK Association for the Conservation of Energy, February 2002, <http://www.ukace.org/wp-content/uploads/2012/11/ACE-Fact-Sheet-2002-02-UK-Fuel-Poverty-Strategy-and-the-Warm-Homes-and-Energy-Conservation-Act-2000.pdf>.

14 Fuel Poverty team, Department of Energy and Climate Change, 'Cutting the Cost of Keeping Warm: A Fuel Poverty Strategy for England' (London: HMSO, 2015), p. 20, <https://www.gov.uk/government/uploads/system/uploads/attachment_data/file/408644/cutting_the_cost_of_keeping_warm.pdf>.

15 'Cutting the cost of keeping warm to tackle fuel poverty', press release, Department of Energy and Climate Change, 22 July 2014, <https://www.gov.uk/government/news/cutting-the-cost-of-keeping-warm-to-tackle-fuel-poverty>.

16 The successor government department, the Department for Business, Energy and Industrial Strategy, was contacted but made no comment.

17 'Commentary no. 61' in Andrew Dilnot and Christopher Giles (eds), *The IFS Green Budget: Summer 1997* (London: Institute for Fiscal Studies, 1997).

18 Geoffrey Howe, Budget Statement, 26 March 1980, in *Hansard,* vol. 981, 1474–7, <http://hansard.millbanksystems.com/commons/1980/mar/26/income-tax>.

19 'Digesting the Budget', BBC News, 10 March 1999, <http://news.bbc.co.uk/1/hi/events/budget_99/news/294083.stm>.

20 'Brown cuts basic tax rate by 2p', BBC News, 21 March 2007, <http://news.bbc.co.uk/1/hi/uk_politics/6472999.stm>.

21 See, for example, Graham Ruddick, 'Asda raises price paid to dairy
    farmer as value of milk sales plummets', *Guardian*, 13 August
    2015, <https://www.theguardian.com/business/2015/aug/13/
    value-uk-milk-sales-plummet-pressure-mounts-dairy-farmers>.

22 See generally William R. Berends, *$ Price & Profit %: The Essential Guide
    to Product & Service Pricing and Profit Forecasting* (Oakville: Berends &
    Associates, 2004).

23 See generally Toby C. Rider, *Cold War Games: Propaganda, the Olympics,
    and US Foreign Policy* (Champaign: University of Illinois Press, 2016);
    Steven Ungerleider, *Faust's Gold: Inside the East German Doping Machine*
    (CreateSpace, 2013); Michael Krüger, Christian Becker and Stefan Nielsen,
    German Sports, Doping, and Politics: A History of Performance Enhancement
    (Lanham: Rowman & Littlefield, 2015).

CHAPTER 4

1   Conversation with Michael Spence, recorded on 10 June 2016.

2   'A. Michael Spence – Biographical', NobelPrize.org, <http://www.nobelprize.
    org/nobel_prizes/economic-sciences/laureates/2001/spence-bio.html>. See
    also Michael Spence, 'Job Market Signaling', *Quarterly Journal of Economics*,
    87:3 (August 1973), 355–74.

3   George A. Akerlof, 'The Market for "Lemons": Quality Uncertainty and the
    Market Mechanism', *Quarterly Journal of Economics*, 84:3 (August 1970),
    488–500.

4   Michael Rothschild and Joseph Stiglitz, 'Increasing Risk: I. A Definition',
    Journal of Economic Theory, 2:3 (September 1970), 225–43.

5   Perhaps the earliest paper in this field is that of Kenneth J. Arrow,
    'Uncertainty and the Welfare Economics of Medical Care', *American
    Economic Review*, 53:5 (December 1963), 941–73.

6   See generally Brian Hillier, *The Economics of Asymmetric Information* (New
    York: Palgrave Macmillan, 1997).

7   Charles Darwin, letter to Asa Gray, 3 April 1860. Available via the Darwin
    Correspondence Project: <https://www.darwinproject.ac.uk/letter/DCP-
    LETT-2743.xml>.

8   See, for example, David Catchpoole, 'Peacock tail tale failure: Charles
    Darwin's "theory of sexual selection" fails to explain the very thing
    Darwin concocted it for', Creation.com, 6 June 2008, <http://creation.com/
    peacock-tail-tale-failure>.

9   Charles Darwin, *The Descent of Man, and Selection in Relation to Sex*
    (London: John Murray, 1871).

10 See Amotz Zahavi, 'Mate Selection – A Selection for a Handicap', *Journal of
    Theoretical Biology*, 53:1 (October 1975), 205–14; Amotz Zahavi and Avishag
    Zahavi, *The Handicap Principle: A Missing Piece of Darwin's Puzzle* (Oxford:
    Oxford University Press, 1997); and Alan Grafen, 'Biological Signals as
    Handicaps', *Journal of Theoretical Biology*, 144:4 (June 1990), 517–46.

11 The seminal work in this field was Vincent P. Crawford and Joel Sobel, 'Strategic Information Transmission', *Econometrica*, 50:6 (November 1982), 1431–51.

12 For a useful account and critique of the economics of cheap talk, see Joseph Farrell and Matthew Rabin, 'Cheap Talk', *Journal of Economic Perspectives*, 10:3 (summer 1996), 103–18.

13 Alex Konrad, 'Even With Record Price, Expect a $10 Million Super Bowl Ad Soon', *Forbes*, 2 February 2013, <http://www.forbes.com/sites/alexkonrad/2013/02/02/even-with-record-prices-10-million-spot/#7df2842d2f02>.

14 This kind of account of advertising started with Phillip Nelson in 'Information and Consumer Behavior', *Journal of Political Economy*, 78:2 (March–April 1970), 311–29, and 'Advertising as Information', *Journal of Political Economy*, 82:4 (July–August 1974), 729–54. See also Evan Davis, John Kay and Jonathan Star, 'Is advertising rational?', *Business Strategy Review*, 2:3 (autumn 1991), 1–23.

15 For example, it might be that more efficient producers have lower costs and can thus afford to advertise more.

16 Tülin Erdem and Joffre Swait, 'Brand Equity as a Signaling Phenomenon', *Journal of Consumer Psychology*, 7:2 (December 1998), 131–57.

17 'Actress Catherine Zeta-Jones Signs with T-Mobile International as Global Spokeswoman', T-Mobile press release, 11 June 2002, <https://newsroom.t-mobile.com/news-and-blogs/actress-catherine-zeta-jones-signs-with-t-mobile-international-as-global-spokeswoman.htm>.

18 T-Mobile were shown a draft of this section, but had no comment other than to stress that 'referring to consumers as "dim" and/or "naive" doesn't fit at all with how we talk about or perceive consumers as a company'.

19 Zeta-Jones's presence in the ad might tell us that people who like Catherine Zeta-Jones are the sort of people who might like T-Mobile. I would regard that as a likely account if a choice of mobile phone provider was conspicuously consumed, and had elements of fashion or taste around it like the choice of dress or car. But it isn't in this category. And I suspect that T-Mobile's target market was rather wider than that of Zeta-Jones types or their followers.

20 See, for example, Joel Sobel, 'Signaing Games', *Encyclopedia of Complexity and Systems Science* (New York: Springer Science+Business Media, 2015), pp. 8125–39.

CHAPTER 5

1 'Teachers in Space: A Chronology', *Education Week*, 17:20 (28 January 1998), p. 12.

2 John C. Wright, Dale Kunkel, Marites Pinon and Aletha C. Huston, 'How Children Reacted to Televised Coverage of the Space Shuttle Disaster', *Journal of Communication*, 39:2 (June 1989), 27–45.

3 Conversation with Steve Nesbitt, recorded on 10 December 2016.

4 'Challenger timeline', Spaceflight Now, <http://spaceflightnow.com/challenger/timeline/>.

5 'Full Metal Jacket (1987) Quotes', IMDb, <http://www.imdb.com/title/tt0093058/quotes>.

6 'Apologetic Jackson says "costume reveal" went awry', CNN, 3 February 2004, <http://edition.cnn.com/2004/US/02/02/superbowl.jackson/>.

7 It has made appearances in Friends, Mad Men and The Grinch Who Stole Christmas. See, for example, the TV Tropes website <http://tvtropes.org/pmwiki/pmwiki.php/Main/OhTheHumanity>.

8 Further reading: Mark T. Conard and Aeon J. Skoble (eds), Woody Allen and Philosophy: You Mean My Whole Fallacy Is Wrong? (Chicago: Open Court, 2004), p. 162.

9 'The Queen in Ireland: Dublin Castle speech in full', Daily Telegraph, 18 May 2011, <http://www.telegraph.co.uk/news/uknews/queen-elizabeth-II/8522318/The-Queen-in-Ireland-Dublin-Castle-speech-in-full.html>.

10 David Gardner and John Murray Brown, 'The Queen in Ireland: A sovereign's debt', Financial Times, 20 May 2011, <https://www.ft.com/content/eafb3d4e-8319-11e0-85a4-00144feabdc0>.

11 Further reading: Sarah Hyndman, Why Fonts Matter (London: Virgin Books, 2016).

12 Thomas Erskine May, A Treatise upon the Law, Privileges, Proceedings and Usage of Parliament (1844; Cambridge: Cambridge University Press, 2015), p. 203.

13 For a balanced, critical article on PC language from the early nineties see Michiko Kakutani, 'The Word Police', New York Times, 31 January 1993, <http://www.nytimes.com/1993/01/31/style/the-word-police.html?pagewanted=all>. On American school textbook policing: 'Language police bar "old," "blind"', CNN, 28 May 2003, <http://edition.cnn.com/2003/EDUCATION/05/28/life.language.reut/index.html?iref=mpstoryview>.

14 As the actor Benedict Cumberbatch did in January 2015, for which he faced some criticism on social media. See Daniel Welsh, 'Benedict Cumberbatch's Comments About "Coloured" Actors Have Landed Him In Trouble on Twitter', Huffington Post, 26 January 2015, <http://www.huffingtonpost.co.uk/2015/01/26/benedict-cumberbatch-coloured-actors-backlash-twitter_n_6547906.html>. See also Dot Wordsworth, 'What Benedict Cumberbatch didn't understand about "coloured"', Spectator, 31 January 2015, <http://www.spectator.co.uk/2015/01/what-benedict-cumberbatch-didnt-understand-about-coloured/>.

15 John Humphrys, Lost for Words: The Mangling and Manipulating of the English Language (London: Hodder & Stoughton, 2004), p. 13.

16 Ibid., p. 164.

17 Ibid., p. 259.

18 Ibid., p. 261.

19 George Orwell, 'Politics and the English Language' (1946), <http://www.orwell.ru/library/essays/politics/english/e_polit/>.

20 The six rules are: '1. Never use a metaphor, simile, or other figure of speech which you are used to seeing in print. 2. Never use a long word where a short one will do. 3. If it is possible to cut a word out, always cut it out. 4. Never use the

passive where you can use the active. 5. Never use a foreign phrase, a scientific word, or a jargon word if you can think of an everyday English equivalent. 6. Break any of these rules sooner than say anything outright barbarous.'

21 Steven Pinker, *The Language Instinct* (New York: Harper Perennial Modern Classics, 1994), p. 18.

22 For accounts of one of the most well-known practitioners of the art of using the retail environment to attract a young demographic, see Emine Saner, 'Abercrombie & Fitch: for beautiful people only', *Guardian*, 28 April 2012, <https://www.theguardian.com/fashion/2012/apr/28/abercrombie-fitch-savile-row>; Nicolai Jørgensgaard Graakjær, 'Dance in the store: on the use and production of music in Abercrombie & Fitch', *Critical Discourse Studies*, 9:4 (November 2012), 393–406.

23 Colin Marrs, 'The Top 10 funniest TV ads of all time', *Campaign*, 4 December 2008, <http://www.campaignlive.co.uk/article/top-10-funniest-tv-ads-time/865453>.

24 For example, in Britain's EU referendum the Leave campaign managed to give two conflicting impressions: to the country at large, it was suggested that immigration would fall if the UK left the EU; to voters of South Asian heritage, the impression was left that there could be more immigration from Asia once the large number of EU migrants had been cut. While not logically inconsistent (you could reconcile the contradiction by having a little extra Asian immigration and a big drop in EU immigration), the two messages were clearly discordant. See Jim Pickard, 'Vote Leave woos British Asians with migration leaflets', *Financial Times*, 19 May 2016, <https://www.ft.com/content/94adcefa-1dd5-11e6-a7bc-ee846770ec15>.

25 For an interesting account of the relationship between Donald Trump and WWE, see Aaron Oster, 'Donald Trump and WWE: How the Road to the White House Began at "WrestleMania"', *Rolling Stone*, 1 February 2016, <http://www.rollingstone.com/sports/features/donald-trump-and-wwe-how-the-road-to-the-white-house-began-at-wrestlemania-20160201>.

26 See, for example, <https://www.youtube.com/watch?v=MMKFIHRpe7I&list=RDMMKFIHRpe7I#t=11>.

27 In 1989, 'spokesmen for the World Wrestling Federation testified ... before the New Jersey Senate that professional wrestling is just "entertainment" and that participants are trained to avoid serious injuries'. They declared it to be 'an activity in which participants struggle hand-in-hand primarily for the purpose of providing entertainment to spectators rather than conducting a bona fide athletic contest'. See Peter Kerr, 'Now It Can Be Told: Those Pro Wrestlers Are Just Having Fun', *New York Times*, 10 February 1989, <http://www.nytimes.com/1989/02/10/nyregion/now-it-can-be-told-those-pro-wrestlers-are-just-having-fun.html>.

28 See Katherine J. Cramer, *The Politics of Resentment: Rural Consciousness in Wisconsin and the Rise of Scott Walker* (Chicago: University of Chicago Press, 2016).

29 Jeff Guo, 'A new theory for why Trump voters are so angry – that actually makes sense', *Washington* Post, 8 November 2016, <https://www.

washingtonpost.com/news/wonk/wp/2016/11/08/a-new-theory-for-why-trump-voters-are-so-angry-that-actually-makes-sense/>.

30 Speech to New York Economic Club, 15 September 2016. Reported in Patrick Gillespie, 'Donald Trump check: Has NAFTA "destroyed our country?"', CNNMoney, 16 September 2016, <http://money.cnn.com/2016/09/16/news/economy/donald-trump-nafta-mexico-china-tariff/>.

31 Campaign speech in Minneapolis, 6 November 2016. Reported in Tessa Berenson, 'Donald Trump: Minnesota Has "Suffered Enough" Accepting Refugees', *Time*, 6 November 2016, <http://time.com/4560078/donald-trump-minnesota-somali-refugees/>.

32 Salena Zito, 'Taking Trump Seriously, Not Literally', *The Atlantic*, 23 September 2016, <http://www.theatlantic.com/politics/archive/2016/09/trump-makes-his-case-in-pittsburgh/501335/>.

33 Richard Fording and Sanford Schram, '"Low Information voters" are a crucial part of Trump's support', *Washington Post*, 7 November 2016, <https://www.washingtonpost.com/news/monkey-cage/wp/2016/11/07/low-information-voters-are-a-crucial-part-of-trumps-support/>.

CHAPTER 6

1 '2005 General Election Manifesto', The Official Monster Raving Loony Party, <https://www.loonyparty.com/history-4/loony-archive/2005-general-election-manifesto/>.

2 Robert M. Schindler and Patrick N. Kirby, 'Patterns of Rightmost Digits Used in Advertised Prices: Implications for Nine-Ending Effects', *Journal of Consumer Research*, 24:2 (September 1997), 192–201, <http://dept.camden.rutgers.edu/business/files/Schindler-Kirby-1997.pdf>.

3 Conversation with Robert Schindler, recorded on 3 June 2016.

4 'Number of qualifications obtained in Psychology', Higher Education Statistics Authority. The actual figures are 1995/96: 7345, 2015/16: 27,370.

5 Higher Education Statistics Agency (HESA), Students by subject 2015/16, <https://www.hesa.ac.uk/data-and-analysis>. The numbers starting full-time degrees are psychology 21,530, physics 5110.

6 'The Sveriges Riksbank Prize in Economic Sciences in Memory of Alfred Nobel 2002', Nobelprize.org, <http://www.nobelprize.org/nobel_prizes/economic-sciences/laureates/2002/>.

7 See generally Peter Diamond and Hannu Vartiainen, *Behavioral Economics and its Applications* (Princeton: Princeton University Press, 2012).

8 Stefano DellaVigna, 'Psychology and Economics: Evidence from the Field', *Journal of Economic Literature*, 47:2 (June 2009), 315–72, <http://www.aeaweb.org/articles.php?doi=10.1257/jel.47.2.315>.

9 Richard H. Thaler and Cass R. Sunstein, *Nudge: Improving Decisions about Health, Wealth, and Happiness* (London: Yale University Press, 2008).

10 Leo Benedictus, 'The nudge unit – has it worked so far?', *Guardian*,

2 May 2013, <https://www.theguardian.com/politics/2013/may/02/nudge-unit-has-it-worked>.

11 Jozef M. Nuttin, Jr, 'Narcissism beyond Gestalt and awareness: The name letter effect', *European Journal of Social Psychology*, 15:3 (July 1985), 353–61.

12 Uri Simonsohn, 'Spurious? Name Similarity Effects (Implicit Egotism) in Marriage, Job, and Moving Decisions', *Journal of Personality and Social Psychology*, 101:1 (July 2011), 1–24, <http://datacolada.org/wp-content/uploads/2015/04/Spurious-Published-JPSP.pdf>.

13 Noah J. Goldstein, Steve J. Martin and Robert B. Cialdini, *Yes! 50 Secrets from the Science of Persuasion* (London: Profile Books, 2007).

14 Robert M. Schindler and Thomas M. Kibarian, 'Increased Consumer Sales Response Through Use of 99-Ending Prices', *Journal of Retailing*, 72:2 (summer 1996), 187–99, <http://dept.camden.rutgers.edu/business/files/Schindler-Kibarian-1996.pdf>.

15 Daniel Kahneman, *Thinking, Fast and Slow* (London: Penguin, 2012).

16 Constance L. Hays, 'Variable-Price Coke Machine Being Tested', *New York Times*, 28 October 1999, <http://www.nytimes.com/1999/10/28/business/variable-price-coke-machine-being-tested.html>.

17 Mr Ivester's departure was not related to the episode described here. See Betsy Morris and Patricia Sellers with Natasha A. Tarpley, 'What Really Happened at Coke: Doug Ivester was a demon for information. But he couldn't see what was coming at the showdown in Chicago', *Fortune*, 10 January 2000, <http://archive.fortune.com/magazines/fortune/fortune_archive/2000/01/10/271736/index.htm>. He was contacted for comment, but no response was received.

18 Jon Lewis, 'Walnut the whippet has gone for his final walk and there wasn't a dry eye on the beach', *Plymouth Herald*, 12 November 2016, <http://www.plymouthherald.co.uk/not-a-dry-eye-on-the-beach-hundreds-of-dog-lovers-join-walnut-the-whippet-for-his-final-walk/story-29889665-detail/story.html>.

19 'Did the new John Lewis advert make you cry?', KVA Digital, 10 November 2016, <http://kvadigital.co.uk/index.php/voice/item/349-did-the-new-john-lewis-advert-make-you-cry>.

20 Walter R. Fisher, *Human Communication as Narration: Toward a Philosophy of Reason, Value, and Action* (Columbia: University of South Carolina Press, 1987).

21 'hello, we're innocent', Innocent Drinks, <www.innocentdrinks.co.uk/us/our-story>.

22 Richard Reed, one of the company's founders, does point out that the pot was 'the very antithesis of all microwave meals – made from nothing but fresh vegetables and wholegrains, they were made fresh each day, contained three portions of veg, were high fibre, low in salt and no sugar added, with zero processing, or additives of any kind'. The pots are no longer on sale.

23 Ronald Reagan, 'Address to the Nation on Tax Reform', 28 May 1985, <http://www.presidency.ucsb.edu/ws/?pid=38697>.

24 William F. Lewis, 'Telling America's story: Narrative form and the Reagan presidency', *Quarterly Journal of Speech*, 73 (1987), 280–302.

25 Ronald Reagan, 'Inaugural Address', 21 January 1985, <http://www. presidency.ucsb.edu/ws/?pid=38688]>.

26 Many argue Vladimir Putin is a prominent promoter of the myth of the Russian strongman and the authoritarian model to legitimise undermining democracy. See Miguel Vázquez Liñán, 'History as a propaganda tool in Putin's Russia', *Communist and Post-Communist Studies*, 43:2 (2010), 167–78, <http://dx.doi.org/10.1016/j.postcomstud.2010.03.001>; Emil Persson and Bo Petersson, 'Political mythmaking and the 2014 Winter Olympics in Sochi: Olympism and the Russian great power myth', *East European Politics*, 30:2 (2014), <http://dx.doi.org/10.1080/21599165.2013.877712>. This is not a new phenomenon either. See Jane Derose Evans, 'The Legends of Early Rome used as Political Propaganda in the Roman Republican and Augustan Periods (Numismatics, Painting, Sculpture)' (1985), Dissertations available from ProQuest, AAI8523409, <http://repository.upenn.edu/dissertations/AAI8523409/>.

27 Goldstein, Martin and Cialdini, *Yes!*, p. 9.

28 Further reading: Robin Mordfin, 'Why long lines can be good for shoppers, and business', *Chicago Booth Review*, 15 June 2015, <http://review. chicagobooth.edu/magazine/fall-2014/why-long-lines-can-be-good-for-shoppers-and-business>.

29 A famous example is the private polling of the Liberal Democrat Party in the run-up to the 2015 general election. See 'Lib Dem private polling', UK Polling Report, 20 February 2015, <http://ukpollingreport.co.uk/blog/archives/9259>.

30 See, for example, K. A. Neuendorf with T. Fennell, 'A social facilitation view of the generation of humor and mirth reactions: Effects of a laugh track', *Central States Speech Journal*, 39:1 (1988), 37–48.

31 See Robert R. Provine, *Laughter: A Scientific Investigation* (London: Penguin, 2001); T. A. Nosanchuk and Jack Lightstone, 'Canned laughter and public and private conformity', *Journal of Personality and Social Psychology*, 29:1 (January 1974), 153–6.

32 Jennifer Keishin Armstrong, 'Where does canned laughter come from – and where did it go?', BBC Culture, 26 September 2016, <http://www.bbc.co.uk/culture/story/20160926-where-does-canned-laughter-come-from-and-where-did-it-go>.

33 Quoted in '60 years ago today, "The Hank McCune Show" debuted on NBC – ushering in the laugh track on network TV', Archive of American Television website, 10 September 2010, <http://emmytvlegends.org/news/60-years-ago-today-the-hank-mccune-show-debuted-on-nbc-ushering-in-the-laugh-track-on-network>.

34 Jacob Smith, *Vocal Tracks: Performance and Sound Media* (Berkeley: University of California Press, 2008), p. 43.

35 Ibid., p. 47.

36 Ibid., p. 36.

37 Christine Emba, 'Confirmed: Echo chambers exist on social media. So what do we do about them?', *Washington Post*, 14 July 2016,

<https://www.washingtonpost.com/news/in-theory/wp/2016/07/14/
confirmed-echo-chambers-exist-on-social-media-but-what-can-we-do-
about-them/?utm_term=.871dcb711524>; Filippo Menczer, 'Fake Online
News Spreads Through Social Echo Chambers', *Scientific American*,
28 November 2016, <https://www.scientificamerican.com/article/
fake-online-news-spreads-through-social-echo-chambers/>.

38 Featured in Reid Hastie and Robyn M. Dawes, *Rational Choice in an
Uncertain World: The Psychology of Judgement and Decision Making*
(Thousand Oaks: Sage Publications, 2001), p. 103.

39 Fritz Strack and Thomas Mussweiler, 'Explaining the Enigmatic Anchoring
Effect: Mechanisms of Selective Accessibility', *Journal of Personality and
Social Psychology*, 73:3 (1997), 437–46, <http://bear.warrington.ufl.edu/
brenner/mar7588/Papers/strack-mussweiler-jpsp97.pdf>.

40 Amos Tversky and Daniel Kahneman, 'Judgement Under Uncertainty:
Heuristics and Biases', *Science*, 185:4157 (September 1974), 1124–31, <http://
links.jstor.org/sici?sici=0036-8075%2819740927%293%3A185%3A4157%3C11
24%3AJUUHAB%3E2.0.CO%3B2-M>.

41 Dan Ariely, George Lowenstein and Drazen Prelec, '"Coherent arbitrariness":
stable demand curves without stable preferences', *Quarterly Journal of
Economics*, 118:1 (February 2003), 73–105, <http://web.mit.edu/ariely/www/
MIT/Papers/CA.pdf>.

42 George Lakoff, *Don't Think of an Elephant! Know Your Values and Frame the
Debate: The Essential Guide for Progressives* (White River Junction: Chelsea
Green, 2004).

43 The Dyson press office was invited to comment, but declined to do so.

44 Marc Prieto, 'Do Amateur Sellers Adopt the Professionals' Price Ending
Formats? Lessons from the Used Car Market', *Journal of Applied Business
Research*, 30:2 (2014), 387–96.

45 Jason Stanley, *How Propaganda Works* (Princeton: Princeton University
Press, 2015).

46 Jason Stanley, 'Beyond Lying: Donald Trump's Authoritarian Reality', *New
York Times*, 4 November 2016.

47 Ibid.

CHAPTER 7

1 T. Petanidou, D. Vokou and N. S. Margaris, 'Panaxia quadripunctaria in the
highly touristic Valley of Butterflies (Rhodes, Greece): conservation problems
and remedies', *Ambio*, 20:3–4 (1991), 124–8.

2 Discussion of short-termism in business: Roger L. Martin, 'Yes, Short-
Termism Really Is a Problem', *Harvard Business Review*, 9 October 2015;
Laurie Fitzjohn-Sykes, *Playing the Long Game: How to Save the West from
Short-Termism* (Luton: Andrews UK, 2015); Alfred Rappaport, *Saving
Capitalism from Short-Termism: How to Build Long-Term Value and Take
Back Our Financial Future* (New York: McGraw-Hill, 2011).

3 George Bush, 'Address Accepting the Presidential Nomination at the Republican National Convention in New Orleans', 18 August 1988. Transcript available via the American Presidency Project: <http://www.presidency.ucsb. edu/ws/?pid=25955>.

4 Sharon Waxman, 'After Hype Online, "Snakes on a Plane" Is Letdown at Box Office', *New York Times*, 21 August 2006, <http://www.nytimes. com/2006/08/21/movies/21box.html>. See also James Silver, 'How to flog a turkey', *Guardian*, 3 October 2005, <https://www.theguardian. com/film/2005/oct/03/pressandpublishing.sun>; Spencer Kornhaber, '"Snakes on a Plane," 5 Years Later', *The Atlantic*, 18 August 2011, <https://www.theatlantic.com/entertainment/archive/2011/08/ snakes-on-a-plane-5-years-later/243790/>.

5 New Line (Warner Bros) were invited to comment, but declined to do so.

6 There has been sporadic tongue-in-cheek talk of a sequel. Samuel L. Jackson is reported to have said of the idea, 'I don't know. If there is, I wouldn't mind doing it. I'm down with that.' Tambay A. Obenson, 'Samuel L. Jackson On "Snakes On A Plane 2," Dressing In Drag, Not Giving A F*ck & Doing TV', IndieWire, 18 December 2012, <http://www.indiewire.com/2012/12/samuel-l-jackson-on-snakes-on-a-plane-2-dressing-in-drag-not-giving-a-fck-doing-tv-139300/>.

7 Although there are some dysfunctions. For example, notoriously there is an incentive for the advertisers to quote selectively from reviews. Film critic Mark Kermode devoted a blog to this topic and quotes a review of his that said 'Sadly, *The Most Fertile Man in Ireland* is every bit as hilarious as the title suggests', which found its way on to the DVD box as 'Every bit as hilarious as the title suggests'. Mark Kermode, '*The Most Fertile Man in Ireland*', *Observer*, 22 June 2003, <https://www.theguardian.com/film/News_Story/ Critic_Review/Observer_review/0,4267,982428,00.html>. See also Benjamin Lee, 'How my negative review of *Legend* was spun into movie marketing gold', *Guardian*, 9 September 2015, <https://www.theguardian.com/film/ filmblog/2015/sep/09/legend-review-movie-marketing-false-advertising>.

8 Gideon Rachman, 'A survey of wine: The globe in a glass', *The Economist*, 16 December 1999.

9 For examples see the Pinterest pages 'Explore Honda Advertisement', <https://uk.pinterest.com/pin/322007442077454704/>, and 'Explore Old Hyundai Ads', <https://uk.pinterest.com/pin/532339618424069066/>.

10 Further reading: Koichi Shimokawa, *The Japanese Automobile Industry: A Business History* (London: Athlone, 1994).

11 P. A. Geroski and A. Murfin, 'Entry and industry evolution: the UK car industry, 1958–83', *Applied Economics*, 23:4 (1991). See also James Walker, 'Determinants of the Decline of British Leyland: The Roles of Product Quality, Advertising and Voluntary Export Restraints (1971–2002)', London School of Economics PhD thesis, <http://etheses.lse.ac.uk/1846/1/U206329.pdf>.

12 See generally James Ruppert, *The British Car Industry: Our Part in Its Downfall* (Bradenham: Foresight, 2008).

13 John R. Graham, Campbell R. Harvey and Shiva Rajgopal, 'The Economic Implications of Corporate Financial Reporting', *Journal of Accounting and*

Economics, 40:1–3 (2005), 3–73, fig. 6 and table 7, line 2. Available at: <https://faculty.fuqua.duke.edu/~charvey/Research/Published_Papers/P89_The_economic_implications.pdf>.

14 Peter F. Drucker (ed. Rick Wartzman), *The Drucker Lectures: Essential Lessons on Management, Society, and Economy* (New York: McGraw-Hill Education, 2010), p. 238.

15 See also M. P. Narayanan, 'Managerial Incentives for Short-term Results', *Journal of Finance*, 40:5 (December 1985), 1469–84.

16 Data from the American Presidency Project, <http://www.presidency.ucsb.edu/data/popularity.php>.

17 'Liberal Democrats: Say goodbye to broken promises', Liberal Democrats YouTube channel, uploaded 13 April 2010, <https://www.youtube.com/watch?v=jTLR8R9JXz4>.

18 Edward C. Banfield, *The Moral Basis of a Backward Society* (1958; New York: Free Press, 1967), p. 10.

CHAPTER 8

1 The *Oxford English Dictionary* defines 'literally' as 'In a literal, exact, or actual sense; not figuratively, allegorically, etc.', but gives its opposite as an additional, colloquial, definition: 'Used to indicate that some (freq. conventional) metaphorical or hyperbolical expression is to be taken in the strongest admissible sense: "virtually, as good as"; (also) "completely, utterly, absolutely"'.

2 See Tom Geoghan, 'The CV detectives', BBC News, 22 August 2005, <http://news.bbc.co.uk/1/hi/magazine/4167204.stm>. In academic studies, CV exaggeration comes under the term 'impression management' – see Stephen B. Knouse, 'Impressions of the resume: The effects of applicant education, experience, and impression management', *Journal of Business and Psychology*, 9:1 (September 1994), 33–45, <http://link.springer.com/article/10.1007/BF02230985>.

3 Carla Riemersma, *What Are the Odds: The Likelihood of Finding Love and Romance in Cyberspace* (Indianapolis: Dog Ear Publishing, 2008), p. 67.

4 See Elizabeth Wright, *From Fancy Pants to Getting There* (Luton: Andrews UK, 2014), ch. 15.

5 Monica T. Whitty, 'Revealing the "real" me, searching for the "actual" you: Presentations of self on an internet dating site', *Computers in Human Behavior*, 24:4 (July 2008), 1707–23, <https://www.loja.elsevier.com.br/bibliotecadigital/arquivo/artigo_sdol.pdf>.

6 Ibid.

7 Nicole Ellison, Rebecca Heino and Jennifer Gibbs, 'Managing Impressions Online: Self-Presentation Processes in the Online Dating Environment', *Journal of Computer-Mediated Communication*, 11:2 (January 2006), 415–41.

8 See also Nicole Ellison, Jeffrey T. Hancock and Catalina L. Toma, 'Profile as promise: A framework for conceptualizing veracity in online dating self-presentations', *New Media & Society*, 14:1 (June 2011), 45–62.

9   See, for example, Henrik Brumm and Sue Anne Zollinger, 'The evolution of the Lombard effect: 100 years of psychoacoustic research', *Behaviour*, 148:11–13 (November 2011), 1173–98.

10 Étienne Lombard, 'Le signe de l'élévation de la voix', *Annales des Maladies de l'Oreille et du Larynx*, 37:2 (1911), 101–19.

11 On Lombard's life and career see Harlan Lane and Bernard Tranel, 'The Lombard Sign and the Role of Hearing in Speech', *Journal of Speech, Language, and Hearing Research*, 14 (December 1971), 677–709, <http://jslhr.pubs.asha.org/article.aspx?articleid=1749461>; Marcel Lermoyez, 'Obituary: Étienne Lombard (Paris, 1869–1920) (A Translation)', <https://www.cambridge.org/core/services/aop-cambridge-core/content/view/S0022215100021575>.

12 Conversation with Andrew Parkin, recorded on 24 May 2016.

13 See Leandro Herrero, '"Simplify, then exaggerate": a saying from journalism, with different versions in our organizations', leandroherrero.com, 22 November 2014, <https://leandroherrero.com/first-simplify-then-exaggerate-a-journalism-saying-with-different-versions-in-our-organizations/>.

14 See Bill Saporito, 'The Conspiracy to End Cancer', *Time*, 1 April 2013.

15 Petroc Sumner, Christopher D. Chambers et al., 'The association between exaggeration in health related science news and academic press releases: retrospective observational study', *BMJ*, 349: g7015 (2014).

16 See Peter Preston, 'More popular than the populars: quality papers see circulation rise', *Guardian*, 24 April 2016, <https://www.theguardian.com/media/2016/apr/24/march-abcs-quality-newspapers-increase>; 'BBC Radio 1 loses a million listeners as Radio 4 hits new high', BBC News, 4 August 2016, <http://www.bbc.co.uk/news/entertainment-arts-36965649>.

17 Fan R., Zhao J., Chen Y. and Xu K., 'Anger is More Influential Than Joy: Sentiment Correlation in Weibo', *PLoS One*, 9:10 (October 2014).

18 See, for example, Ryan Holiday, *Trust Me, I'm Lying: Confessions of a Media Manipulator* (New York: Portfolio/Penguin, 2012), and his summary, 'I Helped Create the Milo Trolling Playbook. You Should Stop Playing Right Into It', *Observer*, 7 February 2017, <http://observer.com/2017/02/i-helped-create-the-milo-trolling-playbook-you-should-stop-playing-right-into-it/>.

19 *The Untouchables* (1987). For quote, see <http://www.imdb.com/title/tt0094226/trivia?tab=qt&ref_=tt_trv_qu>.

20 Mark Lilla, 'The End of Identity Liberalism', *New York Times*, 18 November 2016.

21 This account was put forward for example by the CNN political analyst Van Jones on the night of the presidential election. See 'Emotional Van Jones: How do I explain this to my children?', CNN, 9 November 2016, <http://edition.cnn.com/videos/politics/2016/11/09/van-jones-emotional-election-results-sot.cnn>.

22 See, for example, Ian Leslie, 'There's one word that explains why I got it wrong over Brexit and Trump', *New Statesman*, 15 December 2016, <http://www.newstatesman.com/politics/uk/2016/12/there-s-one-word-explains-why-i-got-it-wrong-over-brexit-and-trump>.

23 For a good summary of some evidence on this, see German Lopez, 'Research says there are ways to reduce racial bias. Calling people racist isn't one of them', *Vox*, 15 November 2016, <http://www.vox.com/identities/2016/11/15/13595508/racism-trump-research-study>.

24 Chris Neiger, 'To honk or not to honk', BBC Autos, 13 November 2014, <http://www.bbc.com/autos/story/20141030-to-honk-or-not-to-honk>.

25 Paul A. David, 'Clio and the Economics of QWERTY', *American Economic Review*, 75:2 (May 1985), 332–7; Paul A. David, 'Understanding the Economics of QWERTY: The Necessity of History' in William Nelson Parker (ed.), *Economic History and the Modern Economist* (New York: Basil Blackwell, 1986). See also 'The QWERTY myth', *The Economist*, 1 April 1999, <http://www.economist.com/node/196071>.

26 S. J. Liebowitz and Stephen E. Margolis, 'The Fable of the Keys', *Journal of Law and Economics*, 33 (April 1990), <http://www.utdallas.edu/~liebowit/keys1.html>.

27 Dan Ariely, *The (Honest) Truth About Dishonesty: How We Lie to Everyone – Especially Ourselves* (New York: HarperCollins, 2012).

28 See, for example, Jim Pickard, 'Jeremy Corbyn debuts his new style of people's PMQs', *Financial Times*, 16 September 2015, <https://www.ft.com/content/c599a046-5c67-11e5-9846-de406ccb37f2>; Emily Ashton, 'People Prefer Jeremy Corbyn's New Style of PMQs, Poll Suggests', BuzzFeed, 14 October 2015, <https://www.buzzfeed.com/emilyashton/people-prefer-jeremy-corbyns-new-style-of-pmqs-poll-suggests?utm_term=.dn5lB6K7Q#.egxJ68nab>; Isabel Hardman, 'How Corbyn failed to transform PMQs', *Spectator*, 1 March 2017, <http://blogs.spectator.co.uk/2017/03/just-answer-question-public-thinks-pmqs/>.

29 James B. Stockdale and Sybil Stockdale, *In Love and War: The Story of a Family's Ordeal and Sacrifice during the Vietnam Years* (New York: Harper & Row, 1984).

30 Conversation with Taylor Stockdale, recorded on 25 July 2016.

31 Jim Collins, *Good to Great: Why Some Companies Make the Leap ... And Others Don't* (New York: HarperCollins, 2001).

32 M. J. Stephey, 'Top 10 Veep Debate Moments – Perot's Tongue-Tied Running Mate', *Time*, undated, <http://content.time.com/time/specials/packages/article/0,28804,1846388_1846409_1846427,00.html>.

CHAPTER 9

1 Dr Nicola Rooney and Dr David Sargan, *Pedigree Dog Breeding in the UK: A Major Welfare Concern?* (Horsham: RSPCA, 2009), <https://www.rspca.org.uk/ImageLocator/LocateAsset?asset=document&assetId=1232712491490&mode=prd>.

2 See Felicity Lawrence and Helen Pidd, 'It's time to junk the junk food', *Guardian*, 10 March 2005, <https://www.theguardian.com/education/2005/mar/10/schoolmeals.schools>. See also Jamie Oliver's UK school dinners campaign website <http://www.feedmebetter.com>.

3 See generally Andrew Ross Sorkin, *Too Big to Fail: Inside the Battle to Save Wall Street* (London: Penguin, 2010); Robert J. Shiller, *The Subprime Solution: How Today's Global Financial Crisis Happened, and What to Do about It* (Princeton: Princeton University Press, 2012).

4 See generally Colin Read, *The Corporate Financiers: Williams, Modigliani, Miller, Coase, Williamson, Alchian, Demsetz, Jensen, Meckling* (New York: Springer, 2014).

5 William A. Barnett and Robert Solow, 'An Interview with Franco Modigliani', *Macroeconomic Dynamics*, 4:2 (June 2000), 222–56.

6 For a rich resource of material about Psychological Operations and Warfare, see <http://www.psywar.org>.

7 John Bradshaw, *In Defence of Dogs: Why Dogs Need Our Understanding* (London: Allen Lane, 2011).

8 To avoid having to incorporate the fee in the headline price, Ryanair used to charge additional fees for using any card except for its own obscure pre-payment card. This practice ended after an investigation by the Office of Fair Trading. See 'Airlines/Payment Surcharges: Investigation into pricing practices by 14 airlines', <http://webarchive.nationalarchives. gov.uk/20140402142426/http://www.oft.gov.uk/OFTwork/consumer-enforcement/consumer-enforcement-completed/card-surcharges/>. See also Ed Monk, 'End to Ryanair debit card tricks as budget airlines forced to include payment fee in ticket price', *Daily Mail*, 5 July 2012, <http://www.thisismoney.co.uk/money/holidays/article-2169087/End-Ryanair-debit-card-tricks-budget-airlines-forced-include-payment-fee-ticket-price.html>.

9 Opinion is divided as to the nature and operation of compassion fatigue. For a useful discussion of these ideas and a summary of the evidence, see David Campbell, 'The Myth of Compassion Fatigue', david-campbell.org, February 2012, <https://www.david-campbell.org/wp-content/documents/DC_Myth_of_Compassion_Fatigue_Feb_2012.pdf>.

10 David Halpern, the head of the Behavioural Insights Team set up by the British government, sets his watch three minutes fast. Mr Halpern has argued that it does work to put your watch a few minutes fast on the occasions that you are not consciously thinking hard about your timing. He has said of it, 'Periodically I think "this is really stupid" and set [my watch] to normal time, the right time, and then I miss my train.' See Nick Miller, 'Nudge-unit trials reveal best ways to prod people', *Sydney Morning Herald*, 29 August 2015, <http://www.smh.com.au/world/nudgeunit-trials-reveal-best-ways-to-prod-people-20150826-gj7yoo.html>.

11 'In Conversation with Daniel Kahneman', London School of Economics, 1 June 2012, <http://www.lse.ac.uk/website-archive/newsAndMedia/videoAndAudio/channels/publicLecturesAndEvents/player.aspx?id=1502>.

12 Ted J. Kaptchuk et al., 'Placebos without Deception: A Randomized Controlled Trial in Irritable Bowel Syndrome', *PLoS One*, 5:12 (2010), e15591.

13 See, for example, Boris Johnson's attempt to expose the comedy quiz show *Have I Got News for You*: 'I was stitched up', *Spectator*, 1 May 1998, <http://archive.spectator.co.uk/article/2nd-may-1998/16/i-was-stitched-up>. As one

who has been on the show, it felt to me more spontaneous than Mr Johnson's article implied.

14 The IPA documents outline many criteria for the Effectiveness Awards, including 'Scale of task: How difficult is the communications task undertaken?' This could be interpreted as looking at the quality of the product being marketed, although the guidance does not interpret it that way. See '2016 Effectiveness Awards writing pack', IPA, 25 January 2016, <http://www.ipa.co.uk/document/2016-effectiveness-awards-writing-pack>.

15 Jonathan Salem Baskin, 'How Come Bad Ads Sell Good Products, But Good Ads Can't Sell Bad Ones?', *Forbes*, 28 November 2012, <http://www.forbes.com/sites/jonathansalembaskin/2012/11/28/how-come-bad-ads-sell-good-products-and-good-ads-cant-sell-bad-ones/#36111e9d260e]>.

16 Paul Krugman, 'The Populism Perplex', *New York Times*, 25 November 2016, <https://www.nytimes.com/2016/11/25/opinion/the-populism-perplex.html>.

17 An example of someone doing this is the economist Simon Wren-Lewis, who wrote a blog about the 2015 British general election that suggested it was myths about Labour and Conservative economic competence – propagated or not falsified by the media – that '*probably* had a decisive role in winning [the Conservatives] the election'. He suggests that 'Political scientists need to reflect on what this means for their models of how elections are won and lost'. Professor Wren-Lewis could be right, or it could be that the public framed their views on economic policy very differently to the way he would. Simon Wren-Lewis, 'Recognising the success of macroeconomic myths', Mainly Macro blog, 29 May 2015, <https://mainlymacro.blogspot.co.uk/2015/05/recognising-success-of-macroeconomic.html>.

18 See John R. Baldwin, Stephen D. Perry and Mary Anne Moffitt, *Communication Theories for Everyday Life* (London: Pearson, 2004); Richard E. Petty, Thomas M. Ostrom and Timothy C. Brock (eds), *Cognitive Responses in Persuasion* (Mahwah: Lawrence Erlbaum Associates, 1981).

19 For the earliest published article on the Overton window for a general audience, by the research institute of which Joseph Overton was vice-president, see Nathan J. Russell, 'An Introduction to the Overton Window of Political Possibilities', Mackinac Center for Public Policy, 4 January 2006, <http://www.mackinac.org/7504>. John Lanchester famously referred to it with respect to the Brexit debate: 'Brexit Blues', *London Review of Books*, 38:15 (28 July 2015), 3–6.

20 See Doni Bloomfield and Noah Buhayar, 'Buffett Follows "Avarice" Warning by Keeping $100,000 Salary', Bloomberg, 13 March 2015, <https://www.bloomberg.com/news/articles/2015-03-13/buffett-follows-avarice-warning-by-sticking-to-100-000-salary>.

21 All these quotations are taken from the transcript of my own interview with Mr Buffett, filmed on 27 August 2009 for a BBC documentary, *The World's Greatest Money Maker*. There was too much material in the interview to be used in the broadcast, and so quotations used here may not have appeared in the programme.

22 In fact, I have quoted him myself in the notes to Chapter 7.

23 *The World's Greatest Money Maker*, BBC, 26 October 2009.

24 *2011 Annual Report*, Berkshire Hathaway Inc., 2012, pp. 4, 5, <http://www.berkshirehathaway.com/2011ar/2011ar.pdf>.

25 Warren E. Buffett, 'An Owner's Manual: A Message from Warren E. Buffett, Chairman and CEO', Berkshire Hathaway Inc., January 1999, <http://www.berkshirehathaway.com/owners.html>.

26 For a discussion of Pinochet's reputation see Luis Eduardo Barrueto and Carlos Sabino, 'Was Augusto Pinochet a Villain or Hero for Chile?', *Panam Post*, 24 February 2015, <https://panampost.com/panam-staff/2015/02/24/was-augusto-pinochet-a-villain-or-hero-for-chile/>.

CHAPTER 10

1 See Harry G. Frankfurt, 'Donald Trump Is BS, Says Expert in BS', *Time*, 12 May 2016, <http://time.com/4321036/donald-trump-bs/>; Michael Kinsley, 'Why It's Pointless To Fact-Check Donald Trump', *Vanity Fair*, 8 February 2016, <http://www.vanityfair.com/news/2016/02/politics-media-gaffes-lies>.

2 This is commonly held to be out of the playbook of campaign expert Lynton Crosby. See, for example, Jon Quinn, 'Seven lessons from the Tory election campaign', Charity Comms, 26 May 2015, <http://www.charitycomms.org.uk/articles/seven-lessons-from-the-tory-election-campaign>.

3 'Government forced to publish list of "priority investors" given lion's share of Royal Mail shares – Chuka Umunna', LabourPress, 30 April 2014.

4 'Response to updated Help to Buy figures', LabourPress, 23 March 2014.

5 'Report further highlights need to act as quickly as possible to reform consumer credit market – Stella Creasy', LabourPress, 24 March 2014.

6 'Response to FCA report on pension annuities – Gregg McClymont', LabourPress, 14 February 2014.

7 'NAO Progress Report on the Regional Growth Fund – Response from Toby Perkins', LabourPress, 25 February 2014.

8 'Ministers have got their sums badly wrong and left a black hole in the student finance budget – Umunna', LabourPress, 22 March 2014.

9 'The State of the NHS – speech by Andy Burnham', LabourPress, 3 February 2014.

10 'Power and One Nation Jon Cruddas' Speech to the NLGN Annual Conference', LabourPress, 12 February 2014.

11 'New consumer powers for open competition, not broken competition – Miliband', LabourPress, 19 January 2014.

12 Donald J. Trump, speech at a rally in Des Moines, Iowa, 8 December 2016. See <https://www.youtube.com/watch?v=OfzRlvR83M0>.

13 'Transcript: Donald Trump on NATO, Turkey's Coup Attempt and the World', *New York Times*, 21 July 2016.

14 Barney Henderson, 'Donald Trump savages Japan, saying all they will do is "watch Sony TVs" if US is attacked and threatening to "walk" away from treaty', *Daily Telegraph*, 6 August 2016, <http://www.telegraph.co.uk/news/

2016/08/05/donald-trump-savages-japan-saying-all-they-will-do-is-watch-sony/>.

15 The CNN poll can be found at <http://edition.cnn.com/election/results/exit-polls>. The question *Is Hillary Clinton honest and trustworthy?* saw responses of 36 per cent yes, 61 per cent no. The question *Is Donald Trump honest and trustworthy?* yielded 33 per cent yes and 64 per cent no.

16 Further reading: Charles Tilly, *Popular Contention in Great Britain, 1758–1834* (Boulder: Paradigm, 2005); Frances Fox Piven and Richard A. Cloward, *Poor People's Movements: Why They Succeed, How They Fail* (New York: Vintage, 1979); Nicholas John Cull, David Holbrook Culbert and David Welch, *Propaganda and Mass Persuasion: A Historical Encyclopedia, 1500 to the Present* (Santa Barbara: ABC-Clio, 2003).

17 Further reading: Charles Duhigg, *The Power of Habit: Why We Do What We Do, and How to Change* (London: William Heinemann, 2012).

18 Ian Leslie, *Born Liars: Why We Can't Live Without Deceit* (London: Quercus, 2011).

19 Paul Boyle has made this point on various occasions, including at a conference of the Institute of Chartered Secretaries and Administrators on 2 October 2008. The precise text quoted here is taken from an email exchange with Mr Boyle.

20 Although this line is also attributed to John Maxwell, Roosevelt would have come earlier – though there isn't any record of it in the online archive of his presidential library.

21 Mark Schmitt, 'It's Not What You Say About the Issues . . . ', The Decembrist, 14 September 2004, <http://markschmitt.typepad.com/decembrist/2004/09/its_what_the_is.html>.

22 Ezra Klein, 'What Donald Trump understands that Hillary Clinton doesn't, and vice versa', *Vox*, 26 January 2016, <http://www.vox.com/2016/1/26/10833028/donald-trump-hillary-clinton>.

23 Robert Phillips, *Trust Me, PR is Dead* (London: Unbound, 2015).

24 Henry Mance, 'Review: Trust Me, PR is Dead by Robert Phillips', *Financial Times*, 24 June 2015, <https://www.ft.com/content/172832e4-18c8-11e5-8201-cbdb03d71480>. In the review, Mr Mance offers the Thomas Cook example as a counter to the argument of Phillips's book. He says it suggests that a good communications strategy *is* important. For me, it makes the case that a good communications strategy should focus on the overall impression of the organisation, rather than winning the specific point.

25 Jonathan Guthrie, 'Thomas Cook shows how to turn private tragedy into public outrage', *Financial Times*, 20 May 2015, <https://www.ft.com/content/0300ee10-ff18-11e4-84b2-00144feabdc0>.

26 Further reading: James H. Gilmore and B. Joseph Pine II, *Authenticity: What Consumers Really Want* (Boston: Harvard Business School Press, 2007); Charles Taylor, *The Ethics of Authenticity* (Cambridge, MA: Harvard University Press, 1991).

27 Further reading: Jerry Vass, *Soft Selling in a Hard World: Plain Talk on the Art of Persuasion* (Philadelphia: Running Press, 1998).

28   In a debate about the UK's nuclear deterrent, Mr Corbyn argued against the
      renewal of the Trident missile system, even though it was his own party's
      policy. Several of his backbench MPs urged him to follow the party line but
      he refused. One exchange went as follows:

>   Kevan Jones: Like me, my right honourable friend stood in May
>   2015 on the basis of a party policy which had been agreed at our
>   conference, through our mechanisms in the party, and which
>   supported the renewal of our continuous at-sea deterrent. He now
>   has a shadow Front Bench and a shadow Cabinet in his own image,
>   who, I understand, agreed last week to present that policy from the
>   Front Bench. Is he going to do it, or will it be done by the Member
>   who winds up the debate?
>
>   Jeremy Corbyn: My honourable friend is well aware of what the policy was.
>   He is also well aware that a policy review is being undertaken, and he is
>   also well aware of the case that I am making for nuclear disarmament.

      See *Hansard*, vol. 613, 18 July 2016, <https://hansard.digiminster.com/
      commons/2016-07-18/debates/7B7A196B-B37C-4787-99DC-098882B3EFA2/
      UKSNuclearDeterrent>.

29   Appearance on David Axelrod's podcast *The Axe Files*, 9 May 2016.

30   BBC World Service *Newshour* interview with John Kerry, 6 January 2017. An
      excerpt that includes the quoted material is available at <http://www.bbc.
      co.uk/news/world-us-canada-38538589>.

31   See Stephen G. Post, 'Altruism, Happiness, and Health: It's Good to Be Good',
      International Journal of Behavioral Medicine, 12:2 (2005), 66–77; Elizabeth
      W. Dunn, Lara B. Aknin and Michael I. Norton, 'Spending Money on Others
      Promotes Happiness', *Science*, 319:1687 (2008).

32   'Q & A: Open Refrigerator', Ask the Van: Department of Physics, University
      of Illinois at Urbana-Champaign, 23 April 2008, <https://van.physics.illinois.
      edu/qa/listing.php?id=1790>.

CHAPTER 11

1   'Evan Davis meets Rob George', *One to One*, BBC Radio 4, 8 November 2011,
      <http://www.bbc.co.uk/programmes/b016wxtz>.

2   'Borntoosoon', 'Want to shoot myself in the head', baldtruthtalk, 4 April 2016,
      <https://www.baldtruthtalk.com/threads/23590-Want-to-shoot-myself-in-
      the-head>.

3   The example here assumes an average hair per graft rate of 2.22. A single
      graft normally comprises between two and three hairs, and two-hair grafts
      occur more commonly than three-hair grafts. See Florence Vincent, 'Is a
      hair transplant worth the cost?', OnlineHealth, 3 October 2014, <https://
      onlinedoctor.lloydspharmacy.com/blog/hair-transplant-worth-cost/>.

4   'Effectiveness of 5% Minoxidil in Treating Male-Pattern Hair Loss',
      International Society of Hair Restoration Surgery, 26 August 2012, <www.
      ishrs.org/articles/minoxidil-study.htm>.

5   'Propecia: Five Year FDA Clinical Trial Results', HairLossTalk, undated, <https://www.hairlosstalk.com/treatments/propecia/5-year-trial-results/>.

6   The Belgravia Centre website's page detailing male hair loss treatment says: 'Please be aware that the many products that are advertised for hair loss have no clinical evidence to support their claims for hair loss prevention. The "primary" hair loss treatments that form the core of most of Belgravia's hair loss treatment programmes are medically proven to prevent hair loss or regrow hair and most men who use our treatment combinations will achieve this goal.' The primary treatments listed are Finasteride and Minoxidil. See 'Hair Loss Treatments', The Belgravia Centre, undated, <http://www. belgraviacentre.com/hair-loss-treatment-men/>.

7   The Belgravia clinic also told me via email that 'In terms of continued results – once patients have had the initial regrowth, unless they choose to use additional treatments at a later date (if they are not already using the optimum combination for them), it is unlikely density will continue to improve after the first 12 months. After this period the hair density will be maintained, or may thin over time, but at a much slower rate than if they weren't using treatment.' The implication of this is that it is unlikely that the long-term success stories would be more impressive than the shorter-term ones on display. The clinic says it is now looking into getting follow-up success stories. It has not done so hitherto, mainly because once it has taken photos of a happy customer, it doesn't usually go back to ask the same client for another photo later.

8   '7 Best Laser Combs for Hair Regrowth – Which is Best?', Nicehair, <http:// www.nicehair.org/worlds-best-laser-combs-for-hair-growth-which-is-best/>. Spelling of triphosphate has been amended.

9   Mostafa M. El-Bermawy, 'Your Filter Bubble is Destroying Democracy', *Wired*, 18 November 2016, <https://www.wired.com/2016/11/ filter-bubble-destroying-democracy/>.

10 For a brilliant example of this, look no further than Karl Popper, *Conjectures and Refutations: The Growth of Scientific Knowledge* (London: Routledge and Kegan Paul, 1963). In it he famously describes an anecdote involving the psychotherapist Alfred Adler: 'Once, in 1919, I reported to him a case which to me did not seem particularly Adlerian, but which he found no difficulty in analyzing in terms of his theory of inferiority feelings, although he had not even seen the child. Slightly shocked, I asked him how he could be so sure. "Because of my thousandfold experience," he replied; whereupon I could not help saying: "And with this new case, I suppose, your experience has become thousand-and-one-fold." What I had in mind was that his previous observations may not have been much sounder than this new one; that each in its turn had been interpreted in the light of "previous experience," and at the same time counted as additional confirmation.' (From p. 46 of the 2002 paperback reprint.)

11 See William Haltom and Michael W. McCann, *Distorting the Law: Politics, Media, and the Litigation Crisis* (Chicago: Chicago University Press, 2009), p. 215. The Liebeck case was also used by Republicans who were pushing for tort law reform. Republican Representative Michael Oxley said: 'Whenever

the public reads about a woman who spills coffee in her lap and gets $3 million, most people say this doesn't make a whole lot of sense.' (Ibid., p. 279.) The Republicans' 'Contract with America' reforms were the result. See also 'Are lawyers burning America?', *Newsweek*, 20 March 1995, <http://europe.newsweek.com/are-lawyers-burning-america-180680?rm=eu>.

12 Bonnie Bertram, 'Storm Still Brews Over Scalding Coffee', *New York Times*, 25 October 2013, <http://www.nytimes.com/2013/10/28/booming/storm-still-brews-over-scalding-coffee.html>.

13 Stephen Greenspan, *Annals of Gullibility: Why We Get Duped and How to Avoid It* (Santa Barbara: ABC-Clio, 2008), p. 181.

14 This argument has been made from a liberal perspective by the *Guardian* columnist Nick Cohen. See his 'Trump's lies are not the problem. It's the millions who swallow them who really matter', *Guardian*, 5 February 2017, <https://www.theguardian.com/commentisfree/2017/feb/05/donald-trump-lies-belief-totalitarianism>.

15 'Word of the Year 2016 is . . .', Oxford Dictionaries, <https://en.oxforddictionaries.com/word-of-the-year/word-of-the-year-2016>. The announcement that 'post-truth' had beaten other contenders also contains a brief history of the word, which traces its origin back to 1992.

16 The £285 million per week figure comes from the attachment to a letter from Sir Andrew Dilnot, the Chair of the UK Statistics Authority, to the Liberal Democrat MP Norman Lamb. dated 21 April 2016. The letter was accepted as the best statement of the official view of the cost of British membership of the EU. See <https://www.statisticsauthority.gov.uk/wp-content/uploads/2016/04/Letter-from-Sir-Andrew-Dilnot-to-Norman-Lamb-MP-210416.pdf>.

17 Dominic Cummings, 'Dominic Cummings: How the Brexit referendum was won', *Spectator*, 9 January 2017, <blogs.spectator.co.uk/2017/01/dominic-cummings-brexit-referendum-won/>. In the piece, Mr Cummings sets out the key Leave argument as being 'The official bill of EU membership is £350 million per week – let's spend our money on our priorities like the NHS instead', which was clearly rather different from the stronger formulation that was much used in the campaign: 'We send the EU £350 million a week'.

18 'Immigration is now the top issue for voters in the EU referendum', Ipsos MORI Political Monitor – June 2016, 16 June 2016.

19 'UK Statistics Authority statement on the use of official statistics on contributions to the European Union', UK Statistics Authority, 27 May 2016.

20 For one example, see Binyamin Appelbaum, 'Conflicting Policy From Trump: To Keep, and Remove, Tax Cut', *New York Times*, 16 September 2016, <https://www.nytimes.com/2016/09/17/us/politics/trump-tax-plan.html>.

21 For historians who explore this interpretation, see: Joachim C. Fest, *Hitler* (Boston: Houghton Mifflin Harcourt, 2013); Ian Kershaw, *Hitler* (London: Longman, 2000).

22 The Institute of Fiscal Studies found that in 2014/15 mean income had finally returned to its 2008/09 level. See Chris Belfield, Jonathan Cribb, Andrew Hood and Robert Joyce, *Living Standards, Poverty and Inequality in the UK:*

2016 (London: IFS, 2016), <https://www.ifs.org.uk/uploads/publications/comms/R117.pdf>.

23 On the Rhodes Must Fall campaign, see Jessica Elgot, '"Take it down!": Rhodes Must Fall campaign marches through Oxford', *Guardian*, 9 March 2016, <https://www.theguardian.com/education/2016/mar/09/take-it-down-rhodes-must-fall-campaign-marches-through-oxford>. For the Germaine Greer controversy, see Heather Saul, 'Germaine Greer defends "grossly offensive" comments about transgender women: "Just because you lop off your d**k doesn't make you a ******* woman"', *Independent*, 26 October 2015, <http://www.independent.co.uk/news/people/germaine-greer-defends-grossly-offensive-comments-about-transgender-women-just-because-you-lop-off-a6709061.html>.

24 On the Black Lives Matter movement, see Wesley Lowery, 'Black Lives Matter: birth of a movement', *Guardian*, 17 January 2017, <https://www.theguardian.com/us-news/2017/jan/17/black-lives-matter-birth-of-a-movement>. On the transgender bathroom debate, see Jeannie Suk Gersen, 'The Transgender Bathroom Debate and the Looming Title IX Crisis', *New Yorker*, 24 May 2016, <http://www.newyorker.com/news/news-desk/public-bathroom-regulations-could-create-a-title-ix-crisis>.

25 Dominic Cummings, 'Dominic Cummings: how the Brexit referendum was won'.

26 For one accusation of fake news being used as a deflection tactic, see Eli Stokols, 'Trump accuses Obama of "wire tapping" Trump Tower phones', *Politico*, 4 March 2017, <http://www.politico.com/story/2017/03/trump-obama-wire-tapping-trump-tower-phones-235679>.
    See also Karim Traboulsi, 'Assad adopts Trump's "fake-news" defence to dismiss war-crimes accusations', *Al-Araby: The New Arab*, 13 February 2017, <https://www.alaraby.co.uk/english/blog/2017/2/13/assad-adopts-trumps-fake-news-defence-to-dismiss-war-crimes-accusations>.

27 Ross Douthat, 'The Tempting of the Media', *New York Times*, 22 January 2017, <https://www.nytimes.com/2017/01/21/opinion/sunday/the-tempting-of-the-media.html?_r=0>.

28 Interview on BBC *Newsnight*, 23 January 2017.

29 In the UK there is Channel 4's FactCheck (<https://www.channel4.com/news/factcheck>), the BBC's Reality Check (<http://www.bbc.co.uk/news/topics/267ada11-b730-4344-b404-63067c032c65/reality-check>) and Full Fact, 'the UK's independent fact checking charity' (<https://fullfact.org/about/>). Similarly, in the US there are standalone organisations like Factcheck (<http://www.factcheck.org/>) and services within established media organisations such as the *Washington Post*'s Fact Checker (<https://www.washingtonpost.com/news/fact-checker/>). For an account of the rise of this type of journalism in the US, see Lucas Graves, *Deciding What's True: The Rise of Political Fact-Checking in American Journalism* (New York: Columbia University Press, 2016).

30 Liz Spayd, 'When to Call a Lie a Lie', *New York Times*, 20 September 2016. Liz Spayd is the public editor of the paper.

31 Gerard Baker, 'Trump, "Lies" and Honest Journalism', *Wall*

Street Journal, 4 January 2017, <https://www.wsj.com/articles/
trump-lies-and-honest-journalism-1483557700>.

32 The airline industry's transition from a 'blame' to a 'learning' culture is
widely cited in change management texts. See, for example, Peter Brandl,
*Crash Communication: Management Techniques from the Cockpit to
Maximize Performance* (New York: Morgan James, 2016).

33 Washington DC political commentator and founding editor of *Slate*, Michael
Kinsley, is widely credited with this particular definition, so that a 'Kinsley
gaffe' is 'when a politician tells the truth – or more precisely, when he or she
accidentally reveals something truthful about what is going on in his or her
head'. See Michael Kinsley, 'Gaffes Can Be Deceiving', *Time*, 2 February 2007,
for a development of Kinsley's earlier ideas on the subject. See also his *Curse
of the Giant Muffins: And Other Washington Maladies* (New York: Summit
Books, 1987), p. 272.

FINAL WORDS

1 See, generally, Robert Shogan, *No Sense of Decency: The Army–McCarthy
Hearings: A Demagogue Falls and Television Takes Charge of American
Politics* (Lanham: Ivan R. Dee, 2009).

2 Available to watch online at <https://www.youtube.com/watch?v=K1eA5bUzVjA>.

3 See, generally, Arthur Herman, *Joseph McCarthy: Reexamining the Life and
Legacy of America's Most Hated Senator* (New York: Simon and Schuster,
2000).

4 Michelle Dean, 'A mentor in shamelessness: the man who taught Trump the
power of publicity', *Guardian*, 20 April 2016, <https://www.theguardian.com/
us-news/2016/apr/20/roy-cohn-donald-trump-joseph-mccarthy-rosenberg-trial>.

ACKNOWLEDGEMENTS

Countless people – family, friends, journalists, a few politicians and quite a few people in the business of public relations – have helped stimulate my thinking for this book, and they have often done so without realising it. I shall not attempt to name them all here, but do want to acknowledge their wisdom and open-mindedness.

I owe a special debt to James W. Ramsay, who worked as my research assistant on the book and was invaluable in seeking out the facts on my behalf, often having to investigate whether they fitted the story that I had already started to write. It was sometimes tiresome work, and he did it intelligently and uncomplainingly.

I must also thank my colleagues at the BBC, and at *Newsnight* and the *Bottom Line* in particular. One couldn't ask for a more stimulating group of professionals to work with. There are few people who think harder about how to handle bullshit constructively than those who work at the corporation.

The BBC of course takes no responsibility for the contents of this book, but I'm grateful to Jo Carr for making it possible for me to write it. And especially to Malcolm Balen, who read it with a careful eye, and who gave extremely useful comments in a timely fashion. He didn't just find problems, he invariably offered solutions to them as well. Lucy Lunt was the producer of four interviews that focused on the subject of honesty in the Radio 4 *One to One* series; they contributed to my understanding of the issues before a word of this text had been typed.

My long-time friend Anne Coyle deserves acknowledgement as someone who was more helpful than she probably ever realised. Ian Leslie, too, gets my thanks. In the course of one lunch he managed to unload a huge number of useful insights that found their way into the text.

Michael Spence, Andrew Parkin, Steve Nesbitt, Robert Schindler, Chris Voss and Taylor Stockdale all generously gave their time, patiently answering my questions and offering their thoughts. They have all played a part in shaping the contents of the book.

Others who have helped in one way or another, or from whom I have stolen ideas or good lines, are David Weston, Charles Gant, Randeep Sidhu, David Wilkinson, Owain Fitz-Gibbon, Petr Prokopík, Peter Rollings, John Willman, Ben Page, Robert Philips, Rob George and Paul Boyle.

I am also grateful to those who have commented on particular sections of the book: Tracey O'Brien, John Humphrys, Lord Armstrong of Ilminster, Torsten Bell, Lord Howard of Lympne, Richard Reed and Jonny Harris.

The book would never have been started without the encouragement of Claire Conrad. And it would never have been finished without the support of my agent Will Francis, and Tim Whiting of Little, Brown. It was conversations between the three of us that gave a structure to the book and which brought discipline to the process of writing it.

Zoe Gullen had the thankless task of editing the text, so the least I can do is to thank her for the way she went about that.

Everyone mentioned here has been invaluable, and there

would be many errors in the book but for their help. Remaining mistakes are, unfortunately, my own responsibility.

Of course, the most special thanks go to my partner Guillaume. While it is often exciting to write a book, it is nothing but tedious to watch someone else doing so. And he has been wonderfully patient and supportive throughout.

INDEX

1600 Penn (NBC sitcom) ix
acoustic engineers 189–91, 199
actions and gestures: and
    allegiance 112–14, 115–20,
    149; broad judgements on
    narrow signals 63–6; corporate
    social responsibility (CSR)
    programmes 57; in corporate
    sphere 57; Dame Carcas
    myth 53–5, 76; dressing
    for the occasion 112, 201;
    hidden charges 62–3, 226;
    and message sending 55–7;
    in political sphere 57–62;
    projections of status 56–7;
    role of understatement 102–4;
    signalling theory 67–76, 77–84,
    85–7; smiles in photographs
    56; Trump and WWE 115–16;
    up-front prices vs ongoing
    charges 63, 127
adverse selection 71*
advertising and marketing xiii;
    celebrity endorsements 82–3;
    corporate brands xvi, 165–6,
    169, 173–5, 262, 263; evidence
    for success of 231–2; favoured
    bullshit of target market
    113–14; and framing 153–4;

hollow brand slogans xvi;
    IPA Effectiveness Awards
    231–2; prevention of outright
    lies 8; and quality of product
    231–2; signalling theory 80–4,
    85; subtle cues/dog whistles
    113–14
Advertising Standards Authority
    283
airline industry 226, 296
Akerlof, George 71
animals 68, 225
Annie Hall (Woody Allen film,
    1977) 98–9
Anthony Trollope, *The Way We
    Live Now* (1875) xiii
Apple 80
Ariely, Dan 202
Armstrong, Sir Robert 13–16
AT&T 123
authoritarian rhetoric 156–8

Baker, Gerard 292
baldness cures, male 276–9
bandwagon effect 145–9, 156, 197,
    224
Banfield, Edward, *The Moral Basis
    of a Backward Society* (1958)
    182–4

Barclays Bank, Annual Report
    (2007) 35–7, 38, 39, 243
BBC 43–5, 46–9, 194, 238–9, 294
behavioural economics 126–32,
    134–5
Behavioural Insights Team at
    Downing Street 127
Belgravia Centre 278
Berkshire Hathaway 239–40
Berlusconi, Silvio 232
Bilbao 64–5
biomedical science 193
Black, Max, 'The Prevalence of
    Humbug' 10–11
Black Lives Matter campaign 287
Blair, Tony 181; Case for Iraq War
    24–8
Bosi, Andrew 19
Boyle, Paul 258–9
Brexit 7, 137*, 288–9; see also EU
    referendum campaign, UK
British Leyland 175–6
Brown, Gordon 62, 149–50
Buffett, Warren 166*, 236–42, 243,
    246
bullshit: and 'cheap talk' theory
    75–6, 77–9, 85–7; collective
    responses 275–6, 283–6, 288,
    289–94; and costly signals
    73–5, 76–7, 78–9, 80–4, 85–6;
    deception through self-
    delusion 24–5, 28–9, 257–9;
    definitions of xiv–xv, xviii–xix,
    33–4; fact-free assertions
    of populists xi–xiii, 31–3,
    40; forms that hoodwink us
    123–34, 135–51, 152–6, 224,
    276–9; Harry G. Frankfurt
    on xv, 33–4, 38; gibberish
    49–50; gratuitously complex
    language 51; and gullibility
    xx, 84, 119, 125, 230–6, 279,

282–3; and habituation
    224–7; hope-mongers 276–9;
    latitude of acceptance/
    rejection 233–4; Lombard-
    type feedback effects 190, 191,
    192–200; Lovett on ix–xi, xiv;
    media reaction to 289–94;
    mental defences against
    224–30; over-confidence
    of PR professionals 216–17,
    222–3; and recognition 224–5,
    227–30; role of individual
    recipients 275, 276–83; and
    signalling theory 67–76, 77–84,
    85–7; target audience's pre-
    disposition 119–20, 152–4,
    158, 216, 229–30, 233, 235, 244,
    276–87; through disproportion
    23–4; transparency of 51–2;
    'your call is important to us'
    refrain xvi; see also actions
    and gestures; mendacity and
    deception; nonsense and
    gibberish; obfuscation
Burke, Edmund 13, 15
Burnham, Andy 250–1
Bush, George H. W. 163*, 180
Bush, George W. 180
BuzzFeed 5–6

Caesar, Sid 147
Capital Transport Campaign 19
car alarms 225
car manufacturers 165–6; British
    car industry 175–6; gaming
    of emission test results 11–12;
    Japanese and Korean 174–5
Carcassonne 53–5, 76
Carling Black Label lager 113–14
Carter, Jimmy 180
Challenger space shuttle disaster
    (1986) 92–6, 97–8

Charlemagne, Emperor 54, 76
Chiaromonte, Italy 182–4
Chicago, University of 75, 124
Chilcot Inquiry 25–8
Child Poverty Act (UK, 2010) 58
Churchill, Winston 302
Circle line, redesign of (2009)
    16–19, 255
the Citadel (military college, South
    Carolina) 207
Clark, Alan 16
Clegg, Nick 181
Climate Change Act (UK, 2008) 58
Clinton, Bill 8–11, 180
Clinton, Hillary 32, 254, 267–8,
    269; child sex ring stories
    xiii; Lilla's account of 198;
    obfuscation on Israel 43
Coca-Cola 84, 134–5, 139
Cohn, Roy 300–1
college education 73–5
comedy quiz shows 229
communication ix–xx; and
    allegiance 112–14, 115–20,
    223; as always changing
    299–302; Warren Buffett's
    style 237–42, 243; bullshit
    as always with us 298; and
    choice of font 104; and context
    91–8, 99–104, 105–8; critics
    of obtuse expression 108–11;
    embedded social norms 182–4,
    185–8, 191–203, 208–11, 223,
    224; failure of public discourse
    215; feedback effects 188–92,
    200; formal language in public
    signs 107–8; forms of idiom
    112; general culture and norms
    of 39, 185–8, 191–203, 208–11;
    hidden messages 101–7,
    109; and identity/aspiration
    111–20, 149, 287; lags between

assertion and verification
    164–5; language and message
    99–108; managerial style of
    300; and narrative structures
    138–44, 156, 224, 280;
    non-verbal 53; Orwell on
    insincerity 110–11; Pinker's
    view of language 111; plain
    speaking as exaggerated virtue
    99–105; politically correct
    language 106–7; 'public-
    sector English' 108–9; role of
    indirect language 102–11; role
    of understatement 102–4, 111;
    signalling of tribal allegiance
    115–20, 137, 149, 196–7; social
    norm of being loud 200–1, 203;
    and time-frames 162–84, 232;
    Trump's style xix, 31–3, 117–19,
    246–7, 252–4, 300; types of
    language 105
communications industry x, xi;
    academic work on persuasion
    233–6; and bad reputations
    241–5; and bandwagon
    effect 145–9, 156, 197, 224;
    comparisons with finance
    sector 222–3, 236; emotional
    appeals 135–8, 142–4, 155,
    224; empty assertion by
    35–8; focus on character over
    policy 260–4, 266–7; and
    framing 152–4; hard sell as
    counterproductive 264–6, 271;
    Labour's 'cost-of-living crisis'
    (2013/14) 248–51; lessons of
    populism's emergence 247–8,
    254–72; managed expectations
    149–50, 151, 224; message
    discipline 248–52; over-
    confidence of PR professionals
    216–17, 222–3; and power of

communications industry – *cont.*
    social habit 19, 256–7; and
    psychological mechanisms
    124–5, 134–8, 142–6, 149–58;
    Source credibility 144–5; target
    audience's pre-disposition
    152–4, 158, 216, 229–30, 233,
    244, 276–87; tendency to try
    too hard 247–52
confirmation bias 28, 258, 279,
    280–1
Conservative Party 252
conspiracy theories xii–xiii, 40–1,
    283
Corbyn, Jeremy 46–9, 203, 268–9
corporate sphere: character
    and trust 262–4; corporate
    brands xvi, 165–6, 169,
    173–5, 262, 263; corporate
    social responsibility (CSR)
    programmes 57; short-termism
    in 178–9, 184, 237
Cosby, Bill 153
Cramer, Kathy 116
Creasy, Stella 249
Cruddas, Jon 251
Cummings, Dominic 285, 288–9

Dame Carcas 53–5, 76
Darwin, Charles 68, 76; *The
    Descent of Man, and Selection
    in Relation to Sex* (1871) 77
deception, *see* bullshit; mendacity
    and deception; spin
DellaVigna, Stefano 127
Dilnot, Sir Andrew 285
door-to-door salesmen 228
Douglass, Charles 146
Douthat, Ross 290–1
Drucker, Peter 179
Durant, Alan 15–16
Dyson, James 154

'economical with the truth' phrase
    13–19, 27–8
economics: asymmetries of
    knowledge xv, 67–8, 70–6,
    77–84, 85–6; 'babbling
    equilibrium' 86–7, 169;
    'cheap talk' 75–6, 77–9, 85–7;
    equilibrium 86–7; Eddie
    George on monetary policy
    23–4, 46; human capital
    theory 75; and psychological
    mechanisms 126–32, 134–5;
    psychological pricing 121–4,
    130–2, 134–5, 155–6, 231;
    rational model xv, 85–7, 123,
    126, 130, 131, 286, 298, 299;
    reduced income tax band
    60–2; revolutions in 68–70;
    signalling theory 67–76,
    77–84, 85–7; spinning of
    economic figures 20; Trump
    on unemployment rate 31–2,
    35, 39, 40, 41, 117; volatility of
    data 193–4; World Economic
    Forum, Davos 50
Edelman (PR agency) 262
Eisenhower, Dwight D. 180
Elizabeth II, Queen 102–4, 111
Enron Corporation 57
environmental issues: CFC-infused
    aerosol hairsprays xi–xii, 7;
    Climate Change Act (UK,
    2008) 58
Epictetus 207
EU referendum campaign, UK
    xii, 246, 271, 288–9; Brexit 7,
    137*, 288–9; Vote Leave's '£350
    million a week' claim 12–13,
    284–6, 292
evolutionary science 68; the
    peacock's tail 76–7; sexual
    selection 68, 77

expert opinion: and facts 7, 22;
scepticism of xi, xiii, 31, 32,
275, 286, 291

facts: and direct lies 3–8; and
expert opinion 7, 22; as matters
of judgement 6–7, 25–6; near
lies 8–13; as rhetorical devices
31–3; selective (economy with
the truth) 13–19, 27–8; *see also*
spin
fake news stories xii, 165; examples
5–6; media responses to 289,
291; speed of dissemination 5
fascism, Italian 183
film industry 168–71, 173
Financial Reporting Council 258–9
financial sector: asset-backed
securities 218–19; Barclays
Bank, Annual Report (2007)
35–7, 38, 39, 243; and Warren
Buffett 236–42, 243; City's bad
reputation 242–3; comparisons
with PR trade 222–3, 236;
financial engineering 218–22;
Lloyds Bank Annual Report
(2007) 37–8, 39
Finasteride 277
Fisher, Walter, 'narrative paradigm'
138, 142
Ford, Gerald 180
Frankfurt, Harry G., *On Bullshit*
(2005) xv, 33–4, 38
Franklin, Benjamin 257–8
Friedman, Milton 68–9
Friedman, Thomas 291
fuel poverty 59–60, 76
Full Metal Jacket (Stanley Kubrick
film, 1987) 95

game theory 78*
Gehry, Frank 64–5

general election, British (1992) 163*
George, Eddie 23–4, 46
George, Rob 273–5, 276
German Democratic Republic 64
gibberish, *see* nonsense and
gibberish
Gladwell, Malcolm 138
Gore, Al 208, 209
Gove, Michael 21
Graham, Benjamin, *The Intelligent
Investor* (1949) 236
Graham, John 178
Greenspan, Stephen, *Annals of
Gullibility* (2008) 282–3
Greer, Germaine 287
groupthink 149, 197, 290
Gulf of Tonkin incident 204–5, 207
gullibility xx, 84, 119, 125, 230–6,
279, 282–3

Hanoi Hilton (prison) 205–6
Harvey, Campbell 178–9
healthcare 72, 273–5, 276
Hindenburg airship disaster (1937)
96–7
Hitler, Adolf 233, 286–7
Honda 174–5
honesty and frankness: the case
for 255–72; as the exception
not the norm xviii, 298; and
levels of accountability 296–7;
long-term reputation 161,
162–3, 165–6, 173–6, 240–5,
260–1, 262–3, 266–7; and
open-mindedness xx, 259,
266–7, 280–2; public responses
to 295–7; and James Bond
Stockdale 203–11; and time-
frames 162–84, 298–9
house prices 194*
Howard, Michael 43–5, 48
humbug 10–11

Humphrys, John, 46–9; *Lost for Words* (2004) 108–9, 110
Huntley, Ian 3–5, 6–7, 39
Hussein, Saddam 25–6
Hyundai 174–5

identity politics xx, 120, 137, 149, 155, 287; backlash concept 197–8; competitive 196–8, 199–200; Lilla's account of 198–9, 200; and zero-sum arguing 199
implicit egotism theory 128
Innocent Drinks 139–41
Institute for Fiscal Studies (IFS) 61
Institute of Practitioners in Advertising (IPA) 231–2
insurance market 71, 72
Iraq War 24–8
Ireland, Queen's visit to (May 2011) 102–4, 111
Israel 43
Ivester, Douglas 134, 135

James Bond movies 169, 229
Japan 253
jobs market 70–1, 72, 73–5; CV massaging 186
John Lewis Christmas ads 136, 229–30
Johnson, Boris 21
Johnson, Lyndon B. 180, 204–5
Jones, Paula 9

Kahneman, Daniel 126, 133, 228
Kansas City 65
Kay, Katty 269
Kennedy, John F. 180
Kerry, John 269–70
Keynes, John Maynard 68–9, 270
Kibarian, Thomas 130
Kissinger, Henry 43

Klein, Ezra 261–2
Krugman, Paul 232–3

Labour Party 248–51, 268–9
Lakoff, George, *Don't Think of an Elephant!* (2004) 152–3
Las Vegas 191
latitude of acceptance/rejection 233–4
legal system 5, 8
Leslie, Ian 28–9, 257–8
Lewinsky, Monica 8–11
Lewis, William 142
liberalism–populism divide xii, 198–200, 232–3, 287–8
Liebeck, Stella 281–2
Lilla, Mark 198–9, 200
Lloyds Bank Annual Report (2007) 37–8, 39
Lombard effect 189–91
Lovett, Jon xiv, ix–xi
lying, *see* mendacity and deception

managed expectations 149–50, 151, 224
Mance, Henry, 262–3
marketing, *see* advertising and marketing
Marks & Spencer 263
May, Erskine, *Parliamentary Practice* (1844) 105
May, Theresa 269–70, 271–2
McAleese, Mary 103–4
McAuliffe, Christa 92
McCarthy, Senator Joseph 300–2
McClymont, Gregg 249
McDonald's 281–2
McMahon, Vince 115
media world x; BBC 43–5, 46–9, 194, 238–9, 294; bullshit through disproportion 23–4; canned laughter 146–9;

competitive shouting in 192–4; mainstream use of spin 22–4; need for competing impartial sources 293; need for diversity 294; reaction to bullshit 115, 289–94; use of word 'lie' 291–2; word 'gaffe' 296

mendacity and deception: absence of relevant information 13–19, 27–8; 'alternative facts' 5; cheating as contagious 202; convenient beliefs 28–9; embedded culture of 182–4, 185–8, 223, 224; empty assertion compared to 38–40; flagrant lying 3–8; Gulf of Tonkin incident 204–5, 207; legal and reputational penalties 7–8; lying as not necessary for deception 8; mental process of self-justification 11; and missions to persuade 27–8, 30; near-lies 8–13; politicians' traditional behaviour 114–15; and power of social habit 19, 256–7; selective facts (economy with the truth) 13–19, 27–8; self-deception 24–5, 28–9, 257–9; and short-term horizons 159–62, 163–5, 166–73, 176–84, 222, 223–4, 232, 298–9; and sincere belief 25, 26; socially mandated lying 99–101; in UK parliament 8; white lies xvii, 99–101; *see also* spin

message discipline 248–52
Miliband, Ed 251
Miller, Charles 239
Miller, Merton 220–2
Minoxidil 277
Modi, Narendra 21–2

Modigliani, Franco 220–2
Monster Raving Loony Party 121
Morrison, Herbert (US journalist) 96
movie industry 168–71, 173
Munger, Charlie 237

narrative structures 138–44, 156, 224, 280
NASA 91–6, 97–8
NATO 253
negotiation 151
Nesbitt, Steve 91–6, 97–8
Nescafé, 231
New Labour 300
Nixon, Richard 41–3, 180
nonsense and gibberish xiv; empty assertion 35–40, 117–19; reasons for wanting to believe 40–1; responding to 40–1, 45, 157–8, 199–200; three types of guff 34–52; wine reviews 49–50
Nudge (Richard Thaler and Cass Sunstein, 2008) 127
Nuttin Jr, Jozef M. 128

Obama, Barack 5, 6, 180
obfuscation x, 41; and bad health news 273–5, 276; constructive ambiguity 43; in diplomacy 41–3, 164; honest deflection as preferable 48–9; and Humphrys–Corbyn interview 46–9; Paxman–Howard interview 43–5, 48; responding to 45
oncology 193
online dating 186–8
Oriel College, Oxford 287
Orwell, George, 'Politics and the English Language' (essay, 1946) 110–11

Osborne, George 20
Overton window 234–5

Parkin, Andrew 189–91, 199
Paxman, Jeremy 43–5, 48
payment protection insurance
    (PPI) 36
Penny, Laura, *Your Call Is
    Important to Us: The Truth
    About Bullshit* (2005) x
People's Republic of China (PRC)
    41–3, 195–6
Pepsi-Cola 134
perjury 8
Perkins, Toby 249–50
Perot, Ross 208
Phillips, Robert, *Trust Me, PR is
    Dead* (2015) 262
Pinker, Stephen, *The Language
    Instinct* (1994) 111
placebo effect, 228–9
Podesta, John xiii
politically correct language 106–7
politics: actions and gestures
    57–62; anger at elites xx, 24,
    215; and appeals to emotions
    137–8, 156–7; breakdown of
    left–right spectrum xii, xx;
    British adversarial system
    203; Conservative 'long-term
    economic plan' 252; critics
    of obtuse expression 108–11;
    different messages to different
    groups 114–15; division
    and tribalism in West xx,
    115–20, 137–8, 149; focus on
    character over policy 260–2,
    263–4, 266–7; and framing
    of issues 152–3; hard sell as
    counterproductive 264–6,
    271; Labour's 'cost-of-living
    crisis' (2013/14) 248–51; laws

enshrining targets 58–60,
    76, 255; 'my honourable
    friend' convention 105; and
    narrative structures 141–4,
    156; Overton window 234–5;
    peddling of reassuring
    myths 115, 119, 157, 196, 197,
    199; political right's use of
    language 153; populism-
    liberalism divide xii, 198–200,
    232–3, 287–8; public cynicism
    181; reduced income tax
    band 60–2; and short-term
    horizons 162, 163–4, 166,
    177–8, 179–84, 232; signalling
    of tribal allegiance 115–20,
    149, 196–7; sincerity dilemma
    267–70; spin x, 20–1, 226; and
    James Bond Stockdale 207–11;
    techniques of propagandists
    156–8, 233; Trump on
    unemployment rate 31–2, 35,
    39, 40, 41, 117; *see also* identity
    politics; populist politicians,
    new wave of
populist politicians, new wave of
    xi, 181, 211, 232, 287–8; 2016 as
    key year xii, 215, 246–7, 284–8;
    communication styles 252–4;
    Paul Krugman on 232–3; and
    use/creation of anger 117,
    137–8, 156, 157, 232–3, 288; *see
    also* Trump, Donald
'post-truth' term xii, xiii, 30–1,
    284–6; division and tribalism
    in West xx, 115–20, 137–8, 149;
    social media echo chambers
    149, 280
Price, Pamela Vandyke 50
Private Eye, 'Pseuds' Corner' 50
progress, limitations to 217–19
property market 129–30, 228

psychological mechanisms 122–5, 126–7, 129, 223, 224; audience laughter 146–9; 'availability bias' 132–3; bandwagon effect 145–9, 156, 197, 224; cognitive anchoring 150–1; cognitive short cuts 130, 131–8, 152–4; emotions 135–8, 142–4, 155, 156–7, 224; 'endowment effect' 132; framing 152–4, 224; and habituation 224–7; left-hand truncation 131–2; managed expectations 149–50, 151, 224; mental defences against bullshit 224–30; name-letter effect 128; and narrative structures 138–44, 156, 224, 280; psychological pricing 121–4, 130–2, 134–5, 155–6, 231; and recognition 224–5, 227–30; subliminal mental processes 83, 129–30, 148, 153, 224, 228; System One/System Two thinking 133–8, 155, 156, 228–30, 256, 279; techniques of propagandists 156–8, 233
Putin, Vladimir 232

Quayle, Dan 208, 209
QWERTY keyboard model 201

Rainforest Alliance 139
Rajgopal, Shiva 178–9
Reagan, Ronald 142–4, 180
recycling 256
Renzi, Matteo 50
reputation and credibility 260–1, 262–3; long-term, 161, 162–3, 165–6, 173–6, 240–5, 260–1, 262–3, 266–7; penalties for lying 7–8; and short time horizons 159–62, 163–5,

166–73, 176–84, 222, 223–4, 298–9
restaurants, noisy 188–92
retail sector 62–3; nine-ending pricing 121–4, 130–2, 156, 231
Reynolds, Emma 248–9
Rhodes, Cecil 287
Rhodes, Valley of the Butterflies 159–61, 167, 168, 171, 172
Ricke, Kai Uwe 82
Roosevelt, Theodore 261
Rothschild, Baroness Philippine de 173
Russia, military action in Ukraine 35
Rutgers School of Business, New Jersey 123
Ryanair 226

Schindler, Robert 123–4, 130–1, 132, 155–6, 157–8
Schmitt, Mark 261
school dinners 217–18
Schwarzenegger, Arnold 153
science, health-related 193
Scobee, Dick 93
Scott, Ridley 80
second-hand cars market 71, 72, 151, 156
Service, Robert, *A History of Modern Russia* (2013) xvi–xvii
Shanghai Communiqué (1972) 41–3, 164
signalling theory 67–76, 77–84, 85–7
The Simpsons (TV show) 144*, 297
Sina Weibo 195–6
Smith, Jacob 147–8
smoking xii
snake-oil salesmen xviii–xix
Snakes on a Plane (David R. Ellis film, 2006) 170

social media xii–xiii, 115, 170, 227, 247; competitive anger on 190, 195–6; echo chambers 149, 280; 'like' clicks 149; and spread of fake news 5
Soham murders (2002) 3–5, 6–7, 39
Soviet Union xiii–xiv, xvi–xvii, 225–6
Spence, Michael 69–71, 73–6, 77, 79, 85
spin 19–24, 30; academic work on persuasion 233–6; and bad reputations 241–5; bullshit through disproportion 23–4, 46; of companies' financial results 21, 178–9, 255, 258–9; of economic figures 20; and habituation 226; and mainstream media 22–4; managed expectations 149–50, 151, 224; over-confidence of PR professionals 216–17, 222–3; political x, 20–1, 226; psychological pricing 121–4, 130–2, 134–5, 155–6, 231; and two legitimate versions of events 21–2; WMD in Iraq 25–8; world of as binary 22
sporting success 64
Spycatcher trial (1986) 13–16
St Louis 65
Stanley, Jason 156–7
Stanton, Frank 148
Stewart, Jon 269
Stiglitz, Joseph 71
Stockdale, James Bond 203–11
Stockdale, Taylor 205, 206–7, 208, 209–10
Stockdale Paradox 205–6
stoic philosophy 207
sub-prime mortgage market, US 218–19

Sunstein, Cass 127
Super Bowl advertising slots 80
supermarkets 62
swimming relays 125, 244–5

Taiwan 41–3
Taleb, Nassim Nicholas 29
Thaler, Richard 127
Thomas Cook 262–3
T-Mobile 82–3
Topshop 263
tourism 159–61, 171–3
Transport for London (TfL) 16–19, 255
TripAdvisor 171
Truman, Harry S. 180, 301
Trump, Donald: and 'babbling equilibrium' 87; and CFC-infused aerosol hairsprays xi–xii, 7; and Roy Cohn 301; communication style xix, 31–3, 117–19, 246–7, 252–4, 300; 'Drain the Swamp' campaign 252–3; election campaign xii, 117–19, 157, 198–9, 232–3, 246–7, 252–4, 260, 261–2, 275, 286, 287–8; honesty ratings of 32–3, 253; media responses to 289, 290–2; and Overton window 235; and signalling of tribal allegiance xix, 32, 115–19, 260, 261–2; Taylor Stockdale on 210; on unemployment rate 31–2, 35, 39, 40, 41, 117; 'whitelash' argument 199; and WWE 115–16
Turnbull, Malcolm 14–15
Twain, Mark 13
Twitter 195

UK Statistics Authority 285
Umunna, Chuka 248, 250

United Nations (UN) 43*, 58
The Untouchables (Brian De Palma
    film, 1987) 197

Valencia 65
Victorian era xiii
Vietnam War 204–7, 208
Virgin Trains 299*
Volkswagen false-emissions
    scandal 11–12

Warm Homes and Energy
    Conservation Act (UK, 2000)
    59–60
WCRS 113
Welch, Joseph 301

wine reviews 49–50
wishful thinking 279
World Economic Forum, Davos 50
World Wrestling Entertainment
    (WWE) 115–16

*Yes! 50 Secrets from the Science of
    Persuasion* (Noah J. Goldstein,
    Steve J. Martin and Robert B.
    Cialdini, 2007) 129, 145

Zakharchenko, Alexander 35
Zeman, Miloš, xii
Zeta-Jones, Catherine 82–3
Zito, Salena 118